THE TROUBLE WITH LOVE IN THE MOVIES

THE TROUBLE WITH LOVE IN THE MOVIES

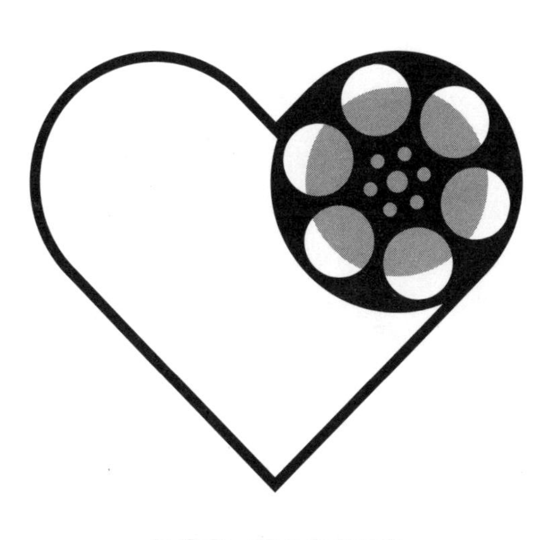

ROB HARRIS

First published 2020

by Zuleika Books & Publishing

Thomas House, 84 Eccleston Square
London, SW1V 1PX

Illustrations: Ivan Ryabokon/Alamy Stock Vector

Story: The Convalescence by Nicola Graydon Harris

Quotes from *My Traitor's Heart* by Rian Malan
reprinted with permission of the author.

British Library Cataloguing in Publication Data

A catalogue record for this book is
available from the British Library

ISBN: 978-1-9161977-5-6

Designed by Euan Monaghan
Printed and bound by
CPI Group (UK) Ltd, Croydon, CR0 4YY

For anyone who's ever been in love
Or been in love with the movies

and

For my companions of the road:
journalist, Paul Lomartire
photographer, Ken Regan
publicist, Marsha Robertson
In memoriam

CONTENTS

PROLOGUE

Go to sleep my weary hobo, let the towns drift slowly by
Can't you hear the steel rails humming
That's the hobo's lullaby

– Woody Guthrie

Twenty years had passed since Ann's death, a few months short of her thirtieth birthday. The breast cancer she'd been battling through most of our four-year marriage had spread to her lungs. Alone in the small hospital room, her assisted breathing increasingly laboured, I sang an old folk song she liked. The attending nurse gave us a few minutes before coming in and shutting off her monitors.

Who do you talk to when you're thirty-five and your wife has died? Not your parents, your siblings, your friends. There were support groups for people who had gone through such tectonic shifts. But I had neither the courage nor the clarity to share my feelings with strangers.

My mother had survived breast cancer. Her prolonged illness defined my childhood.

I disguised my terror with anger in those times. Now, I was angry at Ann's parents for commandeering the funeral arrangements. I was angry at the surgeon for recommending a lumpectomy when a mastectomy might have saved her. When anger flames out, there are only ashes.

A friend recommended a therapist in Santa Monica.

A greying woman in a loose-fitting dashiki top and slacks opened her door and motioned me inside. We exchanged greetings. She studied me.

'Why aren't you breathing?' she began our session.

Ann was pregnant when we discovered the cancer on a routine first-trimester check-up. Her disease was the kind that accelerated with the infusion of progesterone. Her pregnancy was toxic. The baby had to be aborted before she could begin chemotherapy.

Following her diagnosis, I concentrated on her recovery, minimising the grief she felt at the loss of a child, completely suppressing any of my own. It was only in the sorrow of her passing that I could grieve over how much I'd wanted to become a father. To emulate my father. A good man.

In the year that followed, I worked on as many movies as I could fit in, going from job to job, location to location – the further from home, the better. Anything to avoid having to figure out what to do with her clothes.

I remember the year by locations. Grand Junction, Colorado. I took a hundred-mile drive to Wyoming one weekend for Cheyenne Frontier Days. Weekends were the hardest. What was her name? Donna? Donna from Houston. She taught me the Texas two-step in a dance hall. She taught me to move on.

Margaret was singing at a piano bar in Los Angeles. A mutual acquaintance had set us up to meet there. She smiled from the small stage with a nod in the direction of my table as her silken voice filled the room.

I was a week away from leaving for a film in Alabama. We

spent that week together. She was lovely. Warm and kind, spirited and wise, honest and forthright. She was a woman with whom a man could make a good life. But I wasn't ready to fall in love. I needed a fresh start in a new place. I was moving to Seattle.

We corresponded by letter while I was away. Over time, our letters became less newsy, more affectionate. On my return, I scheduled a trip north to find my new home. I invited Margaret to come along. No intention other than a shared excursion.

We'd been three weeks together and five weeks apart. A week into our trip to Seattle, I said this was the way it would be. She was a musician, she reminded me – she understood. I pinned her against a vegetable stand in Pike Place Market and asked her to marry me. We rented a house on the beach, south of the city.

Seven years and two children later, we would move again. This time to Upstate New York. Ithaca. Like Ulysses and Penelope.

You'll recall they didn't have an easy time of it because he travelled too much.

PART ONE: SECRETS AND LIES

CHAPTER ONE: IN A KINGDOM FAR AWAY

I grew up a shy kid on the wrong side of the tracks in the San Fernando Valley, a working-class development north of the railroad that ran along Sherman Way. Yes, it was technically North Hollywood but as far from the glamour of Hollywood as it was to the moon. Movies existed only in the Lankershim Theatre and the Victory Drive-In.

My junior high school was south of Sherman Way where the economic scale tilted slightly upward. Among my new friends there was Stan, whose father worked as a prop man for film and television. One day, he took me into the garage where his dad was storing some set decoration from *The Incredible Shrinking Man.* I remember a pair of salt and pepper shakers as tall as we were. The garage was a wonderland of treasure trunks, holstered pistols, lassos and pieces of things that went with other things that movie stars touched. I never met Stan's father. He was away a lot. But his garage was my introduction to the existence of film crews. Ordinary people, maybe even shy people, supporting a middle-class family on wages from their anonymous contribution to movies. How did that work?

First, the phone rings. Or you get an email inquiring, 'Are you available?'

Your response will require a discussion with your partner. But it's usually you trying to convince him or her that you really can't say no.

How much do we have in the bank?

I know it starts too soon – but it would pay for the kitchen remodel.

If I turn this down, the producer/director/studio executive might never ask me again.

So, you say yes and you wait a few weeks or a few months – hoping the job you've committed to isn't cancelled because, by now, you've turned down two or three others. And cancellations, delays, personnel changes at the top that shift crew preferences down the line are just part of the game.

You put it out of your mind and go on with your daily routines: dinners with family and friends, regular trips to the gym, watching favourite TV series. Maybe you glance at a map of where you'll be filming or idly check out a few names on IMDB. But until you get your travel orders, you don't talk about it. Don't talk about it because you know it could fall through or get pushed. Don't talk about it because then you start thinking about it.

Of course, everyone from your grandmother to your local Starbucks barista wants to know what movie you'll be working on next. So, you tell them. And from the moment the details leave your lips, you're already there. It's now tattooed on your brain. It's the trapdoor in the floor of your life.

A film production is its own ecosystem. All contributing bodies are one body, from the actors to production assistants. Each miniscule amoeba and big fish absorbing, assessing, amassing data, the assimilation and dissemination of which is crucial to the larger organism.

I am a unit publicist. My credit rolls just before the house lights go up and the usher comes to sweep the floor. My job is to tell – or not tell – the public, the press and anyone else who inquires bits of information about the film that's being made. Unit publicist is neither a power position nor a creative one. It is a position of access, a by-product of which can be influence – if you earn it. The unit publicist must be trusted to deliver the right message to the right people, follow through on the studio's promises and strategies, and tread lightly through minefields of conflicting agendas among stars, filmmakers and executives.

I interact with personnel at all levels within the company – from the bosses to the standby painter – gathering enough data and hearsay to read the political playing field and understand what we're making so I can make others understand what we're selling. I interface outside the company as representative to the media, charities, government officials, fans, phonies, the pushy and the powerful seeking access to glitz and glamour. I help sort out those who can be of benefit and try to keep out those who would be a hindrance.

This allows the elves on set to putter and tinker undisturbed, each contributing a piece here, a piece there, to create a toy every child of every age wants to see at Christmas – in summer, or on a date night.

Sound, set decoration, camera, construction, transportation… we all go off with Santa to the North Pole. Sometimes we remember we're just making a toy. Sometimes we think we're making an important toy. Now and then we remember we're not curing cancer.

But here's the difference between making movies and making fairytale castles or bicycles or widgets: for two or three, four, five or six months, we don't just go to work *on* a fairytale castle, we go to work *in* a fairytale castle.

And the unreality of that working environment is difficult to describe to anyone who isn't there.

How was work, dear?

Oh, just another day in the fifteenth century trying to make the dragon breathe fire without incinerating the camera crew.

Do our jobs shape us or do we fall into a line of work that suits who we are? The answer, of course, is both. Ask anyone who works in a correctional institution. Do politicians pontificate around the dinner table? Do athletes have a greater tolerance for mindless repetition? Are we what we do? Do we do what we are?

If we work in a world of illusion – the illusion of control over schedules, over weather, over temperaments and, of course, in a framework of fiction – are we deluded? Do we see life as if it were a movie?

If so, why would any sane person fall in love with a person in film production?

The answer may lie in the adjective.

I rejoice and despair with every job. Early in my career I worked on a movie in Whistler, British Columbia. We were housed at a luxury ski resort surrounded by snow-capped mountains, filming in pristine wilderness with an icon of cinema, Sidney Poitier. I was standing beside Oscar-winning sound mixer Simon Kaye and must have been gushing about how exciting it all was. His not-unkind response was, 'I've got to the point where the most exciting part of any movie is being asked to do it.' The implication being it was all downhill from there.

Permit me to describe the upside of working on a movie: imagine hyper-life. Not so much life on steroids as life on a psychedelic. Having lunch beside a stuntwoman playing a zombie with half her face torn off. Helping a childhood hero with his tummy cinch. Discovering a group of instant intimates, castaways rowing toward the same shore. Working in places where no one else is allowed, in dream worlds no one outside this realm has imagined. Seeing the world on someone else's bank card.

The craic of movie adventure still excites me. But I've come to a better understanding of what Simon meant. It's easy to get excited about the *prospect* of working on a film. It's another thing waking at dawn to put in twelve-hour days for months on end, separated from everything you know and everyone you love.

There are as many reasons that movie marriages have a high failure rate as there are ripples in a pond after a building falls in it. They're probably not much different from the reasons marriages fall apart outside the movie business except for the extremes. You could make an equation: long separations times long hours times long distances equal short marriages.

I loved my wife. I know she loved me. But love is elastic. You can only stretch it as far as it can snap back. If you stretch it too far, it snaps in two.

Throughout our eighteen years together, a series of different marriage counsellors had helped us identify and discuss areas of discontent. Margaret was content with her domestic life: PTA meetings, volunteer work and the occasional singing gig around town. She had her sons to come home to, her sister living next door and friends around her. Her discontent lay mainly with my own.

I needed (note the therapy training in that wording) more of her.

My unhappiness centred around a growing lack of connection when we were together and what I perceived to be her indifference to finding more time to be together. Absence may make the heart grow fonder but there's a tipping point beyond which absence is preferable.

Whose fault was it?

I was never around.

She wasn't emotionally available when I was around.

I wanted us all to be gypsies.

She wanted to make a home.

Whose fault?

I'd married a smart woman who knew how she wanted her life to unfold. She wanted to be a mother and do all the things a mother does. Her own mother had died giving birth to her brother when Margaret was nine years old. Motherhood meant everything to her.

She was raised in Upstate New York, so we moved to Ithaca where we built a house next door to her sister and brother-in-law. I'd become disillusioned with Seattle. Microsoft and Amazon had transformed it from a patchwork of artists, artisans and manufacturing workers to the advance guard of the new century. And there was no film work to be had between the Canadian border and the San Fernando Valley.

Ithaca was a four-hour weekend drive from locations in Manhattan, Toronto and other points east. The alternative was returning to Los Angeles, where they made more movies. But neither of us wanted to live where everyone else in the film business lived.

Exceptionalism has its rewards. We could afford to build a big house on seven acres abutting a state park. Our boys had an outstanding free education in a university town. But a life of exceptionalism requires exceptional efforts. And in recent years, it felt like I was the one making all the effort.

After a courtship shorter than most trial magazine subscriptions, our early years in the Northwest had set us on a voyage of discovery. The sublime joy of holding our newborn children, witnessing their transformation into personalities and loving them beyond all reason overlapped with revelations of fundamental personality differences. She was the girl in the front of the class with her hand up; I was the boy in the back hoping he didn't get called on. I was impulsive; she was methodical. She read instructions; I didn't. I came from a family that hugged a lot; she would break a three-second embrace with a pat on the back. But one thing I thought we had in common was a nomadic spirit: we were travellers.

Now we were a cliché, a couple who were mainly together for the sake of the children. Did I still love her? Love is complicated. And it doesn't exist in a vacuum.

A year and another 3,000 miles ago, I was blithely immersed in the absurdity of Eddie Murphy's *Daddy Day Care* when Margaret phoned to tell me our eldest son had been diagnosed with a rare kidney disease.

Casey was already in the throes of a difficult adolescence. Part of this was a factor of his visual impairment: he was ninety-per-cent blind. One of Casey's doctors believed his blindness and kidney failure might be linked by a little-known condition called Senior-Loken Syndrome.

'He'd have a better chance of winning the lottery than having this,' the doctor told us.

I left the movie and came home with the clear priority of marriage and family.

I passed up bigger pictures to work on a small production called *Wicker Park* in Montreal because that was close enough to Ithaca for a weekend commute. I made that drive faithfully through the sleet and snow of the worst winter Upstate New York had seen in the decade we'd lived there.

Casey would be okay. The need for a transplant wasn't expected for at least twenty years. That's a lifetime to a child. So, any fears he may have had about his health were absorbed by the more immediate traumas of hating school, fighting with his brother and feeling like an outcast.

Meanwhile, Margaret and I worked on our relationship, taking long walks with the dogs through Ithaca's gorges, cross-country skiing when it snowed, seeing the occasional movie. We continued going to counselling every Saturday.

One of the most difficult aspects of movie marriages is the role of 'location wife'. It's an awkward situation for the partner who has no reason for being on a film location, uprooting him/herself for the sake of connecting with the peripatetic spouse. But successful movie marriages make adjustments.

I was about to start work on a long movie. *Troy* was scheduled to film for five months, in three countries, beginning with England. Our sons had two weeks of spring break from school. Margaret would bring them to London for a week.

And here they were.

Our teenagers quickly found a favourite way to pass their days, going off on their own to explore the music stores on Denmark Street in Soho. Sam had been learning saxophone and Casey was becoming proficient on piano. On these outings, Sam shouldered the responsibility of keeping his older brother from bumping into pedestrians or getting hit by a taxi, putting up with his irritability while fighting the urge to push him under a bus.

Another aspect of Casey's difficult adolescence was a fierce independence. He did not like needing other people's help. When he was twelve, I'd taken him sailing and he decided he wanted to be a boat captain so he could live in the middle of the ocean and not have to deal with people. A few years later, he went flying with a friend of mine who had a small plane and landed with a new plan of becoming the world's first blind fighter pilot.

Throughout his early childhood, Casey had handled his visual impairment with impressive equanimity. This was his time for rage. His childhood had transited from 'I'm not different' to 'I'm different, dammit!' Both were necessary for him to graduate to 'I'm different in some ways but not in others. Let's move on.' He wasn't there yet.

Sam was older than his fourteen years. He'd grown up taking care of his big brother. But despite the imbalance in their physical abilities, there was a counterbalance in other aspects of their relationship. In many ways, Casey was Sam's mentor. From his sibling, Sam learned patience and empathy. Casey gave us all lessons in that.

While I was at work and her two independent children were spreading their adolescent wings, Margaret was free to enjoy a cloudless afternoon in Berkeley Square or a stroll through the National Portrait Gallery. It was helpful to have a diversity of settings in which to worry where her sons were in this huge, foreign metropolis.

London is one of the safest big cities in the world for school-aged children to walk and take public transportation. Sam was a responsible young man and Casey wasn't about to run off to find the nearest drug dealer. They'd been travelling with Dad's Circus since they were babies. But this was their first foray without parental interference.

It was understandable that Margaret was worried. But there was more to it than just matters of safety. The boys were changing, as children do, and their mother was strong enough to swallow her own fears and allow that process to take place. I felt an enormous respect for her in the courage that required.

As I drove them to Heathrow Airport at the end of the week, Margaret was relaxed and chatty.

'Well, we're sure going to miss Dad, aren't we?' she said, turning to the back seat. The boys' choir rejoined.

Inside the terminal, my sons squeezed me until their hearts and mine entwined.

I hugged my wife.

One second. Two seconds. Three seconds.

A pat on my back.

She turned and led her children toward the security checkpoint.

My heart sank a little with each step.

CHAPTER TWO: TROY

I'd flown to London well ahead of the start of filming because the media buzz around *Troy* had mushroomed. Insiders were sceptical that a classic theme this expensive – nearly $200 million – would ever be greenlit in an era of budget-busting escapist franchises: *Lord of the Rings, Pirates of the Caribbean, The Matrix, X-Men.*

With an all-star cast featuring Brad Pitt, Warner Bros. decided to roll the dice. They would make this picture through their United Kingdom division. Tax incentives, lower crew costs and a plethora of powerful British actors were among the reasons. To qualify for the tax breaks, the movie had either to start or finish in the UK. After some debate over whether to start filming in Morocco and finish in England or the other way around, the producers decided to launch the project from twenty miles outside central London on the stages of Shepperton Studios.

The reason for this lay in Morocco. To be precise, a little farther east: Iraq. The Second Gulf War had begun two weeks before I arrived in England. The production had already set up a base in the ocean resort town of Essaouira, hoping against the odds that war could be avoided. If the US invaded Iraq, even a moderate Muslim country would be too risky a place to make a Hollywood movie.

A Canadian friend recently visited Morocco and told me about his reception there.

'It was alright, as soon as they found out I was Canadian,' he said. 'But I wouldn't have wanted to be an American there.'

Producer-director Wolfgang Petersen and his team began scouting alternate locations. By late February, war was a foregone conclusion and Morocco no longer a consideration. So, all weapons, props, set dressing and costumes that had been made and warehoused in Essaouira had to be sorted, packed and shipped to a new beachfront encampment in Cabo San Lucas, Mexico. And *Troy* started filming in England.

To anyone unfamiliar with Homer's epic, *The Iliad*, it might help to trace the origins of literature as follows:

Cave drawings.

Homer.

Everybody else.

Others had tried to film *The Iliad* (and its companion *The Odyssey*). In fact, a television movie, *Helen of Troy*, was wrapping as we were beginning production. But ours was going to be made on a scale worthy of its legacy.

And – wait for the pitch – it wasn't an epic *period* movie, it was an epic love story with universal themes as relevant today as they were 3,000 years ago. It was about passion that couldn't be denied, love that defied all reason, a beauty that launched a thousand ships… alright, maybe not as relevant today. Still, corporate marketers strategised they had the male audience with epic (can't use that word enough) battle scenes and breathtaking hand-to-hand combat not witnessed since *Spartacus* (don't mention *Gladiator*, that too-recent spectre of overblown expectations). It was up to the publicity department to figure out how it could also be positioned as a chick flick: *women would relate to being married to the wrong man just when Orlando Bloom comes along!* This was one of many challenges.

Director Wolfgang Petersen was a man in command. Of moderate stature, modest temperament, an impish humour and a spine of steel, at age sixty-two, he was indefatigable. He would need every ounce of energy to complete this film. It was a game of brinkmanship in which he couldn't blink. This would be my fourth movie with Wolfgang, a man I liked personally and admired as a filmmaker. I ran into him as I was leaving the production office.

I think all I said was, 'This one's gonna be interesting.'

'We take everything one step at a time,' he said with a smile. 'If you look at the end, you'll never make it.'

Once you launch, you're leaving gravity. Look down and you fall. I followed him out the door, onto the grounds of historic Shepperton Studios. The pavement rose. I was in orbit, home and family shrinking in the distance as I entered a new surreal reality.

Our main producer, Colin Wilson, had wrestled many big, expensive movies to the mat, most recently *Terminator 3: Rise of the Machines,* budgeted above $200 million.

One of the first people Colin hired for *Troy* was assistant director Gerry Gavigan, veteran of more than a half-dozen James Bond films, among other big movies.

It's the AD's job to break down a script into a shooting schedule. Gerry analysed the screenplay and handed in a schedule. Colin looked at the breakdown.

'It has to be a month shorter.'

'I can make it whatever length you like, but this is the amount of time you're going to need to make this movie.'

A shorter schedule was turned in and the studio – possibly with a wink and a nod or possibly with doe-eyed faces of the innocent – greenlit the project.

Filming began on 17 April 2003.

An international search for the face that launched a thousand ships had received only slightly less speculation than the casting of Scarlett O'Hara sixty-five years earlier.

Bookmakers were taking bets all over England for the actress who would be our Helen. Among the favourites were Claire Forlani (who starred with Brad Pitt in *Meet Joe Black*), Nicole Kidman (the brand name for 'beautiful woman') and even Saffron Burrows (close, but no). Bookies made a killing when the answer turned out to be none of the above.

The wreath landed upon German former fashion model and ballerina Diane Kruger, whose first American picture had been *Wicker Park*. The caprice of the movie gods also plucked Rose Byrne, her co-star in *Wicker Park*, to play Briseis, the high-born priestess who would become Achilles' heel.

Once Diane was selected, the studio publicity machinery had a dilemma. Should they make a big splash of the announcement, including interviews with Wolfgang about what an extensive selection process it had been, TV clips of the screen test and other promotional actions to turn her casting into an event? The alternative was to keep it low-key, taking pressure off the actress and allowing her to be discovered by audiences once they were in theatres. There were arguments to be made in both directions. The studio came down on the side of understatement.

The understatement would be in the form of a single photo released to the international press with a little background on the actress. But we had to get our photo out before some of the former model's former modelling shots started appearing, puncturing the illusion of ancient beauty and undermining our carefully layered publicity strategy.

I climbed the stairs of Stage C annex toward Diane's

dressing room with an armload of test shots she needed to look at for approval.

She greeted me at the door.

'I've got the pictures for you,' she said. It took me a minute to realise she was talking about photos from *Wicker Park* that MGM had sent over only yesterday.

'I was sitting around here for six hours and they never did get to use me,' she said shrugging off her prompt attention to something most actors put off for days, weeks or months. I told her the new shots I had were fairly urgent.

'Do you want to wait while I do them now or can you pick them up later?'

If I could make her into a mould and cast other actors off that assembly line…

A few days later, Colin Wilson came to my office asking if I'd seen the first photo of Diane Kruger as Helen in *Heat* magazine.

'No.'

'Well, she's wearing jeans.' He tossed the open magazine on my desk.

That wasn't the photo we'd sent out!

Diane was wearing a royal purple, Helenesque blouse but the image of antiquity was blown by her designer denims. It was the version of the photo Wolfgang and everyone at the studio had approved; it just hadn't been cropped before it was sent to the press. She looked like a beautiful babe who could've been cooling her heels in a café on the Sunset Strip.

How easily 'publicity strategy' becomes an oxymoron.

For those of us who worshipped the ground that *Lawrence of Arabia*'s camel shat upon, the highlight of our two weeks' filming in London was the start of work for one of the last of the living screen legends, Peter O'Toole, who was cast as King Priam.

Stage C featured a fifty-foot-high statue of Zeus holding a golden sceptre and statues of other deities the size of upright limousines. They would topple when Agamemnon wreaks his bloody revenge. If anyone drew parallels to the looting of the Baghdad Museum that had been news for the past few days, no one said it aloud.

Daniel Petersen, Wolfgang's son, was writing a book about the movie and related a conversation he overheard at the playback monitors as his father and O'Toole waited for cameras to reset in King Priam's throne room.

Peter was talking about his old drinking buddies Richard Burton and Richard Harris and how much they could imbibe back in the day.

'Well, you could never get away with that today,' Wolfgang told him. 'It would be considered very unprofessional for an actor in a film now to come to work drunk or hungover.'

Peter held a beat for the perfect dramatic pause before replying, 'And have you noticed any improvement?'

A charter flight is an airborne crew party. Two hundred *Troy* crew and supporting cast boarded the plane from London to Malta. It was a short flight. Some of our alcoholics took that as a challenge.

Southern England was home to most of *Troy*'s personnel. Malta was the launch of location work. Filming near home means seeing your family on a regular basis. Filming on location means workmates become family: eating, drinking, fighting, laughing and, occasionally, sleeping together. While there are always exceptions – the boastful sibling, the scolding aunt

– a film family are usually the most companionable and entertaining relatives you'll ever have. If you can't play nicely with others, you're not invited back.

It's a paradox how, in most businesses, your work is transparent and your personal life is a closed curtain. It's almost the opposite in the film business. Most departments operate independently and, perhaps because one lives with only slightly more privacy than a shared hospital room, most production people don't keep their private lives private for long.

I sat beside Ana, our script supervisor. She had been crying when she boarded the plane. Recently engaged to be married, she was surprised by how emotional she was about leaving her fiancé.

'I know I'll be seeing him soon but, well, it's a long distance, isn't it?'

I didn't know Ana well but we'd all felt what she was feeling. Her love was new. It was strong. Her partner would become a tether. A partner is a life; a tether is a lifeline. She would return to the former by clinging to the latter.

But many on this ship of fools had neither. And the trouble with love in the movies is not just keeping but finding a love. You're not home enough to build lasting relationships. So, you form relationships of a few months, or a year, or a location. You hope the next location or the next lay-off will open a door to the special someone who can stick. But until then, you end up trading intimacy and permanency for wistful glances in the rear-view and a few good stories. Stories connect us to where we've been and remind us where we're going.

A crew mate leaned across the aisle to reminisce about working with a tribe of pygmies on *Greystoke.* One of the make-up artists shared a bawdy behind-the-scenes tale from *Cutthroat*

Island. Someone groused about how much night work lay ahead until his mate brought up a film they'd recently worked on that had even more.

Ana's tears dried. Moments later, she opened her script and began making notes.

CHAPTER THREE: BEEN HERE, DONE THAT

Malta is a strange little country. A speck in the middle of the Mediterranean between Sicily and Libya, it is genetically and linguistically Arabic and historically Catholic. Ruled for nearly three centuries by zealot relics of the Crusades – the Knights of St John – it boasts a connection to St Paul and celebrates a different saint in a different city fifty-two weeks a year. It was the perfect place to establish our Troy, given the piety that was its undoing.

Downtown Troy was built on ten acres inside a seventeenth-century military compound, Fort Ricasoli. It was the same compound that had been used by *Gladiator* whose setting was approximately 1,300 years more recent. The fortress's walls, towers and tunnels were adaptable to that period. Not so much for this.

So, an entire city had to be built from the ground up. More than 500 Maltese workers were hired and another 200 UK craftsmen were brought to the island. Depth and detail were needed to give the movie scope. Hundreds of clay pots, weaver's looms, leather works and baskets were made to depict an ancient commerce.

But re-entering Fort Ricasoli filled many of us with nostalgia for a different time. Our visual effects supervisor, Nikki Penny, was one of those.

'Everything I do, everywhere I go here reminds me of *Gladiator*,' she said. 'That was just the most amazing movie experience of my life, working with Ridley… and everyone.

Amazing as this movie is, it's like trying to relive your first kiss or pretending you're a virgin again. There are some things that just aren't meant to be done over.'

Shortly after we arrived, Malta was in the news as the hottest inhabited place on the planet: about 111 degrees Fahrenheit (44 Celsius) during the day and still uncomfortably steamy at night. It was just early May. Filming began in an airplane hangar with a tin roof and an improvised air-conditioning system that had to be shut off for sound during every take.

It was a scene in which Paris secretly enters Helen's bedroom. Our technical advisor, Lesley Fitton from the British Museum, marvelled at the authenticity of the set, including the 'genuine Mycenaean door locks'. Unfortunately, the slide bolt was giving Orlando Bloom fits. It required fifteen takes to get the entrance right.

This was a movie with a lot more complications than a door lock. But it was dismissed as a glitch, not a foreshadowing.

'Alright, we've got it.' Wolfgang rose from his chair, wiping sweat from his forehead. 'Turn on the fans. Next set-up.'

I had dinner the following night with a viper from the *Malta Times* who reacted like I'd denied her a heart transplant when I said she couldn't get an exclusive interview with Brad Pitt. She proceeded to make veiled threats and not-so-veiled complaints as she questioned my competence over sea bass.

When I got home, there was an email from the head of Warner's publicity asking if I knew about *Entertainment Tonight* being offered twenty minutes of paparazzi footage from a scene on an atoll with Brad and Julie Christie. It had aired earlier that night on Italian television.

At around 2 a.m., Malta time, I got a follow-up email saying *ET* had agreed not to purchase the footage. This was both ethical and contingent on an agreement that they would be permitted on set to film their own segment another time. I was now tasked with finding that time. Okay. There was a slight problem in getting Brad's publicist to lift her drop-dead prohibition of allowing press on set when Brad was working. But I would appeal to a higher authority.

Wolfgang was a director who liked having press on set so, the next day, I asked if he might want to overrule his star.

'Yes, I will overrule that. *I* don't want any press on set when Brad Pitt is working.'

I spoke with Margaret infrequently during our early weeks in Malta. She was in Nashville, recording her first album in nearly twenty years. I checked in regularly with Casey and Sam, home alone taking care of our dogs, Gershwin (a big Rottweiler mix) and Oliver (a mixed terrier). Gershwin would look out for their safety while Margaret's sister and brother-in-law came by nightly to cook them dinner. Though some members of the PTA might want us arrested, the boys would be fine.

Sam was doing some recording of his own with a band called Pocket – named after their favourite sandwich. My youngest mainly wanted to play me his songs when I called. Perhaps it was the phone lines but they sounded like a car crash with lyrics sung through a megaphone. Casey was devouring audiobooks at the rate of nearly one a day and had recently read *One Flew Over the Cuckoo's Nest*.

'It's about a guy who values his freedom as much as I do,' he explained. 'But ultimately, when it comes to a choice between his personal freedom and staying to fight an injustice, he realises he can't run away. He has to stay and sacrifice his personal desires in order to do what's right.'

Yeah, the boys would be fine. They'd learned the importance of staying to fight when they felt like running away. Had I taught them that? Had I learned it?

After four weeks away from my family, I was fighting loneliness. Six weeks is usually the pain pinnacle. I tried not to imagine two more weeks of feeling worse before I'd feel better. If I could just take it a day at a time, I'd be fine. We'd be fine.

'It feels so great being back in a recording studio,' Margaret effused when we finally conquered time zones, fatigue and fuzzy phone lines.

That voice that had brightened my nights through so many years was even more radiant now. Doing what she loved, recording an album of originals and classics produced by an old friend who adored her almost as much as I did. If I had a fleeting thought about any involvement with him that wasn't professional, it ran a very short distance and hit a wall at any real concern. I knew her heart and it wasn't made for going there.

The conversation began with a quotidian, 'How are you?' I'm fine, I lied. Then I let her talk because it was what she needed in her foreign but familiar circumstances. And she knew it was what I wanted. Just to hear her voice. Married people sense each other's needs. The instincts of coupledom fill unarticulated cavities. If I'd wanted to say more, she would've been happy to give her attention. Sometimes I'd pass along an anecdote from the day's filming and she would listen as if to something important. It was rarely important. What was important was the silver thread of her voice weaving the tapestry of our home life. What our boys were doing. What our friends were up to. Descriptions of our dog Gershwin playing in the snow. Things that mattered less in substance than the soft blanket of her voice.

'Well, I guess I should go now.'

No, wait, tell me more. And she'd think of something more to tell.

She talked and I listened, my spirit replenished. Temporarily.

Our first day on the sea left many of the crew queasy from rough currents and, though it was calmer the next day, the heat made work go slowly. Wind forced us off the water on the third day – forcing a schedule change. The blazing sun at Fort Ricasoli sent our cinematographer, Roger Pratt, to the hospital with heat prostration. Another half-day lost.

There was a mutiny on the Mediterranean a day later.

We were back in the boats under blistering heat when, after lunch break, the fifty Maltese extras playing Achilles' oarsmen refused to return to work.

Extras – more respectfully referred to as background actors – are the movie world's underclass. Their treatment is always less than that of the crew, certainly less than that of the cast. Background actors are usually prohibited from snacking at the main craft service tables, consigned to port-o-potties instead of having access to base-camp bathrooms, given inferior meals at lunch, kept in a tent or 'holding area' apart from main cast and crew, and generally treated like migrant day labourers.

While production personnel were ferried to the lunch boat for a catered buffet, the oarsmen were stuck on the picture boat, a single-mast bireme (two lines of rowers) with a flat deck and no shade. A small cabin concealed a compartment of urinals below deck.

There wouldn't have been sufficient space on the lunch boat to add fifty hulking men with rubber armour, but adding a second craft would've been expensive in two ways: the obvious was the cost of renting another kitchen-equipped vessel with bench-style tables; the less obvious expense was time. Getting the oarsmen off the picture boat would've required transporting them both ways, with additional minutes spent removing and refitting their breastplates and wigs.

So, a motorboat was dispatched to bring box lunches to the bireme. Production assistants distributed them and tried to encourage the background actors to keep their armour and hairpieces in place. Under the broiling sun. This didn't go over well. Neither did the lunches – a sandwich, a pack of crisps and some cookies. But it wasn't until word got out that the extras were being charged three Maltese pounds (about $8/£5) each for their meals that a spontaneous uprising began.

The PAs were taken off the boat to save them from being thrown overboard. The mutineers used their breastplates for shade and sat under them for the rest of the day. The production lost at least $100,000 (the approximate cost of a half-day's filming) to save about $400. I'll admit to sending up a quiet cheer for the proletariat.

Eventually, the extras were removed from the boat. Colin fired the ringleaders of the mutiny and shooting resumed the next day. Without the box lunch charge.

Less than halfway through our filming in Malta, pressure was starting to get to everyone. Deliveries were delayed because the production office was saving shipping costs and important documents weren't being processed because the office staff were overworked and under-experienced. Work hours were getting longer because there was a lot to do on set and, even with over 400 full-time crew, we were understaffed. Word was circulating that some of our key personnel were on the verge of quitting the movie because they were putting in seven-day weeks to keep up.

Filming moved to the Ivy Temple, which stood on a rock cliff against a spectacular view of the Mediterranean. The scene was swordplay between Achilles and Patroclus, Achilles' young cousin, who was played by Garrett Hedlund in his film debut.

Garrett was a talented young actor who was cast, in part, for his similar look to Brad, which comes into the story later. A Midwest farm boy who'd followed his dreams to Hollywood, he claimed to have lived on the streets before being offered this role on his first audition. The mean-streets-to-big-screen tale might have been slightly apocryphal, but it was hard to tell when Garrett was putting you on. He was a prankster.

The production returned from lunch and was under pressure to make the day. As cameras were being set, Garrett suddenly ran away holding his nose. It didn't take long for the sulfuric stench to reach the nostrils of the rest of us.

Brad stood alone on his mark with an embarrassed look and hands in the air.

'I'm sorry, guys. It must've been something I had for lunch.'

Laughter rose with the fumes of the stink bomb Hedlund had set off.

'My wife used to fancy you,' one of the grips finally said. 'She's going to be very disillusioned to learn about your intestinal problem.'

Movie making is seriously hard but it's hardly serious. We're in the toy factory, kids. Paint a smile and push on.

Despite a budget that practically had him clipping coupons, Colin had agreed to a 'companion flight' in my deal. It was a fairly outrageous request on my part, wheedling an extra business-class airfare because I knew I was in a bargaining position. Of course, neither of us suspected at the time just how parsimonious the production would become. But I'd asked and he agreed.

'I can't put it in writing,' he said at the time, 'but I'll give you my word.'

Good to his word, Margaret got a ticket to join me for five days in Malta. This was reduced to four days when US Attorney General John Ashcroft, in one of his Friday Night Fright modes, issued an orange alert. No one really knew what that meant but it was just one shade under red, which meant the world was ending. Somehow Margaret's name showed up on a no-fly list and her ticket was confiscated. It took a full day for the bureaucrats to figure out that my wife, though a Democrat, wasn't a terrorist and Ashcroft allowed her to leave the country.

It was good of her to come – though after arm-twisting our producer to get her here, it would have been really bad for her not to come. But it wasn't a great visit for either of us. She arrived with a cold. A battle with the stills photographer had escalated into a memo war that reached the studio, making it look like we couldn't play nicely together and sapping precious time and attention from both my job and my wife.

It wasn't until day three of her trip that Margaret got over her sniffles and jet lag and our creative producer, Diana Rathbun, negotiated a truce in the publicity department. I took Margaret to the beach set, introduced her to Brad, Eric Bana (our Hector) and some of my crew mates. We had dinner in the ancient capital of Mdina and visited the Hypogeum, a wondrously preserved 5,000-year-old necropolis. Then she flew home. The brevity of her trip was more frustrating than revitalising for both of us. We didn't fight. We rarely even argued anymore. You need time to work through arguments.

My father gave up a good job with exotic travel after he married my mother. I wasn't that selfless. Margaret went into our marriage with eyes wide open but when reality struck, in the form of two children, in the cold glare of what her life would be attaching herself to my perpetual road trip, she saw things differently. I blamed her for backing out of our vows to be together, for richer or poorer, in Paris or Peoria. She'd signed a blank cheque. I should have known better than to fill in an unrealistic payment.

But doesn't love conquer all? Only in the movies. In the real world, love is a hydra-headed beast that needs constant feeding. It feeds mainly on two things: the desire and the time to be together. You can keep love alive with the former, but it wastes away without the latter.

There are defining moments in relationships. Snapshots of a dynamic. Ordinary. So insignificant in the instant, they only crystallise on reflection.

I'd returned home from a long location and Margaret told me she was going grocery shopping. I love grocery shopping. 'I'll come with you,' I said. Her shoulders slumped and she rolled her eyes. Rolled her eyes. It was nothing. Why would I even remember something so trivial?

'Okay, come if you want to.' It was a purely pragmatic response. It didn't require two people to push a grocery cart. She was used to doing it alone.

Did I want to be with her more than she wanted to be with me? I brushed it off.

My hope now was for a lengthy family reunion in Mexico. There were three months of summer break from school and many of the crew were already planning to bring their families for the duration of our stay. Margaret and I could nourish our love with time there. I'd make it a special memory for us all. Time would feed desire.

CHAPTER FOUR: BEST LAID PLANS

The turnaround from shooting days to nights is brutal. To make the adjustment in sleeping patterns, cast and crew must keep themselves awake into the wee hours before their report time switches from dawn to dusk. We were working six-day weeks, a scheduling necessity perhaps but not a popular one.

'You reach a point of diminishing returns after five days,' Brian Cox, our Agamemnon explained. 'When you start shooting six, you only get four and a half.'

While the main unit was on night shift, second unit continued covering various angles of the Greek captains, Achilles, Agamemnon, Atlas, Menelaus, Odysseus and their soldiers, landing and disembarking.

Second unit – sometimes called 'the action unit' or 'stunt unit' – is a separate entity with its own director that shoots independently, though often concurrently, with the main unit. Our second unit filming began on Golden Beach, a popular public recreation spot. The director was Simon Crane, whose long list of credits included *Braveheart* and *Titanic*.

The second unit normally works without stars. But many of the scenes in this film required Brad to do his own stunts. His double, David Leitch, would step in for the long shots but much of the action in this sequence would track Pitt from Achilles' ship to the Trojan beachhead. The Greek invasion and attack on the Temple of Zeus would be filmed in Mexico. We would shoot the landing in Malta.

My job here was waiting around for something to go wrong. Brad Pitt on a public beach was an obvious formula for media mischief. I'm not a security guard but it's my responsibility to safeguard the production's embryonic marketing efforts. Whoever controls the images controls the impact, and studios hate losing that control. Since our star hadn't approved one of a thousand unit-photographer shots submitted ('I don't like any of them'), Warner Bros. was helpless. The movie's important first-look photo – the image that would represent *Troy* in the run-up to release – was open to anyone with a long lens.

The paparazzi were being kept at bay by our security team on Golden Beach. But they couldn't control an entire public beach. Splashed across newswires the next day was a picture of Brad, in full battle armour as Achilles, talking on his mobile phone. Not releasing our own photo before this was a major fumble. (Idiot alert: all publicity is not good publicity.) But stars rule the movie galaxy with the power of gods and we here on Earth can only serve what's given us through contractual photo approval.

Maybe we could reposition the film as a time-travel adventure.

Brad had a day off to make his turnaround to the main unit, having spent the previous week leaping from his warship. For this and other stunts our star performed, he was well trained by assistant stunt coordinator Wade Eastwood. However, the background actors playing Achilles' fighting men were untrained and under strict orders not to heroically leap off the boats. These were strong, athletic men, and several of them couldn't resist. Two of them broke their legs.

Warner's had *Time* magazine targeted for its first press visit. Writer Jeff Chu was based in London and was having trouble finding an available date. That was fine with me because there hadn't been a revised shooting schedule published in weeks, which meant I didn't know when you-know-who was you-know-where.

I got a late-night phone call saying Jeff had a sudden window over the next two days. I scrambled to get approvals and he was on set for our first day inside the walls of Troy – absent Achilles, of course. *Time*'s arrival opened the gates.

The studio had been pressing me to schedule days for an international press junket that would involve a dozen territories. They had to arrange flights from Europe, Japan, Australia, so they needed advance notice. I'd spun a wheel on the calendar and it landed on the second day of *Time*'s visit. With help from my assistant Lizzi, we managed to get eight actors, plus Wolfgang, for interviews between filming breaks and during lunch.

The third column of media invaders, the Germans, for whom Wolfgang was more popular than bratwurst, had already crashed through my barricade. I gave *Stern* magazine an opening – not knowing whether you-know-who was… you know – because the writer promised his story was exclusively on Wolfgang. Holm Dressler, from German television network ZDF, was another friend of our director and had flown to the island to film portions of a Petersen documentary. He was phoning daily to see when he might get his crew on set. I overlapped his visit with *Stern* magazine.

Another front opened in the person of Kate O'Toole, Peter's daughter, who was invited by her father to do a profile on him for the Irish edition of the *Mail on Sunday*. It was only a profile and who could say no to a legend? Not that he gave me a choice. It turned out her agenda wasn't exactly as stated and her *Ireland on Sunday* piece was the first production story to come out – breaking Warner's agreement with other publications that consented to hold their articles for the release of the film. I was the patsy who'd passed along Kate's disingenuous assurances.

The London *Daily Mail* printed a story about Brad being 'dark' and 'stormy' on set because he was on steroids. After a flurry of phone calls – from me, his personal publicist and his lawyer – they retracted it but not before the *New York Post* picked it up.

Studio-sanctioned press visits – along with swarms of paparazzi, tabloids and local press whenever we shot outside the fort – would continue without pause for our remaining four weeks in Malta. The next two weeks were in the undiminished heat of days. Then we returned to nights to finish our filming here and nearly the crew along with it. More than a third of those who'd flown in from Britain were on antibiotics.

I was determined to stay healthy for Mexico, watching my diet and alcohol intake, exercising at the Fort Ricasoli gym as much as I could. We all work through illness, then allow our bodies to collapse when the job is over. But this movie was months from ending and I had to be on form for summer when my family arrived. So much was riding on that. We'd never been together for a full summer. If it was a positive experience, there would be more. I already wanted more.

I skipped the turn-around party, in which cast – including Brad – crew and even Wolfgang stayed out dancing in Paceville until 4 a.m. to reset their body clocks for night work. I managed to sleep 'til late morning. With a 4 p.m. crew call, I had the afternoon free and decided to drive to the capital city of Valletta for some sightseeing. I was inside the sixteenth-century St John's Cathedral, staring at one of the two magnificent Caravaggios on display there, when I got a phone call from producer Diana Rathbun.

George Camilleri was a 39-year-old bodybuilder and former Mr Malta. He was one of the extras who'd broken his leg while jumping from Achilles' boat. The other extra had fully recovered but Camilleri's leg clotted, causing a heart attack. Sometime after being released from hospital he suffered another heart attack. He was rushed to intensive care where he died of an embolism.

It didn't take long for the press to be all over this and embellish the story from Camilleri being a background actor to being one of the stars of the film to being close friends with our star. Specious news articles continued as Warner Bros. negotiated compensation. Rathbun asked me to spend the day at the second unit set on Golden Beach. The police were due to stop by for 'questioning' and who knew how many press would follow?

'I can't wait to get off this damn beach,' Simon Crane voiced my sentiments. He'd been up half the night talking with nervous Warner executives about the stunts Camilleri and other extras had done against his orders.

No media accompanied the police but stories and anecdotes about the deceased's 'close' relationship with our star cropped up throughout the week. Nothing I could do about them. To deny is to perpetuate.

I have never been a dad who came home every night, but I'm a full-time father when I am home and I've tried to be a daily presence in my children's life over the phone. The six-hour time difference combined with a heavy workload, frequent day/night shifts and covering two units made me less successful on this trip.

At 2 a.m., Margaret called. She was upset.

My office window at our house in Ithaca overlooked a detached garage that had a loft I'd designed as a kind of clubhouse for my boys. A previous attempt at converting a deer blind into a treehouse was a doomed experiment in Upstate New York winters. Casey, in another declaration of independence, had moved his bedding from our house into the loft and begun camping there. Eventually, I helped him move his bed and a dresser.

Margaret was phoning from my office where she happened to look out the window into the loft where Casey and Sam had some friends over. She saw them smoking marijuana.

Restraining a mother's instinct to leap through double-paned glass across a fifty-foot span of driveway to grab them by their delinquent throats, she asked me to talk to them – our version of 'wait 'til your father gets home!' My wife and I had differing views on the severity of this transgression. I suggested she take a few deep breaths and sleep in confidence that her designated disciplinarian would deal with it tomorrow.

The next afternoon, at an arranged time, I found a quiet place with mobile reception behind the Temple of Apollo. Both boys were contrite. I had to tell Sam to stop beating himself up over it.

'I'll never do it again, Dad.'

Don't say that. But wait until you're older.

'Maybe after I turn fifteen this summer.'

Maybe a little older.

'Will you be here for my birthday?' he changed the subject.

Absolutely I will. (Movie-speak for 'I hope so.')

Casey sensed his freedom was at stake.

'I don't want to have to move back into the house.'

With freedom comes responsibility.

'I know. I'll tell my friends never to bring it to where I live.'

Both signed off by telling me how much they missed me.

Oh, how I was missing them.

The homecoming parade for Hector and Paris through Troy's main thoroughfare reminded me how long it would be until my own homecoming. We were less than a third of the way through filming. But the boys' school was nearly over and our summer in Mexico was fast approaching.

On Monday night, the ancient city slept as Odysseus and his men – Sean Bean and Simon Crane's stunt performers – crawled out of the belly of the wooden horse and opened the gates to let in the Greek soldiers. The streets were about to become an inferno.

Agamemnon's men burned and pillaged through the rest of the week. Stuntmen ran through fires and break-away façades, stuntwomen fought off rapists and were thrown from towers, stunt performers stabbed, punched, tumbled down steps, fell over balconies and hung from the sides of buildings.

Our last night of shooting in Malta, Brad finished his close-ups before midnight, then stayed past 3 a.m. to sign autographs for the Maltese crew. He also stood for a special photo with the daughter of one of our drivers. She would be leaving for a series of leukaemia treatments in London and the crew had taken up a collection to fly her family out with her.

After Brad was gone, we burned his wax dummy in a funeral pyre.

Farewell, brave Achilles. See you in Mexico.

CHAPTER FIVE: GROUNDWORK

The first thing a crew does upon arrival in any new location is complain about their accommodations. My room's too small, I want a higher floor, I don't want to be next to the ice machine, I want to be next to so and so, I don't want to be anywhere near him or her, etc. These complaints are funnelled through the production office – where the rush to change rooms during our first few days in Mexico resembled a ninety-per-cent-off sale at Walmart.

There were two main hotels: the Estancia, for actors, filmmakers and key department heads; Villa del Palmar for the main crew. I was offered a small room at the Estancia and was in the production office with my suitcase five minutes after seeing it.

Villa del Palmar was a mid-range, beachfront resort with 1980s rock music blaring from 11 a.m. until 10 p.m. It had a two-tiered swimming pool dividing children's side from adults by an arched wooden bridge. The children's pool featured a slide in the form of a killer whale. The one-bedroom suites had a full kitchen, a balcony with plastic furniture and an unobstructed ocean view. It was a comfortable place to bring the whole family.

That was the one thing I found depressing about it.

Margaret and I usually conferred about everything of importance. When offered a job, I'd ask her before saying yes to it. If the boys needed something significant, she'd confer with me before saying yes or no. When we'd discussed them all coming to Mexico for the summer, she'd said, 'Let's see,' but in my mind, it was only a question of dates.

Our first conversation from Cabo San Lucas changed that.

Margaret had enrolled our sons in a month-long music camp in Los Angeles. It was limited enrolment and they had to send an audition tape to get in, she told me. They'd just received their acceptance. They were excited about it, she added, sounding very excited for them. She would bring them to visit me for one week in late August.

One week.

'We all can't wait to see you!'

There once was a time when I would've screamed, 'Do you know what this means to me? To us? To our family?' But the years had taken that fight out of me.

Instead, I asked if she could come ahead of them.

Her answer took the heart out of me.

'I've already made other plans,' was how it started. 'Sorry' was in there somewhere. But I'd stopped listening.

I'm here to work, I reminded myself when we'd hung up. That's the only reality I have. My wife and children are a pleasant fantasy, disembodied voices on a phone line. Keep them in your heart but not on your mind. Work. Everything else is quicksand. Work.

With military advisor Richard Smedley as ballast on my quad bike, we set off across the dunes to scout the Greek encampment at the beach.

The four-wheeled motorbikes were not easy to manage on this terrain. If you didn't accelerate into the hills, they'd get stuck. If you leaned the wrong way over one of the mounds, you were in danger of rolling and bringing the bike down on top of you. On an early scout, we nearly lost Wolfgang when his bike teetered and toppled over a dune. He managed to jump out before it landed on him, but a less agile director might have been finishing the movie on crutches.

The bikes were not only tricky to handle, they were tricky to distribute. There were only fifty-two of them and production had tried to assign them to departments based on need. The greatest need was for those working on the beach rather than three miles away at the wall. Our base camp was set up behind the wall and most departments – grip, camera, props, wardrobe – needed regular transport to and from their equipment trucks throughout the day. Bike hijackings were a regular occurrence, as were fights over whose bike it was anyway.

A film crew runs on two things: catering and transportation.

These are departments I make quick friends with on a production. Part of that is based on empathy. Catering and transport work the longest hours, receive the most complaints and – along with the publicity department – are marginalised because they're considered tangential to the actual filming.

Another reason I make a special effort to get to know the people in catering and transportation is that they can be valuable allies. While they may sometimes need me at the end of a show to get them autographed pictures of the stars or souvenir hats that the production office distributes to everyone on set but rarely remembers to give anyone on the lunch wagon or in a transport van, I need them almost daily.

My lunch hours are irregular. Sometimes I'll eat early with the drivers, sometimes I'll have to ask for a takeaway to eat at my desk because lunchtime might be the right time to do business with an actor or director. Sometimes, I'll forget to remind the caterers that a press junket of fifteen is joining us today. So, my relationship with catering is important.

And the transportation department – that group of tireless professionals on whom we all depend for safe passage from points A to B – was never more crucial than on this vast set.

Welcome to our collective nightmare.

No one could figure out why these people were working on this movie.

All the drivers and three – count them, *three* – transportation captains were locals with virtually no movie experience. Another cost-saving measure or something slightly more sinister? Perhaps *un sacaron*: an arrangement in which individuals of persuasive means or connections are awarded monetary considerations for doing nothing except not getting in the way. Whatever it was, it was dysfunctional – emphasis on the *fu*.

One got the feeling that the hands of the American transportation coordinator (head of the department) were tied. Mario was a highly experienced guy, albeit with a surly nature and monosyllabic vocabulary, who had been captaining or coordinating for twenty-five years. There seemed to be a two-tiered system and the one for moving heavy equipment – cranes, cherry pickers, sand-smoothing rake trucks – worked pretty well. The one for moving crew between base camp and two remote sets was a broken-down oxcart.

It was with naïve bonhomie that I approached the transportation trailer for the first time, a few days into the shoot. The bars on the 'reception' window should have served as fair warning but I just regarded it as a funky piece of equipment with which a production makes do in a developing country.

Discovering the photographer had absconded with our department's quad bike, I needed a ride for my EPK cameraman to cover the Trojan archers' assault on the Greeks at the beach.

I didn't yet know about transportation's impenetrable matrix, so I tried the door. It was locked. A woman's face appeared behind the barred window.

My high-school Spanish was about as colloquial as a robot butler but I always thought an attempt at something other than English showed a certain grace and humility. I wanted her to like me and made a sacramental offering of my bad accent and horrible grammar.

Yo tengo trabajo en la playa – I have work on the beach and we need – *nosotros necessitamos* – a ride.

'Who are you?'

Well, I'm a member of the crew, I should've said. See, I have this crew badge that we all wear around our necks to distinguish us from the tourists.

Instead, I introduced myself and my videographer.

'Come back later. We got nobody here now.'

Don't you have a radio? Couldn't you call somebody?

She walked away. A long minute later, I heard her on a transmitter talking with someone in Spanish. She returned to the window.

'Wait there.' She pointed to some vague spot in the middle of the road.

After about fifteen minutes, a driver pulled up and piled us into a jeep.

This was going to be a tough bunch to charm.

Small things can make a big difference in the life of a film crew: clean bathrooms at base camp, an appetising vegetarian option for lunch, a hotel bar that stays open late. A shooting schedule. First and second units finally got a printed outline of the work ahead, from mid-July through early September.

In addition to enabling all departments to plan supplies and equipment, our schedule gave us an idea of how we might plan for our post-*Troy* lives. It gave us a wrap date. The last page is the first page any of us turns to when handed a shooting schedule. The new end date had been revised from 2 September to 8 September.

A word about wrap dates: don't count on them.

A film ends when it ends, not when the schedule says it's going to end. At best, an end date is a goal. It's also a bit of trickery for the psychological well-being of cast and crew and the pacification of a studio.

Most people who choose a life of itinerant labour in the fields of film production have low boredom thresholds. If they wanted high-paying jobs without an end date, they would have gone into banking or BMW repair. As much as we all put our hearts, heads and backs into the job at hand, we all – at some point during filming – start looking forward to its conclusion. And we start lining up our next movie.

Leaving a movie before it wraps is one of the cardinal sins of the film business. Unless you've notified a producer or director in advance of being hired that you have a hard 'out' date, you risk being labelled disloyal. Not only does that screw you for future employment with your current director/producer, the word spreads.

So, when a movie goes over schedule you're faced with a choice: remain loyal and cancel a job you've been offered in hopes you don't default on your mortgage while waiting for the next one or shut the door on your relationship with your current employers. A film that exceeds its end date is not just a problem for the studio and the producers, it's a dilemma that affects everyone on a production.

And September in this part of the world was hurricane season.

Arriving at our base camp around lunch hour on Friday were Warner Bros. top three executives: studio President and Chief Operating Officer Alan F. Horn, President of Production Jeff Robinov and my friend Dawn Taubin, President of Marketing. Dawn was a social friend, not just a business acquaintance. I knew her family, and our kids played together whenever my sons were in LA.

The executives met for three hours with Wolfgang, Diana Rathbun and Colin Wilson. The conversation was ostensibly to discuss potential release windows for the movie. Heads of a studio don't fly a thousand miles for something they could discuss in a thirty-minute conference call. When they emerged from the meeting, I had a few moments to talk with Dawn before the limousine whisked them off to Warner's private jet. I knew better than to ask about the meeting. However, I did have one question: 'You think I'll make it home in time for Sam's birthday on 26 September?'

'I hope so,' she said in a tone that sounded more hopeful than reassuring.

A producer's job is to put all the money on the screen. You can skimp on stationary but not on scenery, use cheap replica set dressing where you can but real antiques where you must, employ as many local resources as possible but import what you need to make the movie look right.

Colin had consulted with Wolfgang and Simon Crane and they'd concluded that the Mexican extras would be fine for long shots and group movement but for anything closer, they'd need athletes with a Mediterranean complexion and legs that looked good in short skirts. So he contacted an athletic club in Bulgaria.

Two hundred and sixty muscular young men arrived in Cabo San Lucas, lured by the promise of a two-month Mexican fiesta – and a little bit of acting. They weren't being paid much – and a percentage of their salaries went to the company that contracted them – but they wouldn't mind working all day in the hot sun, provided they were free for a hot time at night.

Anticipating his Bulgarian press gang would be drinking themselves to insensibility if they were anywhere within crawling distance of a cantina, Colin arranged for housing in the middle of nowhere, ten miles out of town, with crew buses only to and from location. The young men might have come to party but the filmmakers had brought them here to perform.

Strong-willed, resourceful, sex-starved lads would find their way to share in the fun, pooling taxi rides into town on weekends. Some would also end up getting rides from women on the production. It's not only male crew who go for sexy extras in short skirts.

Our location commute was a twenty-minute drive from the hotels to an unpaved turn-off marked by signage directing vehicles over a rutted dirt road through one of the poorest villages any of us had seen in any part of the world. It had a handful of generator-powered cement houses, but the majority were scrap shacks without plumbing or electricity. The dust that blew over our vegetation-stripped set whenever a breeze kicked up was full of God-knows-what bacterial elements from a lack of sanitation in the village.

The day of Patroclus's dying scene found Garrett Hedlund lying in a pool of fake blood on the sand near Apollo's Temple. He'd just had his throat cut by Hector.

It was probably a cameraman who noticed it first: the sand was moving.

Garrett stayed on his mark until the cameras had got the shot, then jumped up, striped off his breastplate and started brushing off what he could reach of his back. Shocked crew came to his aid.

The spot on which Patroclus had been slain was crawling with maggots.

How do you say 'don't drink the water and don't breathe the air' in Bulgarian?

Regular emails from my boys brightened my inbox. They were having a good time at music camp, each in his own band, learning new chops and collaborating with other talented young musicians. I had to concede it was probably the right choice for them. Margaret, meanwhile, was spending the month with friends in Seattle and her brother in Idaho. Phone calls were out of sync and we'd be out of contact for days. She was always on my mind but I felt her absence – and a tinge of resentment – most deeply at night when the crew would gather at the poolside bar and increasing numbers of spouses and girlfriends were introduced into our film family.

I was feeling lonely. Not horny-lonely, certainly not without-companionship-lonely, but unconnected, unanchored, uncared-for-lonely.

I had breakfast Sunday morning with Brian Cox. He was also feeling a little uncared-for. All the actors were. They were peeved about being called to set by the ADs only to 'sit around all day' and be told just before wrap, 'You're not needed.'

'I think it's left over from the British class system,' he said. 'Here to serve your lordship. American films don't do that.'

Really, it just was *that time* in the movie for all of us. Hump time. Curse-it-and-get-over-it time. Exhale and suck it in. Repeat as needed until it's fun again.

Like most complaints about production peccadillos, Brian's masked a deeper suffering. He had a year-old son who, along with his wife, Nicole, he was aching to see. He was roaring like a caged tiger, not because the zookeepers were rude but because he was separated from his mate and cub.

That primal ache had dulled in me. Still, as July crept toward August, I cast longing glances at the date of my family's arrival. That vision sustained me through days of press demands, unrelenting heat, an unpredictable schedule and the silliness of chores that cause us to lose our sense of the absurd.

CHAPTER SIX: TWO UMBRELLAS, PLEASE

When I first interviewed my assistant Lizzi, I saw a tight-lipped young woman with a tough shell and no sense of humour. Not long after we started working together, the shell cracked and the humour showed up droll and sly.

Lizzi was half-Maltese and half-Australian, a fairly common combination I later learned, as many Maltese had escaped to Australia during and after WWII. She was slightly built with a pretty face that featured sharp cheekbones and big brown eyes. Her toughness revealed itself as a stubborn self-respect. She was dedicated to her job, willing to apply herself to whatever tedious or ridiculous tasks she was assigned. So she wasn't fazed when I handed her an umbrella and asked her to keep the crickets quiet in the bushes near our EPK interview area.

Arranging actor EPK interviews during production requires several things: a quiet space near the set that shows some of the filming background, a twenty-minute span between scenes when the actors are available and willing to talk, coordination with the ADs to ensure the subjects aren't needed elsewhere, coordination with hair, make-up and wardrobe to make sure they look good. Sometimes it requires a little luck.

Opportunity knocked shortly after we arrived at location as a threatening overcast delayed filming. The production decided not to fight the weather and rigged a tent to shoot a cover scene. That left about a half-dozen actors who were supposed to be on the battlefield, sitting around stewing, wondering why they weren't released to go back to the hotel. That wasn't something the AD department were willing to do. They were therefore delighted to use EPK interviews as a means of keeping the talent occupied. First AD Gerry Gavigan set his assistants in motion getting our subjects ready.

I borrowed some high-backed chairs from the props department and behind-the-scenes cameraman Steve Wacks set up at the side of Troy's immense wall. Lizzi went to tell the ADs we were ready for the first actor, Brendan Gleeson.

Just as Brendan sat down, a light drizzle appeared. Not a big problem. I sent Lizzi for umbrellas. I held one over the interview chair to keep our subject dry; Lizzi held one over the camera. Wacks rolled tape. Producer Sam Hurwitz asked his first question.

Unfortunately, you could hear neither the question nor Brendan's answer because a swarm of crickets in a nearby thicket of sage started having a party. Allen, the soundman, suggested that if you stood near the sage and opened and closed an umbrella, it would shut them up long enough to get some decent audio. So, Lizzi trotted off into the thicket in her low-top sneakers. A single 'ouch' as a thorn tore into her ankle was the only sound we heard.

Starting again. First question…

The misty rain continued, Lizzi snapping away on cricket duty while I kept my umbrella over the head of our subject and Wacks covered his camera body in plastic. In the middle of Hurwitz's third question, a roar went up from another part of the vast open space. The Mexican extras were engaged in a game of tug of war.

Interview paused again while I announced, '*Silencio por favor. Hacemos un interview*,' as nicely as I could.

Alright, camera ready? Umbrellas ready? Action.

Then the quad bikes started.

We moved our set-up so the Great Wall would buffer most of that sound.

Okay, all reset. Brendan, can you tell us…?

The rumble of a fifty-foot crane moving into place behind the wall halted Hurwitz in mid-sentence. The rigging crew began lifting lights onto the parapet.

We thanked Mr Gleeson for his time and Lizzi went to tell the ADs our interviews were over. The next day, I visited the production office to see if we might reserve a quiet room at the actors' hotel. The interviews wouldn't have a sexy on-set backdrop but at least we wouldn't need umbrellas.

Lizzi and I drove to the location Friday morning to get some make-up supplies and a couple of director's chairs to take back to the Estancia where our assistant coordinator, Boo Motjuoadi, had arranged an empty penthouse suite in which we could do our interviews.

Cruising along the main road north, we passed a lengthy cortège of well-built, half-naked men walking in the opposite direction.

Back at the office, I started receiving phone calls from local press – despite begging the production office not to give out my phone number (email only! *Por favor*). They were asking about the big parade. I could honestly respond with, '*Yo no se' nada*.'

I phoned Diana Rathbun.

Our Bulgarian extras had walked approximately thirty miles from the set to their hotel in protest over their wages. They were earning $30 per day, plus a small per diem, and found out the Mexican extras were getting $50. Rathbun was not unsympathetic. These were skilled athletes and their demand for equal salary sounded reasonable to her. However, she was not the producer in charge of negotiating such things.

I avoided further media inquiries until I could speak with Colin. He was understandably busy. I was in mid-dinner with the EPK guys when he returned my call to explain production's side of the story.

The Bulgarians were provided housing – albeit a little remote and shared – and had been flown to Mexico at great expense. Our producer had made his deal through a subcontractor – ironically called Bright Ideas – and if the employees had a beef, it should be with them, not us. As far as Colin was concerned, they were in breach of their contracts – though he was light on detail about how that might be enforced.

Meanwhile, messages from local press were piling up. The unit publicist is not authorised to speak on behalf of the studio about matters like these without consultation. But tomorrow was Saturday and the studio was closed at this hour. I did make the decision to ignore the press messages that kept coming all night based on basic publicity logic: it was too late to stop the few broadcasts on the evening news and, at the time they went on air, there was nothing to report but an unusual sighting along Route One. As for print press, lacking information to turn an item into an article, newspapers would forego publishing on Saturday and gather string to break a bigger piece on Sunday.

I spent the night putting together a statement that I ran by the producers the next day. Diana thought it was a little too harsh; Colin thought it was a little too soft. But Wolfgang approved it with only minor amendments.

I sent it to the studio VP on her day off.

The message came back: we don't want you to say anything.

Stories ran in all the local papers on Sunday, a newspaper's biggest circulation day, with multiple inaccuracies – calling it 'a riot', misnaming the extras as 'the crew of *Troy*' and, most damaging, claiming they were Mexicans not Bulgarians.

Mexican workers mistreated by Hollywood movie in Mexico!

Ultimately, I was permitted to deny reports the production had shut down. We were 'continuing to work'. That was it. *Nada mas.*

Maybe withholding information was the wisest course, maybe not. But the problem with production publicity being run from corporate offices by people who don't know beans about production is that they don't know beans about production. Bad press on location hurts. Locations are sensitive – especially small towns. An influx of hundreds of outsiders with per diem in their pockets, even in a resort hub accustomed to the go and flow of rich *Yanquis*, will be welcomed by some and not by others. There was already a groundswell of resentment toward the film crew amongst some of the locals. It would eventually erupt.

Various misrepresentations of the extras' walkout continued running in the local newspapers all week. Those stories bled into local impact articles. Some positive: jobs created and money spent here by the production. Some negative: not every shop and restaurant owner was singing our praises. If two decades in the publicity racket had taught me anything, it was that few people remember positive stories.

Colin solved his problem by firing 'the ringleaders' and shipping them back to Sofia on the next plane out. The public-relations problem continued festering. More negative stories about environmental impact and misbehaving crew began to appear in the local press.

Warner's publicity kept lining up a steady stream of American and international visitors, and I was trying to divine dates from an out-of-date schedule to book visits. The month of August looked safe as Brad's work with second unit on the beach was unlikely to change.

Most of the requests that I received directly – that is, not through the studio – were either for general production stories or interviews with Brad. The Pitt press I rejected without studio consultation unless it was something big that could be done after filming wrapped. Some of the more important requests for production stories I sent on to Warner Bros., although they already had most of the key media covered.

One intriguing inquiry came from a journalist for London's *Sunday Times Magazine* about a potential cover story on Peter O'Toole. It had surprised me that there wasn't more interest in him. I'd thought that his return to the epic was one of the most interesting angles we had. This journalist made her pitch just that way: O'Toole returns to the big canvas.

I looked up her previous work and didn't find any film or celebrity features. But I did read a story she wrote about the aboriginal people of South Africa and Namibia. She was a good writer. I forwarded the request to Warner's. They sent back their approval, pending approval of the subject. I ran it by Peter's agent who ran it by Peter who told me on set the next day that he was fine with it, provided the writer didn't expect a lengthy interview during filming. He would have lunch with her in London when he returned home.

The writer's name was Nicola Graydon. She'd included a

phone number. I called her to say I'd try to find an open date when Peter was working – without Brad – probably in September. We talked for a few minutes. She laughed at one of my jokes.

Long separations from one's partner aren't just painful in and of themselves but events occur that are important for husband and wife to share in person, not just over the phone. When you don't spend enough time together, odds are greater that you'll miss those times when only enfolding arms have meaning.

My wife phoned in tears to tell me our dog Gershwin had died. He was in a kennel with our other dog, Oliver, when he collapsed and never got up. He'd been on thyroid medication and needed to drink lots of water. The kennel would claim he'd been given both. He was only eight years old.

It was Gershwin's lethargy in advance of his diagnosis that led us to suspect Casey's ennui might also be health related. It prompted us to visit the clinic in Syracuse where his kidney condition was confirmed. In that way, Gershwin may have saved Casey's life.

I'd got him from an animal shelter in Arizona when I was working on *Tin Cup*. It was a movie on which everyone in the mostly male cast and crew were drinking, wenching and playing golf. I was midway through a year of not drinking – to prove to myself I could do it – was faithful to my wife and didn't play golf. I needed a diversion and some non-drinking, non-golf-playing company. So I got a dog. I told Margaret I was hanging out with Gershwin, who she assumed was a crew member. Gershwin and I flew home during a break.

'Surprise, here's Gershwin!'

'Surprise, he's not staying here with me.' We already had two older dogs.

So Gershwin and I flew to my next location in Texas.

He went everywhere with me. He'd housebroken himself in a few days, knew how to be quiet on set and followed at my heel without a leash. Eventually, he got too big to fit in his shipping crate and Margaret saw how much the boys loved him. He became part of our pack. But he was always my dog. When our two older dogs died, we adopted a little terrier named Oliver who was more Margaret's kind of dog.

Only an animal lover could fathom the weight of the anchor I dragged around for days after his passing. But even an animal lover would be hard-pressed to understand why, in the aftermath of Gershwin's death, my mourning for him was entangled with thoughts of my marriage.

Margaret and the boys arrived at the airport in La Paz the day before my birthday, the third week of August. My spirits soared the moment I saw her, the moment she smiled, the moment I held her again. I was home. I belonged with them, to them. This was my true identity, husband and father. Not movie guy.

I still had my job to do but I would steal hours, entire days if I could, for family time. Wolfgang, my patron, my boss, my friend, would understand. He knew them; he knew what they meant to me. He knew me. And he knew we had precious little time together.

On set, he welcomed them like his own kin. Sam stood beside him at the video monitors. He asked Casey if he was still playing piano. He asked Margaret if she had any trouble crossing the border.

Film families appreciate the importance of nuclear families. Spouses get special greetings: 'Hey, your husband/wife's a great guy/lady.' Children get special treatment: 'You wanna hear this? Put on these headphones.' Most of the time, though, workers must work. Spouses and children don't spend much time on set. Their presence is acknowledged back at the hotel, in popular crew restaurants, in passing on the streets.

It's genuine respect. You've come all this way, knowing you'll be ignored all day, having disrupted your life to wait in a hotel for a partner who'll most likely want to talk shop over dinner and may be asleep before the children. Families are revered for the stability they provide those who have no stability in their work lives. They are our buoys and our beacons.

My life during that week was dedicated to my wife and children. I had a few press chores, which I dispatched as quickly as possible, then turned over to Lizzi. I led my family to the battleground where we watched a bit of the Ajax–Hector fight. Casey drove my quad bike (me steering) and Sam drove another, his mother on the back, down to the beach where I showed them the Temple of Apollo and the Greek ships. I took them to swim with dolphins in La Paz. We took long walks on the sand, body-surfed in the ocean and, at night, with the boys asleep in the living room, I closed the bedroom door, Margaret put on her new negligee and we made love.

On their last full day in Mexico, my work exploded.

We were anticipating turnaround to a week of night shooting on the beach when a voice came crackling over the walkie-talkies.

'Anyone know anything about the phases of the moon?'

They must have found someone because, by the end of the day, the next day's call sheet had to be revised. Apparently, the full moon had been creating tides that were eroding the sand under our heavy warships. The construction department had rigged joists under Achilles' boat but gave notice any further erosion could crack the ship in half. The boats had to be moved further up shore for safety – which made continuity a bit tricky: *weren't there cliffs in the background a minute ago?*

A new schedule was finally printed and the domino effect sent Lizzi and me scrambling to see how our press dates could be salvaged. Brad would now be working on first unit and I'd need to cancel at least one and probably both days of a visit from Asian and Australian journalists. The new schedule also meant that Rose Byrne would not be allowed to fly to Los Angeles to do a photo shoot for *Elle* magazine, which I'd been working for weeks to arrange. And Diane Kruger was now free to fly to London for an awards ceremony I'd previously told the UK office she couldn't attend. I was getting an ultimatum about visit dates from *Entertainment Tonight* and needed to confirm EPK interview dates for O'Toole and Bana before they wrapped filming.

I escaped to be with Margaret and my boys for one hour at Johnny Rocket's, where I wolfed down a hamburger, interrupted by six phone calls.

When I drove my family to the airport, my mind was on work, not on them. It had been a pressurised week of entertaining – rudely interrupted by my job. Once again, there wasn't enough time to establish rhythm and flow to any kind of life together. It was a song and dance for visitors. They were visitors in my life. I'd rarely felt so alone as I did watching them board the plane.

I was hurt and resentful. Surely, she could've found more time to be with me here. I was exhausted and depressed. I saw no point. I saw no future.

CHAPTER SEVEN: STORM WARNINGS

Film families cover up for their own. They will lie for a crewmate to preserve his/her foundation. 'I know he/she's missed you,' they'll say to a cuckolded spouse. They lie because they understand the paradox of loneliness in a crowd, the rootless and transitory nature of the life they've chosen. Contrarily, the appearance of an affair in front of these people you've come to know, shared photos of your kids and maybe even introduced to your partner is at least greeted with a raised eyebrow and sometimes a brotherly/sisterly arm around your shoulder sweeping you off for heart-to-heart counselling.

Sex and the single, or temporarily single, crew member on location can be a caprice, a pattern or a panacea for what temporarily ails you. It can be a passing fancy, an impetuous impulse after one-too-many tequilas or, as happens frequently enough to feed the hopes of the hopelessly romantic, the fated meeting of soulmates.

Like Helen with Paris, a fair number of the female crew were having unhappy hook-ups. Debauches with dissolute stuntmen, brushes with, then brush offs from the glamorous and influential. And there were those hunky Bulgarians. Morning after morning, a different department trailer was shaken by the sobbing of someone who regretted what little she could remember of the previous night.

A remedy was required before behind-the-scenes activities began resembling scenes from *Caligula*. I arrived on set to find one of our make-up artists circulating what looked like a petition. I asked her what it was.

'This movie is driving us mad,' she explained. 'We have a psychic masseuse coming here from England. I'm signing up people for massages. She works miracles. There are only a few appointments left.'

Sign me up, I said.

Back at the hotel, we were about to interview Peter O'Toole. Sam Hurwitz was understandably nervous. Peter had been known to drill those steel-blue eyes straight through a questioner's heart when he didn't like the question.

So Lizzi came up with the idea of buying a couple of bottles of champagne.

There are several actor stereotypes that will stay true to type in interviews: the taciturn too-cool-for-school young Americans from whom you get attitude and the briefest of answers that usually start with 'I dunno', the stiff-upper-lip English who'll respond to your questions like they were facing a military tribunal and the Irish who will take a question, begin telling stories and you just hope your camera battery doesn't run out.

Throw in a glass or two of champagne and I had no worries about Mr O'Toole.

Peter was the brilliant raconteur we'd hoped for and Hurwitz didn't have the opportunity to ask an unacceptable question. Not only did the interview go splendidly but he stayed around our comfortable EPK penthouse suite to finish the bottle and flirt with Lizzi, waiting with us for our next scheduled guest.

Brendan Gleeson was an accomplished fiddle player, as well

as a stellar actor and all-round good egg. He was flying home tomorrow – Hector had killed Menelaus two days ago – and he'd told Peter about a precious violin that had come into his possession. Peter asked him for a tune or two before he left town.

Brendan brought his violin to our interview space, took the instrument from its case, tuned, and as Lizzi, the EPK crew and I sat mesmerised, played a requiem that would melt the coldest heart.

Peter closed his eyes and waved his cigarette holder to the music.

'Exquisite,' O'Toole pronounced at the end. 'Can you play something more lively?'

Brendan obligingly broke into a reel.

Peter started tapping his feet.

Then he got up and began to piston his legs in time with the tune.

Then, ankle over aged knee, hopping, twirling, rapturously stomping like one of Michael Flatley's cloggers, he performed a jig! How amazing to witness the spring that remained in the 71-year-old legs of this chain-smoking sybarite.

His audience was so enraptured they forgot to turn on their camera.

While the publicity team were doing their interviews, the producers were having a closed-door phone conference with the studio bigwigs to determine how much more fuel there was to stoke the engine of this runaway train.

Would it be three more weeks, or five more or…?

The three-hour meeting, eating up a quarter of our filming day, turned into three meetings on consecutive days. Lizzi stood sentinel outside Wolfgang's trailer, hoping to read something from the filmmakers' faces when they emerged.

On the morning of the fourth day, a new, unofficial schedule was given to production designer Nigel Phelps who needed it most desperately to make sure sets were prepared in advance of filming. I looked at it over his shoulder as he moaned, 'I have no prep time between major scenes!'

Colin peered in from behind us. 'It changed at 3 a.m.' He walked away.

Factored into the filmmakers' calculations was an approaching hurricane.

A patch of sunlight sent the make-up department into battle, touching up the Greek troops. Soon though, rain began in torrents.

First unit retreated under a tent to film Achilles being awakened for battle, lying between two naked women. Lizzi had volunteered to be one of the naked women but, unfortunately, got her bid in too late for casting.

Sam Hurwitz and I drove back to the Estancia where his interview camera was set up for Garrett Hedlund, Sean Bean and Eric Bana. Eric had been ill but he fought through it to give us a great interview. After he finished, we stepped onto the balcony to watch the rising seas. It was eerily calm and the air was heavy. Predictions of a category-one hurricane had just reached the production's weather wire. 'I think I need to talk to someone about moving my room,' he said. His room was on the oceanfront side of the hotel. 'I'm worried about my family when this hits.'

At around 2 a.m., Hurricane Ignacio was downgraded to a tropical storm. The storm flooded a concrete basin that spanned the gap between the main road and the hotels. A car full of our crew, driving back from an aborted night's outing, were caught in the flood. They had to climb out windows and wade in waist-deep water to make it across. The car was found washed up on the beach the next day. Our sets withstood the gale-force winds, but some roads had been closed and traffic to our location had to be diverted. I dreaded thinking what the ragtag village on our normal route looked like.

Soon, 2 September, our original wrap date – day 103 of filming – rolled around and several of our crew abandoned ship for 'other commitments'. Wolfgang was not pleased. 'They'll never work on another of my movies.' A feeble threat to a British crew from an American director who made most of his movies in Los Angeles. But probably cathartic.

Colin Wilson's many skills as a producer included keeping information close to his vest and looking busy when approached with questions. He and Gerry Gavigan were working on a new schedule but, possibly because of the recent desertions, possibly due to the sticker shock of how much filming remained, there would be no printed plan forthcoming.

After chasing him relentlessly, he did allow his assistant Jen Teves to give me a glance at the schedule in progress. I found only two days that would be suitable for press. Everything else would have to be called off.

I also looked at the new end date: 26 September. Sam's birthday.

I knew Wolfgang would let me go as soon as my job here was finished. But there was one important task that I'd been told wouldn't happen before filming wrapped.

I found an opportunity to talk to Brad.

Look, I explained, the last assignment for me on this movie will be getting your EPK interview. I'd like to be home for my son's birthday.

'Absolutely. That's important. We'll work it out.'

After consulting with the studio publicity people, I rescheduled *Entertainment Tonight* and the Asian/Australian junket for the two remaining days when Brad wasn't on first unit – praying those days would be locked in. I emailed everyone else on Warner's wish list, telling them we couldn't accommodate.

Nicola Graydon, London *Sunday Times Magazine*, didn't respond.

Instead, I got a strange email – in ALL CAPS – from someone I didn't know.

HI, NICKY AND I ARE LOOKING FORWARD TO SEEING YOU IN MEXICO VERY SOON.

It wasn't until the next day when chatting with one of the make-up team that I learned it was the psychic masseuse. She and the writer were good friends.

I would send a return email and another and another, eventually resorting to ALL CAPS myself.

PLEASE TELL NICOLA THERE IS NO STORY. DO NOT COME!

Finally, I let it go. Psychic Masseuse could work her spells on all who'd signed up for her services – me included – but her pal the journalist could work on her tan by the pool.

I was not in good spirits.

Despite a careful diet, daily gym routine and imbibing mainly wine (*no ice!*), I'd ended up with a mild case of dysentery and an infection from a gash on my leg. I was taking pills for one and ointment for the other but going into my sixth month on this movie, I was clearly breaking down.

Calls home were becoming shorter and less frequent. Margaret was spending her days mixing the songs on her album, so we didn't talk much. I did speak with the boys every afternoon their time – my night. I called as much for my own reassurance as for theirs.

Then came the conversation with my wife I'd been trying to avoid until we could have it in person.

Margaret was telling me about Sam's audition for a new school play, how well Casey was progressing with his piano lessons, how the mixing was coming together on her album. She asked how the movie was going. I told her. In an effort to console, she said, 'All you have to do is stick it out for another ten years and you can retire.'

I suddenly thought of Gershwin.

Life is short.

She read my silence.

'You still want to retire with me, don't you?'

I could hear both umbrage and vulnerability in her question. I'd always been the one asking, 'Where do you think we'll be in ten years? Five years?' And she'd always responded, 'I can't think ahead that far.' Now, she was asking about our future.

'I don't know,' I answered.

A long pause. 'Well, I have to go now,' she said. She didn't want me to hear her cry. It was the first time I'd ever made her cry.

I shut off my phone and stared at my wedding ring. A minute that felt like an hour passed. I twisted the ring off my finger, laid it on the counter. The indentation from the band that had signified eighteen years of love and as many years of loneliness stared back at me. The absence of my ring felt strange. Putting it back on would've felt cowardly. In that instant, I couldn't contemplate what it meant. I only knew how it felt. It felt like I'd stopped fighting for my marriage.

The transportation department continued providing us with something to complain about besides the weather.

Cinematographer Roger Pratt's quad bike disappeared and Mario wouldn't give him another one. He spent the week hitching rides to Apollo's Temple.

The props department, already overworked and exhausted, needed to set up a tent in an auditorium on a day's notice and transport wouldn't get them a truck. They had to unload the prop truck at night, load up the tent, set up the tent, then come back and reload their truck before starting a full day's work on no sleep.

My car battery died and no one in the transport trailer had a pair of jumper cables. Lizzi tracked one down from a security guard two hours after everyone else had gone for the night.

The rain kept falling, followed by enervating heat and humidity. Gerry Gavigan and his amateur meteorology team were glued to weather reports like stranded seamen scanning for a rescue ship.

The actors were making wagers on when their remaining scenes would be shot so they could go home.

Wolfgang, normally the most press friendly of directors, was refusing to do any more interviews because he was in a battle with the studio. ('If I can't say anything nice, I shouldn't say anything at all.')

The production was running out of money and Colin was

ordering more cost cuts and questioning more expenditures, frustrating an already frustrated crew. Complaints turned into shouting matches.

Into this mayhem strolled London *Sunday Times Magazine* writer Nicola Graydon and Psychic Masseuse. It was 11 September. I draw no comparisons.

'We're here!' Psychic Masseuse squealed into my phone at the hotel. 'Can we meet you for a drink at the pool? Nicky's the pretty one.'

That was not going to make a bit of difference.

I'd just returned from another long, hot day shooting the opening scenes in our Thessaly Valley where Agamemnon calls on a reluctant Achilles to battle the Thessalian King's champion. I was tired and my stomach still wasn't right. I was just sitting down to my dinner of a head of lettuce (washed in bottled water) and a bottle of wine. But I wanted to put off this interloper before she could find a way around me and gain set access through cast or crew at the bar.

So, I met them.

Yes, Nicola was pretty: mid-thirties, hazel eyes above a button nose, perfect teeth, medium-length brown hair and a lace-up top with the laces undone just enough for a man in a more generous mood to admire the décolletage.

I was in no such mood.

'You're not getting on set,' I said shortly after hello.

She smiled. 'I know.'

'Oh, now,' Psychic Masseuse chided. She was all brass and flutter, unrefined and not at all the kind of head-in-the-clouds mystic one might imagine a 'psychic healer' – her preferred title – to be.

Nicola gave her a look that registered an end to further pleas on her behalf. She was resigned to her place on the sidelines and seemingly okay with giving up a byline for a few days of sun and surf, hanging out with her friend. I was a bit surprised at how easily she surrendered. With business out of the way, we proceeded to have a lovely evening, as drinks spilled into dinner.

The reason Nicola had turned our correspondence over to her friend was that she'd been in Ladakh.

Where?

It's a state in Kashmir in the Himalayan Mountains. She was there on assignment for *The Ecologist* magazine to report on the impact a globalised economy is having on a society that, not long ago, valued cooperation over competition.

'That's breaking down now because all the young people want to go to India or Pakistan and earn money to buy things.'

She'd been there for a full month.

'I planned to leave after two weeks but they only have flights out twice a month and, well, I missed mine.'

This was the best excuse for non-correspondence I'd ever heard.

She spoke a posh English but her flyaway hair and hippie-chic couture didn't match the lush voice. No doubt she could play the aristocrat – and had many times – but her roots were in the earth, like her South African father.

She was born in Johannesburg. Her parents moved back to London, her mother's home, when she was a toddler but they returned to South Africa regularly on holiday. Her fondest childhood memories were of camping in the bush with her family.

'One year we were by the Vaal River and my brother and I took a boat out. When we came in, we threw the oars to land.

But there was nothing for us to grab hold of. So we drifted out into the current. Dad ran toward us and the land shelved beneath his feet. All six foot four inches of him disappeared under water! We were terrified – until we saw his arm come up, holding his camera.' She laughed a full-throated laugh. 'My sister dove in to save us.'

It wouldn't be accurate to say she was unlike any woman I'd ever known. She seemed the composite of every woman to whom I'd ever been attracted: smart, self-deprecating, engaged, curious, outspoken, outrageous, courageous. Can someone's eyes really sparkle when they laugh? We talked about Africa. We talked about horses. We talked about everything but the movie. I became aware that my right hand was rubbing the indentation on the third finger of my left.

Back in my room I looked at tomorrow's call sheet: we'd have a second day at Thessaly with Brad. Then, after the weekend, weather permitting, we'd shoot the scene in which the Trojans find the wooden horse on the beach. With Peter O'Toole.

I called our *Sunday Times* journalist.

'Lemme talk to Peter. Maybe Monday.'

Was I compromising my publicity principles to ingratiate myself with this woman?

Piss off. It's a good story.

CHAPTER EIGHT: DANCING

Our sword master, Richard Ryan, was the latest to be hospitalised after passing out from heatstroke. He had plenty of company. Two of our department heads were being treated for typhoid, one of the make-up girls was recovering from a kidney infection and dysentery was running rampant. Brad nearly joined the ranks of the fallen when his chariot horse ran away with him up a sandy slope to Apollo's Temple. He managed to jump off without injury, but it was another trauma to his aching legs.

I had a hacking cough, but a soothing psychic massage helped. The massage was a little weird – as in stripping invisible demons from my 'soul body' – but it relieved some of the mounting tension in my shoulders. *Carrying the world on your shoulders?* Only my small world but I was dragging. I still had *Entertainment Tonight* and a dozen Asian journalists to take care of this week, along with a half-dozen more EPK interviews – including Brad, who had promised to do his on an expected day off, Friday the nineteenth.

It felt like the last stage of a race. Sam's birthday was the excuse I gave myself but the added impetus was the seismic crack I'd put in my marriage with the 'retirement' conversation. Was it repairable? Was I asking for a divorce? What did I want? And what were these feelings awakened by Nicola?

Psychic Masseuse was booked for the evening, so I had Nicola to myself.

This wasn't the first movie she'd been on, she told me. The one other was a John Boorman picture about the Truth and Reconciliation Commission in South Africa last year. She'd been working as a senior commissioning editor for the *Mail on Sunday* when the *Times* called and asked if she wanted the freelance assignment. When her boss at the *Mail* refused to let her go, she went anyway.

'It was a first-class ticket. I couldn't turn that down.'

She'd never been married but had two live-in relationships in her twenties and thought she'd found the love of her life at age thirty. 'He was beautiful and spiritual. It turned out he was also bipolar and off his meds.' She was thirty-nine now, no boyfriends, just a series of lovers in the intervening decade.

She asked about me.

I'd been married for eighteen years, I told her. Two terrific teenage boys.

Then I crossed the Rubicon. 'But… there are issues.'

'I know. My friend told me.'

I may have let something slip during my massage.

I had a second night with Nicola. This time Psychic Masseuse came along.

Theirs was a sisterly relationship – with the occasional twist of epistemological scholars discussing how many angels could fit in a salt shaker. The two would fall into what I can only call spirit-speak, filled with references to 'the ancestors'. They were both big into the ancestors. I'd just kind of nod until they changed the subject.

It was Saturday night and the bars were overflowing with *Troy* personnel. After dinner, we ran into Sean Bean, our Odysseus, and invited him to join us at a dance club.

The Aqua Bar was loud and crowded with the kind of techno music I hate. But the ladies wanted to boogie. Hips swaying, body undulating, head thrown back to the rhythms, I couldn't take my eyes off Nicola. After the second margarita, I didn't even mind the music. Soon though, the dance floor became impossibly crowded and, after she quickly downed her third margarita, the four of us moved on. Psychic Masseuse attached herself to Sean Bean like a barnacle.

The What's Up? Bar was a favourite of our film gang. It was a true local joint with Mexican music and karaoke. It had pool tables at the back and plenty of room at the counter. The locals were given preference at the karaoke mike, but now and then a gringo we knew would take a turn. I'd switched from margaritas to ginger ale just to sustain consciousness. In the back – alright, the forefront – of my mind was the possibility of Nicola, and I wanted to be able to respond should the opportunity arise. (Dog catches bus?)

Then she disappeared into the pool room. *Hey, give her a little space.* I retreated to a table where Orlando's friend Nick and a couple of the ADs were seated. I was content there for about an hour, chatting, listening to the karaoke – including a fair version of Eminem's 'Cleanin' Out My Closet' by Garrett Hedlund and a fully attitudinal rendition of 'New York, New York' from Owain Yeoman.

It was past 2 a.m. and my mind kept wandering back to Nicola. So I bought us each what I hoped was a last drink and headed off toward the pool tables.

There she was with our production designer, Nigel, her hand on his chest, her face inches away from his.

At that moment, PM passed by.

'Here,' I said, handing her both drinks. 'Tell your friend I left.'

It was nearly noon when I awoke on Sunday in need of a long walk to clear my head.

Who was that middle-aged moron last night hanging around like a stray after scraps? Nobody I recognised. I hadn't dated in twenty years. Did I even know *how* to be a single man in my fifties? What could have motivated me to make a fool of myself over a woman who could drink me under the table, whose best friend was a psychic masseuse and who apparently had no interest in me other than exploiting me for a story?

I was haemorrhaging self-doubt. It wasn't too late to reconcile myself to the sanctuary of marriage. Mine wasn't so bad. It was just unfulfilling. What is fulfilment? Getting up every morning should be fulfilling enough. Did I want to have affairs? Could I handle that? I'd not had much past luck at compartmentalising my love life but maybe with a little practice I could have satisfying flings and still stay married. Look at the French!

I needed a complete re-evaluation of my life.

I was almost out the door when my hotel phone rang.

'You disappeared last night.' There was a slight crack in her voice.

I had no reason to stay, I said, calmly as I could. I was under the impression we'd made a personal connection. But don't worry, our professional relationship is still fine.

A beat before she asked, 'What are you doing today?'

I'm about to go for a walk on the beach.

'Can I come with you?'

The beach stretched for miles in both directions from our hotel but was cut off to the west by resorts and bisected by a marina. On the other side of the marina was a sandy cove, above which was a house owned by Brad Pitt and Jennifer Aniston. We walked the length of the beach, around the marina toward the cove. She sprinkled chatter like the sea spray, none of it meaningful: *Quite a night, wasn't it? Sean was such a gentleman. I think I spoiled a pool game by 'potting' the black ball.*

I didn't say much.

She was shaky. Probably all the tequila. But there was something else.

'Why did you leave?' Her voice quivered.

I saw you pawing Nigel in the pool room. (To be honest, Nigel was the last guy I'd be jealous of in a room full of men, but he did outrank me. I suspected she might be working her way up the food chain.)

'I wasn't pawing Nigel. I was asking him things like how many pieces of wood he used to build the horse. And I'm short-sighted.'

Hmm.

We walked in silence for a few minutes. Then things started coming out. She was talking more to the sea than to me.

At age twelve, she'd lost her South African father. He died of a heart attack, but she believed he died from the stress of marrying into a world where he didn't fit.

'My sister holds my grandparents responsible,' she said. 'They were aspiring aristocracy and he was a train conductor's son. My mother remarried – another South African – but this one was a complete monster. I was glad to be away at boarding school in my teens. But I know it messed up my relationships with men.'

I put my arm around her. She fit perfectly. All the apprehension, tension, effort she'd been carrying seemed to melt as my hand rested on the warmth of her bare shoulder. We walked wordlessly for the longest time. At some point, she slipped her arm around my waist.

'I was just hoping to get you into bed last night,' I told her.

She laughed. Not a big laugh.

'I'm afraid I've got so good at putting off advances from men telling me how gorgeous I am that I probably don't even know when I'm doing it anymore.'

'You're not that gorgeous.'

That got her to look up and smile.

'How about we take sex off the table and spend the next few days getting to know each other.' She said okay, glancing up to read my face. Then she snuggled more tightly under my arm.

We continued walking and I told her a few things about the movie I probably shouldn't have. *The director's fighting with the first AD. Orlando's fighting pain from an old back injury. We're weeks over schedule.* Seeds of trust you don't sew in the fields of journalism. But she was no longer just a journalist.

When we arrived at the cove, it was only us and the seagulls.

'Should we go in?' she asked.

She had her swimsuit under her sundress and before I could respond, she was pulling the dress up over her head.

I was caught off guard by her spontaneity. When had I lost that?

God, she was gorgeous.

She dived into the water.

I awkwardly stripped to my briefs and waded in just above my knees.

I turned back toward the cliff and scanned the scattered few houses above us, wondering for a moment if Brad or Jennifer were watching.

The next day I took Nicola to the beach again. This time to our beach set where the Trojan Horse, tall as a house, stood waiting to be filmed. A starry-eyed Peter O'Toole heard advice from his high priest that this was a tribute from the Greeks and a worthy gift for the Trojan gods.

There is a dance that publicist and journalist engage in on a movie set. It can be courtly as a cotillion or clumsy as a couple of boozers in combat boots. The publicist must lead; the journalist has to follow. It doesn't work the other way around. The publicist can't be too stiff or too loose; the journalist must have freedom of movement within the frame the dance partner establishes. Finally, each must be able to signal to and anticipate in the other the turns and flourishes, dips and deviations the music of the set demands. We accomplished this without a misstep. I introduced Nicola to Peter who took her by the hand and led her to his chair, where they chatted for a few moments before I came to lead her away.

Less in step was Psychic Masseuse, who Nicola had coaxed me into bringing along. There are cruder terms for her but 'star stalker' will suffice.

'Stay away from the actors,' I'd warned.

The actors' chairs were under a tarp, a short stroll from the cameras. I could see PM from the corner of my eye, sidling toward the talent. I chased her off twice. But when I wasn't looking, she'd breached the border and stood beside Orlando Bloom, who was trying his best not to pay her any attention.

'Your friend is going to force me to make you both leave,' I told Nicola.

'Oh, I'm sure they're just talking about his massage.'

He'd had one?

Orlando shot me a look.

I led both women off the beach to my quad bike. I tried to hit every bump in the road on the way to base camp to bounce Psychic Masseuse off the back.

'You worry too much,' PM proclaimed in the car en route back to the hotel.

Nicola and I dined alone again that night as PM had another full schedule of massages. After dinner, we sat on the porch of her hotel room until PM reappeared. I took the opportunity for a sweet goodnight kiss while her friend showered.

'I think you gave up too soon,' she said.

Too soon as in…?

'I changed my mind. Come back to my room.'

'No, I think my friend needs me. She takes on so much negative energy when she works.' Then she added, 'Let's wait for tomorrow. It's our last night.'

Leaving tomorrow. No harm, no foul, no promises to keep. Of course, there was one to break. There was that. Backing out was still an option. Backing out, however, was not on my mind as I walked back to my room. *Wipe that stupid grin off your face. Think what it might mean.* But fear of consequences were quickly buried under the fantasy of possibilities.

Tomorrow came. Psychic Masseuse joined us for dinner but was too tired – or intuitive – to intrude beyond that. My imminently departing journalist wanted a farewell tour of our favourite cantinas, ending at the What's Up? Nicola screwed up her courage to register for a karaoke but Mexicans had the mike without break. We waited at a table alone.

'My friend gave me a right chewing out after you left the bar the other night.'

Do tell.

'She said I would flirt with a tree and I'd be single the rest of my life if I didn't straighten up.'

Is that what you want?

'I guess I don't really know what I want. I always thought someone would just come along and sweep me off my feet.'

Where was I with that? Two tequilas into the night, oblivious to the quagmire I could be stepping into. I was light years from wanting to be her 'someone'. Presuming she even threw that pitch in my direction. But it made me question whether I was more than just a lonely guy hoping to get lucky. A one-night stand with someone you liked/didn't love wasn't unheard of back in my single days. But I was starting to feel self-conscious about my naked left hand. She knew I was married – 'with issues'. She was cool with that. I just had to go with the flow. Had my libido completely drowned in a marital ditch?

Two more margaritas, please!

Troy cast and crew started filling the bar around midnight. They were just diving in to their first drinks when Nicola got her turn on the stage.

It had seemed like a lark when she signed up, playing out her popstar fantasies to a crowd of strangers who didn't speak English. Now with Orlando, Garrett and other familiar faces staring at her, all the tequila drained from her body and she gripped the stripper's pole in the middle of the stage to keep her knees from buckling. She squeezed the mike with a trembling fist and the music from Jewel's 'Hands' started playing.

'These hands are small, I know...' Her voice was barely audible.

I didn't have to look at the dead eyes of the locals or the frozen smiles of our movie mates to know it was the Worst.

Choice. Of. Karaoke. Song. Ever. All I saw was a fragile girl mustering enough courage to finish what she now regretted starting. Life in the shadows carries few risks and bravery means doing the things you're most afraid of.

I was intoxicated by her bravery.

She overcame first-verse jitters and got a nice round of applause from our film gang when she finished. She passed Orlando's table where everyone gave her a 'well done' and someone put a margarita in her still-shaky hand.

I was hoping that put the cap on our evening out. But on this, her last night in Cabo, given the choice between my bedroom and a barroom full of boisterous movie lads, she wanted to milk every minute out of her film-crew experience. Sometime around 1 a.m., I switched to ginger ale again. My subtle and not so subtle efforts at getting us headed toward the door were evaded until the last of our movie mates stumbled onto the deserted street.

The stars were 'like fairy lights', she said as we walked back to the hotel, arms around each other. There was starlight in her.

I walked through the dark of my room to a lamp, avoiding the switch at the door, holding her hand. She let go and headed to the bathroom.

I suddenly had no idea what to do with myself.

Should I undress? Should I undress in front of her? Should I put on some music? Should I change the lighting? I was nervous as a schoolboy.

She came out of the bathroom wrapped in a towel. She headed straight to the bed without looking back at me. She dropped the towel and allowed a quick glimpse of her silhouetted nakedness before crawling under the covers.

'I'll just lie here,' she said as she stretched out.

What? And think of England? Was *she* nervous?

I climbed in beside her, my heart pounding. Our eyes met in the dim light of the open curtains. She put her hand on my chest. I breathed. On my exhale, we kissed.

We slept late and made love again in the morning. There was a breeziness in the afterglow now, a lightness that whited-out all thought. I was out of my mind in the best of all possible ways: no past or future. She hadn't existed, even as a fantasy, a few days ago. She was an alien creature who would leave only a vapour trail. She was too gorgeous to be real.

I drove the two women to the airport in La Paz around mid-afternoon.

It was a sweet, sappy, cinematic farewell with lingering looks at the various checkpoints until Nicola's final turn to the boarding gates. There was no sadness, really. I was too filled with the delight of her. There were no promises except keeping in touch about Peter O'Toole. No plans ever to meet again.

Still, something was making me want to do a fandango and buy a sombrero. I had wings on my feet and could fly down the street. Love? What's love got to do with it?

I'd planted a flag of liberation. *Viva mi revolución!*

On the drive back to Cabo, my phone began ringing.

The schedule had changed again. Brad couldn't do his interview this Friday. It would have to be next Friday, the twenty-sixth – Sam's birthday. If we got it done early, I could still make the 5 p.m. flight out. I wouldn't be home on the date but I could be there for his party the following night.

My phone kept ringing. Business. Business. Business. Then…

It was Wolfgang's assistant, Barbara. 'I don't know if you've heard. There was an incident last night at one of the bars.'

Hostilities had been simmering between residents and film personnel since news was erroneously reported about 'Mexican' extras walking out over working conditions and inadequate pay. A few other snarky pieces had appeared in subsequent weeks about our local hires complaining of second-class treatment, some of which may have had a grain of truth but were likely spin-offs from the original story. There was also a report on the death of one of our real Mexican extras who had been hit by a truck walking home from the set. (Brad learned of this and anonymously donated $10,000 to the deceased's family.)

There had been a few complaints of shoddy treatment at restaurants and one or two tales of crew members who had to be pulled away from shouting matches with inattentive bartenders. But all the confrontations I'd heard about were of the vocal variety. Until our last Sunday night in Cabo San Lucas.

Cabo Wabo was the most popular bar in town. I'd been there once and found it too loud, too crowded and too tacky. It was owned by Sammy Hagar from the band Van Halen and played the kind of heavy metal rock I was a generation too late for. But it was a favourite hangout of our stunt team and other party-hard crew types.

Last night, a group of locals – including some of the bar's employees – were lying in wait for *Troy* gringos. A dozen of our crew were ambushed and throttled. Our key grip, Patrick, a gentle giant who never raised his voice, let alone his fists, was dragged into the kitchen and beaten unconscious with pots and pans. He was in the American hospital with a concussion and broken ribs. Other *Troy* crew who escaped through the back door into an alley were met by police and arrested for disturbance.

I drove to the hospital where I found our company nurse checking on the wounded.

'Pat has regained consciousness but we don't know the extent of the damage.'

Others had been treated and released. Eunice, our main stuntwoman was pummelled alongside Patrick when she tried to come to his rescue. Her injuries weren't as severe. She threw out a few more names. Many were my friends. If not for Nicola, I might have been out with them.

I shifted into crisis management mode on the drive back to the hotel. I'd have to find out if any of them were still in police custody. I should call Colin and ask what he knows. I'll get a list of everyone involved and call them individually to see if they're okay. Or might that be misinterpreted as damage control? What about damage control? I should put together our side of the story in case the press runs with this.

My phone rang again.

'Colin?'

'Hi, is this Rob, the publicist?' a sunny female voice inquired.

All I knew about her was she worked for a promotions company in London that threw parties where they wanted celebrities to show up. We'd traded emails when *Troy* was shooting in England but never spoken. None of the actors were interested in her parties but it was a friendly correspondence and I must have written something about going to Mexico and she must have written something like that sounds like fun and I must have said something like, come visit. It wasn't a memorable exchange – at least not for me.

Now she was phoning from the airport in La Paz. She and her friend Amy had just landed.

Uh, I'm kinda busy right now.

'That's okay. Where are you staying?'

A couple of hours later, I got another call, saying she and Amy were at the front desk of our hotel attempting to get a room. There were no rooms. But could I come say hello?

I strode to the lobby, impatient to get this over with. My pace slowed, my patience increased at the sight of a pretty Asian woman with a skirt that barely covered her ass, standing beside a statuesque blonde wrapped in a see-through sarong, long legs shaped by beach-inappropriate heels, leaning on the registration desk. Surprise Guest turned and smiled.

Hel-lo.

They shared my fold-out couch the first night. Amy found a room in town the second night. SG moved into my bedroom.

Shove over Conscience. The singles life might suit me.

SG was an actress, I quickly learned. She seasoned morsels of dialogue with references to parts she'd had in plays I'd never heard of and callbacks she'd had on big commercials in the UK and Europe – just Western Europe though, since 'they were poorly made and paid peanuts' in the East.

Ours were conversations that attempted to fill space:

'How is your meal?'

'This reminds me of a Mexican restaurant I went to in Shoreditch. What did I have there, hmm, let me think…'

There was never anything personal – just like the sex.

Uncomplicated sex had immediately become complicated by my guilt. Even the guilt was complicated. I wasn't sure who I was betraying: Margaret? Nicola? Myself? This lovely lady with whom I'd been delighted to climb into bed then didn't want to be in the same room with? She was already talking about visiting me in LA on the next job.

I kept busy all day wrapping up work chores and checking on our wounded. SG and Amy went boating on a private craft whose pilot kept suggesting they take off their tops.

On night three, Hurricane Marty struck.

It's the wind, not the rain that classifies tropical cyclones. To qualify as a hurricane, winds must be seventy-five miles per hour. Marty was a category two, coming in at around a hundred and heading north-west toward the tip of Baja, California. A portentous calm had sent seabirds and hotel guests to respective shelters. The wind rose in a rumbling bass to a bone-chilling crescendo as tides began to swell and the night turned violent. It sucked water out of the pool and spat it across the hotel patio. It scooped up unsecured furniture like shells on the beach, hurling it against windows and walls. Contortionist trees bent like supplicants.

There were two empty bottles of Merlot on the table next to the one I'd just opened. Surprise Guest was sleeping off her part of the first bottle in my bedroom. I watched the sea pounding lower-level rooms and listened to rain like a thousand tapping fingers on the roof. I felt the exhilaration of the siege, invincible behind a pane of glass, inoculated with a dissociative tranquillity.

The wind narrowed like a scream through a tunnel. Through something hollow. Through me. Listen to the wind. Don't think. There was a stranger in my bed here, Margaret in our bed at home and another woman with whom I wanted to be in bed right now. She was wild as this storm, as unpredictable and maybe…

Okay, that didn't work. Don't think. Just listen. Lose yourself in the wind. Let it blow through you like the hollow man you are. Don't think. Like this storm, regrets, recriminations, current circumstances will pass. Focus on the wind.

I awoke on the couch, cursing the first sunlight I'd seen in days.

The Great Wall of Troy had stretched the length of two football fields. The guard towers were the height of a three-storey building. The double-gated entry was as tall and wide as a pair of vertical billboards. This fortification was built with 200 tons of plaster over fibreglass, a thousand yards of durable mesh bolstered by a mile of rebar, all supported by tubular metal scaffolding. This morning it lay in rubble. Pipe protruded through artificial stone like broken bones through skin. The huge gates, unhinged, leaned upon one another like a couple of drunks in one of the local tequila bars.

The film crew had dutifully reported at call time and were stumbling around the debris that littered our base camp between overturned trailers and trucks, some salvaging what they could, most standing in small groups shaking their heads.

I found Brad Pitt at the wall, photographing the wreckage.

'We were so close to finishing,' he said, lowering his camera.

The airport reopened and I put SG in a taxi. A chaste kiss as I held the cab door. She smiled a movie-star smile, behind which lay the question, 'Did I do something wrong?' No, sweet SG, I'm just a little clumsy at this.

My personal dark cloud swarmed, scolding. Was this how I defined myself? Margaret and I had spoken a few times since the 'retirement' conversation and agreed to return to therapy together. Could I erase the past two weeks and step back into that agreement with any honour? Was the genie already out of the bottle?

Sunset found me in the rented apartment of one of our stuntmen who was selling Troy Stunts T-shirts. There were only a few crew left. Most had taken their scheduled flights home that morning. Mine was delayed by unfiled paperwork. A final fuck you from our office.

My mobile phone rang.

'Hello, my darling. Are you alright?' Nicola wanted to know.

I stepped out on the balcony to take the call.

CHAPTER NINE: RETURN TO NORMALCY

Casey threw his arms around me as Margaret and I met him coming out of Spanish class. He was wearing a jacket, open over a food-stained T-shirt and orange sweatpants. Going on seventeen, he still had a favourite colour. And he refused to wear anything but sweatpants. Jeans were 'too scratchy'.

Oh, my wonderful, quirky, sensitive boy whose joy can light my darkness.

At the airport, a tight embrace and quick kiss from Margaret felt normal. As if we'd never had the retirement conversation. As if the last six months had all been about a stressful movie and now it was over. My infidelities a bagatelle, a lapse isolated from my true nature.

We'd taken Casey out of school early to drive him to the renal clinic in Syracuse. Test results had come in and Dr Welch reported there was no significant decline in his kidney function. He probably wouldn't need a transplant 'until his thirties or forties'.

Margaret was quiet on the ride home. She later confided her fear that 'we may not be around then' to donate our organs.

Missing Sam's fifteenth birthday party meant I'd also missed seeing his brother's gift to him.

'I told him for my birthday present, I'd like him to wear jeans to the party.'

Casey borrowed a pair from Sam.

'How were they?'

'Not bad. I got a lot of compliments from the girls.'

He'd asked his mom to buy him a pair next time she went shopping.

Margaret and I exchanged secret smiles.

Sam was preoccupied. The band he'd formed needed a drummer and a new name. Their former drummer was unreliable. Their former name, Pocket, well, he just didn't like it anymore. For now, they were calling themselves Subject to Change.

'That's a great name!' I told him.

'Dad,' was all he said.

I was in the music room, which doubled as Margaret's office, mixing a tape from my record collection, introducing Sam to some of my favourites from the 1960s. He was on Margaret's computer ordering new mikes for recording.

I played 'Time Has Come Today' by the Chambers Brothers.

'How about some Hendrix?' he asked with his back to me.

Coming right up.

'Great. Got 'em,' he said to the computer. 'See ya later, Pops.'

He was off to the basement before I could drop the needle on 'Purple Haze'.

Life in Ithaca was close to perfect. Alright, it snowed a lot. But in early October, the autumn leaves were blazing, sailboats were still out on Cayuga Lake, the Sunday farmer's market was bustling, Buttermilk Falls was flowing, the downtown pedestrian street – the Commons – was a beehive. Cornell University, Ithaca College, Tompkins Community College doubled the size of this micro-metropolis when school was in session and infused it with youthful zest and intellectual energy.

I had interesting friends: scholars, scientists, architects, artists, boating enthusiasts, even a couple who were professional storytellers.

I eased back into our family routines of Saturday breakfast at the State Diner, going with Sam to buy bagels, newspapers and superhero comics on Sunday morning – though now he wanted *Guitar World, Vibe* and *Spin.* Margaret and I resumed our trail walks through gorges and woodland. But now we were only walking Oliver. And I was feeling rootless in this beautiful place I'd been lucky enough to call home for over a decade.

One night, I drove Casey and three of his friends to a sleepover party at a classmate's house. With the window rolled down, I overheard him say, 'Yeah, my dad's awesome.'

I wasn't feeling very awesome. The wedding ring was back on my finger but it was covering more than just a tan. It was covering shame. It was covering duplicity.

With Casey at his sleepover and Sam away in New Hampshire travelling with a youth choir, Margaret and I assumed our positions reading at opposite ends of the family-room sofa. I'd never taken notice of the physical distance before.

What once had been comfortable routine was less a comfort now and more just a habit. Marriages can get that way and still be viable marriages. But the boys had their own lives in Ithaca, Margaret had her life here and I was just passing through.

We avoided conversations of emotional substance – saving those for sessions with our marriage counsellor – and talked mostly about our sons. We didn't have much time alone. Our social calendar was packed with friends I hadn't seen all year.

At a dinner with one of our favourite couples, he a professor of social psychology, she a therapist, a question came up.

They'd met in college, been married for twenty years and never been apart longer than a weekend.

'How do you guys do it?' he asked about our long periods of separation.

'We have to constantly re-evaluate things,' Margaret responded.

I was in email contact with Nicola. Professional updates on Peter O'Toole were a sidebar. She wrote warm, funny letters, often spiced with a tease that one man or another was pursuing her but she wasn't interested. If these were intended to encourage me, they had the opposite effect. The thought of competing for a woman just made me feel old and grumpy.

Still, hers were the first emails I searched for when I went to my inbox. And their contents provided the illusion of being desired.

Margaret enjoyed being with me. I enjoyed being with her. Did she need me? She had everything she needed right here. What did I need? Was it just sex? Connection? Was it a narcissistic urge to feel desirable? Desire, in its many aspects, was no longer part of our marital agreement.

Margaret served breakfast at the hospice three days a week. She'd leave the house without saying goodbye. I wasn't kissing her good morning to see if she'd notice. It didn't seem she did. Or maybe, like a traumatised war survivor, she was afraid the next bombshell might explode if she got too close. Perhaps she sensed I was too willing to talk and the talk would be about what was wrong. Do people ever talk about what's right? It seemed to me that we used to.

On a brisk, cloudless afternoon, the family gathered in front of our house to plant an oak tree in honour of Gershwin.

Margaret had obtained his ashes and we poured them around the roots.

The short ceremony in which we each shared a memory of our beloved pet was a bonding family event. A celebration of good years together. Whatever I said in my turn was camouflage for the remorse I felt in abandoning him, leaving him not knowing if he'd ever see me again. My pain and remorse transcended the moment. How could I be contemplating doing the same to my family?

On Halloween, Casey went out with a group of friends who'd decided on an *Alice in Wonderland* theme for their costumes. He was the bottle labelled 'Drink Me'. It didn't seem so long ago that Margaret and I were holding the hands of our trick-or-treaters. Now, our eldest was with his own crowd on what was probably his last time performing this childhood ritual.

Rocketing into the primary phase of his sixteenth year – fifteen suddenly sounded so young – Sam considered himself too sophisticated to be going door-to-door asking for candy. He threw his first party in our basement. Ten teenagers showed up and three more 'crashed'. Sam asked permission to let the crashers in. Among them was a sixteen-year-old girl named Olivia with whom he was infatuated.

Margaret and I were exiled to the family room where we watched a reprise double bill of *Chocolat* and *Coming Home*. She fell asleep in the middle of the second feature. We'd had a day of vigorous physical labour, clearing brush behind our detached garage. Working side by side felt so right. Sitting together that night with sounds of screaming teenagers coming up from the basement felt so right. Margaret woke, touched my arm in passing and went upstairs to bed while I finished the movie.

Our farewell at the airport was sweet and a little sad. We embraced well beyond the count of three. I was the one who broke it off. One month hadn't been enough time to replace hurt feelings with healing ones. But it was enough to show me I wasn't ready to give her up.

CHAPTER TEN: A SERIES OF UNFORTUNATE EVENTS

If you haven't read the series of books *Lemony Snicket's A Series of Unfortunate Events*, it's probably because you don't have teenaged kids and are unaware that they also appeal to adults with personality disorders. The books, an unlucky thirteen of them, find their humour in the despair of three orphans whose parents were killed when a mysterious fire destroyed their mansion. In each book, the orphans are dispensed to the care of incompetent guardians and relentlessly pursued by an egomaniacal, homicidal thespian, Count Olaf, who is after their inheritance.

The stories, written by Daniel Handler under the pseudonym Lemony Snicket, are dark satire with laughs that pivot on peril. They are best suited for adolescents who think parents are dangerous idiots. My boys loved them. But co-distributors Paramount Pictures and DreamWorks wanted a family film. It was a cinematic tightrope on which a slip to either side could make the tone too maudlin or too frightening for the wide audience needed to justify their $140 million investment. Initial investment.

'It's a tall order to create as much misery and misfortune as a story like this demands,' the director was quoted in an early press release. 'We have a lot to live down to.'

My first impression of director Brad Silberling was that he looked so young and dreamy-eyed I thought the producers, cinematographer and costume designer surrounding him were placing orders for a coffee run. He wasn't as young as he looked, with shoulder-length hair and John Lennon eyeglasses. He comported himself with a contemplative calm. He was ethereal, soft-spoken and kind.

Jim Carrey was going to eat him for breakfast.

It's the rare comic actor who does not have a reputation for being difficult. Of course, this differs in degree and symptom. Jim expressed his in perfectionism. There was no such thing as too many takes of a scene. He wanted to do them over and over until he – not the director – felt he'd got it right. And then he would want to try it a different way to see if his improvisational skill could lift it a notch higher. Often, it did.

Silberling and the production faced an even greater challenge from the actors playing the Baudelaire orphans. They were in nearly every scene of the movie and they were all under the legal working age of sixteen. California state law permitted no more than four hours' work for the toddlers and eight working hours per day for the older children – which included three hours of school.

The initial shooting schedule called for eighty-four days of filming. The movie would eventually take 119 days to shoot.

I was in no hurry.

Work left little time to dwell on my marriage but thoughts of Margaret lurked at the corner of every action and interaction. We'd made a good life together. Isn't that construct what marriage is about? What if it was marriage itself that I was questioning? Is it love? Is it loyalty?

I tried to express my waverings, weaknesses in an email to my wife. She wrote an angry, defensive response. I phoned her. No better result. We agreed to go back to our therapist when I came home at Christmas break.

Putting in perspective any hardships that either I or the movie would face over the next six months were an unusual number of men and women navigating the streets of America's most auto-dependent city on bicycles. Most of them appeared to be of Latin American descent. A bus strike had made their difficult lives even harder.

Real life went on outside the studio gates.

The disparity of wealth in Los Angeles had always made me despair. I grew up not knowing how poor we were – even when my father was out of work – because we had a house, food and a car. That these necessities weren't handed out at birth didn't enter my consciousness before attending my mixed-race, mostly low-income high school. My father never earned more than a four-figure annual salary. But he always had a car. To those without one, I was the son of a wealthy man.

The bus strike was about driver's health benefits. They surely deserved them. But to the tens of thousands of passengers who depended on LA's truly pathetic public transportation, the drivers were already rich. It's all perspective.

Real life goes on outside the studio gates.

Filming began at the burned-out Baudelaire Mansion, the skeleton of a once-elegant, three-storey Victorian built on Stage 16. All our sets were on sound stages and this movie was occupying more than a third of the total on the lot.

The mansion had been artistically torched beyond repair and special-effects smoke billowed from the char. It was realistically spooky. A little too much so for the toddler triplets alternating in the role of Sunny. They cried during every take.

The triplets wouldn't stop crying and were fired after two days of filming.

'Never work with children or animals,' W.C. Fields had advised while making movies for Paramount many years earlier.

The studio grounds had undergone a number of facelifts during nearly a century of operation but it still felt more like Old Hollywood than any of the others, and it was the only one of the six majors with an actual Hollywood address. It was the fifth-oldest studio in the world, occupying the same grounds at the top of Gower Gulch since 1912.

It was the first lot I'd ever worked on, in the mid-1970s, when Garry Marshall's *Happy Days* spin-offs dominated the networks and I was trying to break into episodic television writing. I recall the blood rush of my first check-in at the security kiosk where a uniformed guard had my name on a list. The iron wings opened and I felt like I was entering the only world that mattered. Funny how perspectives change.

My father drove a bread truck and he would save his deliveries to the commissary at Republic Studios – now CBS Studios – so I could accompany him on Saturdays. Most of my favourite western series and features came from those stages. This was where Roy Rogers and Gene Autry went to work.

I didn't study film at university. I just watched movies. New ones, old ones, in cinemas, on television. There were few film festivals when I was growing up. But LA offered specialty theatres that screened the Janus/Criterion Collection, introducing me to the great international directors – Bergman, Buñuel, Fellini. There was a silent-film theatre in which I remember seeing the Chaplin and Keaton classics. There was the annual LA Film Exposition at the Chinese Theatre on Hollywood Boulevard in which I'd binge for twenty-four hours watching a

Billy Wilder marathon, a Preston Sturges marathon, Lubitsch, DeMille, the Marx brothers.

Wilder made his greatest pictures for Paramount. Lubitsch made his transition from silents to sound here. Sturges rode his bicycle around this lot with a cigarette dangling from his lips. Walking past the DeMille Building, the Pickford Building, the Martin and Lewis bungalows was a stroll through film history.

The Paramount lot had a new commissary now and the alleyways between offices were thoroughfares for golf carts. There were still a few bicycles but most of them were for bored producers.

And there was Jim Carrey riding his Segway to Stage 6.

Real life wouldn't get a visitor's pass.

I needed distractions to keep my mind off my personal life. A friend of mine, Alex Ho, was producing a small movie with which I was keen to become involved. Unfortunately, a unit publicist can only work one movie at a time. So, when Alex offered me *Hotel Rwanda*, I said I could only do it as a consultant. They could hire a local unit publicist in Johannesburg to cover the ten-week shoot; I would supervise him from LA and stay with the picture as an advisor from pre-production through to its fall release. I'd get a flat fee and, most important to me, a voice in the overall strategy for marketing this important film.

Now, I had two jobs.

I continued to phone home, and Margaret and I would exchange news of the day. I'd ask about the progress of her upcoming CD release before she handed me over to the boys.

Sam had found a temporary solution for a replacement drummer.

'But he can't practise with us much because he needs to

study all the time and he's probably going to a different college when he graduates. We need somebody who can commit for the long term.'

He'd gone back to the name Pocket, for lack of anything more inspiring, and hustled up a few club gigs in Ithaca. He'd also nabbed his first date with the 'older girl', Olivia.

His big brother was in demand for his piano playing.

'I played at the ACS [Alternative Community School] spaghetti dinner and a lot of people said they liked it,' he told me. 'And there's this girl group from school who want me to play with them at the talent show.'

He added, 'I can't wait to see you at Christmas.'

Nicola and I hadn't spoken while I was in Ithaca. I waited two weeks after landing in LA before calling her.

'I've missed hearing your voice,' she said. My gut felt an elevator drop, my heart leaped over my head.

'Why don't you come here for a week?'

Was that a casual, 'Come to LA and let's do lunch?' Would she stay at a hotel?

'I couldn't possibly come for less than two weeks.'

Uh… okay.

She was flying in tomorrow.

A portrait of caddishness might be appearing around now. It's not that this self-image hadn't occurred to me and even repelled me. Cue Jeff Goldblum in *The Big Chill* on the importance of rationalisations. I considered myself in an experimental phase, still trying to save my marriage. I know how that sounds. But it was the best excuse for testing the limits of liberation I could come up with. Following them over a cliff remained a distinct possibility.

I drove to LAX to meet her the next morning. My pulse was racing. Anticipation or anxiety? What if we got bored with each other before the end of two weeks? I hadn't made any plans to entertain her. Would it be worse if we discovered we didn't like each other or if we discovered the opposite? Relax. It's a fling. They're rarely fatal.

I paced inside the terminal for an hour, then two hours. No one would confirm if she was on a flight list. She'd bailed. I should have seen it coming. This flaky chick who I barely knew had cost me half a day waiting around for a plane she'd never intended to take. *Couldn't possibly for less than two weeks, blah blah blah.* A big part of me was relieved.

I phoned her, not caring it was six in the morning in London.

'So, where are you?' I asked coldly.

'Still in bed. I can't wait to see you tomorrow. Do you still want me there?'

Tomorrow? It was an overnight flight. She was leaving, not arriving, today.

'Very much,' I said, beginning to realise just how much.

She was waiting outside the International Terminal when I arrived the next day. She wore a waist-length jacket, a long skirt, beat-up leather boots and at least three strands of beaded necklaces. Her hair was tied up in a bandana.

There's the beauty of perfection, cool and encased in its flawlessness. Hers was another kind. A contrast of kinds. Messy and refined; contained and teeming; bold and brittle.

She was a changeling. We embraced. She smelled of incense and lemons.

Nicola hated The Tower, as she called the high-rise apartment Paramount had rented for me in the Fairfax District. While I was at work one day, she bought live plants to replace the plastic ones and a large, wooden Buddha.

'I liked his face,' she said when she introduced me to the statue.

The production had considerately shut down for the next three days to shoot tests of the new baby actors – twins, this time – and get Count Olaf's wig looking right. This, combined with Thanksgiving holiday, gave me a full week off work.

We drove up the coast toward Big Sur, no destination in mind. We ate sandwiches by the side of the road in a 'picnic' area that turned out to be a clear-cut dumping ground. We hiked a trail near Morro Bay at sunset, then stumbled down in the dark, cutting through briar and bramble because she didn't want to walk down the same way we walked up.

We stopped at a filling station outside the Madonna Inn, a resort famous for its kitsch decor. It was late and there was one room available: the old-fashioned honeymoon suite. We laughed and blamed each other for our bizarre surroundings. She took a bath in the claw-foot tub. I applied soap.

Back in LA for Thanksgiving, she wanted us to perform a thanks-giving ritual in the hills at night. We bought sage, candles and flowers, and climbed Sunset Trail below the Hollywood Sign where we shadowed three coyotes running toward a cliff overlooking the Los Angeles basin. There we violated fire laws, burning the sage and lighting the candles, and she made up a ceremony for the Native American ancestors whose spirits, she explained, still roamed these mountains. She conjured a place I felt blessed to visit.

On her last night, she sat by the window working on a story for the *Telegraph Magazine* that was a week overdue. I sat on the sofa behind her, my laptop open on a coffee table writing preliminary production notes for the movie.

Her back to me, she said without turning, 'Don't take this the wrong way but right now, just for this moment, I think I love you.'

CHAPTER ELEVEN: A DISMAL CHRISTMAS

I flew back to Ithaca for Christmas break with only one question in mind: could I be *that* guy who stays married and has a lover?

I slept in the guest room after the boys had gone to bed.

The next day we visited our therapist.

'I don't say this often,' she concluded our session, 'but it sounds like this marriage is over.'

We waited until after Christmas Day to tell the boys. On 26 December, we sat them in the living room.

If there is a Hell, there must be a layer in which the Damned faces his or her children over and over, staring into their expectant eyes and repeating the words… 'Your mom and dad are going to separate. We both love you and we know you love both of us. None of that is going to change.'

Casey welled up. Sam lowered his head and took it all in.

'Are you getting a divorce?' Sam asked.

'We haven't talked about that,' their mother said.

'We just need some time to figure things out,' I told them.

That night, we all behaved as if everything was unchanged. I poured my first glass of red and sat at the kitchen counter while Margaret cooked dinner. We chatted over the National Public Radio six o'clock news. I fed Oliver and he came back begging for more. My heart yearned for Gershwin to amble up for a rump scratching.

We ate at the kitchen table exchanging trivialities. Dinner over, we went our separate ways: Casey to his loft, Sam to the basement, Margaret to what used to be our bedroom, me to the music room. It was all so natural being separate together.

The next morning, I drove Sam to a guitar lesson.

'Ya know, Dad, it's kind of amazing you and Mom were able to keep it together as long as you did.'

I wanted to say, 'Thanks, son. We tried.' But I couldn't get the words out.

It was pointless for me to spend New Year's Eve in Ithaca. There was nothing to celebrate. But returning to LA felt like re-entering Purgatory.

I booked a last-minute ticket to London.

If Malcolm Gladwell is right, that you get eighty per cent of what you need to know about a person in the first fifteen minutes, it may also be true that the last twenty per cent is the deal breaker.

I'd known Nicola for the lifespan equivalent of fifteen minutes.

I had no idea what I was flying into.

I stood on the kerb outside Heathrow Terminal 3 for a half-hour before Nicola's car came screeching up. I'd already learned from our time in LA that punctuality wasn't among her virtues.

She had many others. She didn't shy from intimate conversation. She could challenge without initiating a pitched battle and could respond to a challenge without retreating. She openly embraced a world of spirituality that I'd lost touch with or never had, from the great religions to the magic of fairies. She was affectionate in small ways, resting her head on my shoulder, casual kisses. She made me laugh and made it okay for me to cry.

She was happy to see me. I hadn't given her much notice and was surprised she hadn't made other arrangements. Lyricist-librettist Tim Rice was among the men with whom she'd had a long-running flirtation. Oscar, Grammy and Tony Award-winning *Sir* Tim Rice, if you please. He was still married but then, so was I.

Her flat in West London had high ceilings, century-old cornices and spiritual iconography everywhere. She placed crystals around the bed as I slept off jet lag. In late afternoon, we walked to nearby Holland Park where she told me how she'd started in journalism.

'I was running away from a bad relationship and a woman I met in a bar had an extra ticket to Kenya, so I flew there with her,' she began, as we strolled through the Japanese gardens. Her travel mate was a former Miss Universe contestant whose sexual exploits nearly brought down the Tory government when it was learned she'd been sleeping with a cabinet minister, a notorious arms dealer, a Libyan intelligence officer and two newspaper editors.

In Kenya, Nicola fell in with a group of journalists who were going to Ethiopia to cover the end of the civil war there. She went along, pretending to be filing stories for Reuters.

'I didn't know what I was doing and I didn't write a single story. But I started calling myself a journalist when I realised it got me into interesting places.'

From Ethiopia, she tagged along on a trip to Eritrea. She stayed there for a few months and lived with an Italian businessman's son – until that got sticky.

'He was very possessive and he thought a friend of his was coming on to me. I had no intention of "going there" with his friend but it all got too much.'

She flew back to London where she continued calling herself a journalist. This time, though, she started writing stories and getting assignments. The editor of the *Sunday Times Magazine* took a shine and asked her to pitch him some ideas. She sold him on one about the Bushmen of southern Africa. It was the beginning of a deep connection with those people and her first major byline.

'We have so much to learn from them. About their medicines, their community. And sometimes they're just hilarious little *skellums*,' she said, laughing.

Her laugh was a glass wind chime in a warm breeze.

We kissed on the bridge over the koi pond.

It's very different getting to know someone in their own environment.

The night before New Year's Eve, we went to a party at her friend Anita's flat. Anita was Nicola's only connection to the film business: a line producer who worked mainly on movies directed by the prolific Michael Winterbottom. They'd known each other since boarding school. Anita supplied food and Nicola and I bought the booze. The party ended early and we dropped by the flat of another close friend of hers, Katherine, who lived a few doors away. She asked about our New Year's Eve plans. Nicola told her.

'They are *not* staying at your place, are they?' Katherine voiced concern.

'No, they're staying at Anita's.'

'Thank God.' The subject was quickly changed.

On New Year's Eve, I met Psychic Masseuse's husband, Ghostbuster. Yes, that was what he did for a living. Ghostbuster was a ruddy-faced Irishman, a couple of years older than me, who cleared houses of 'souls that are trapped between worlds'.

Alright, then.

He, like his spouse, had opinions on everything, from 'hidden taxes' and how Jews have an inordinate influence over world politics – *after* he learned I'd been raised Jewish – to classic rock music and Johnny Cash.

'There's nobody like the Man in Black.'

He was very earthy for a person who was only a part-time resident in the land of the living. We had dinner at an expensive restaurant in Holland Park where Ghostbuster explained his theory of the universe and why the Kinks were better than the Stones.

'People who die suddenly or violently are sometimes confused about where to go in the afterlife. I can talk to them and explain why they can't stay where they are. Most of them are happy to leave once they understand. But some of them kick up quite a fuss.'

As for the Kinks: 'They were blues, jazz, rhythm and blues. And there was Ray Davies, my God! "*Girl, you really got me now. You got me so I don't know where I'm go-o-ing.*"'

When the cheque arrived, PM examined it like a legal document and started parsing appetisers. It was annoying. So I picked up the tab. Alright, maybe I was showing off a little. Big spender.

The four of us had our New Year's Eve party at Anita's flat. Anita was staying the night with a friend in Leicester and there was booze left over from the night before. We danced, drank and smoked grass. Ghostbuster busted some moves that resembled a mash-up of Salome's Seven Veils and an epileptic fit. We all kissed at midnight, Ghostbuster pulling me off Nicola to lay one on me. Nicola and I walked home at a little past three. It had been a bizarre welcome to 2004.

Before we went to bed, I phoned home to wish everyone a happy new year. Voicemail took my message.

Nicola's grandparents, now deceased, had purchased a large estate with a grand house and several smaller houses in Bedfordshire during the late 1950s. Nicola, her older sister Sheena, and younger brother Stephen, had partly grown up in a comfortable, not lavish, cottage a short walk from Berrystead, their grandparents place, which they called 'the Big House'.

Her mother was on holiday in the south of France and Nicola had been given permission to use her cottage while she was away. We drove to the country on New Year's Day. PM, Ghostbuster, their three kids and two loads of laundry joined us.

'Our machine just isn't big enough for all these towels,' PM explained.

Nicola and I took a walk alone in late afternoon. She wanted to show me her 'sacred tree' in the deer park, a short walk away. It was a hollowed oak carved by nature like a pipe organ. She ducked inside, sat and patted the ground for me to join her.

'It's beautiful,' I said.

'It's magic,' she said, smiling.

Is this where you used to go as a little girl?

'I would have,' she said. 'But I didn't discover it until I was around thirty.'

We sat in silence until I could feel the magic.

On return to her mother's cottage, we passed Ghostbuster sitting on a woodpile in the dilapidated, open-sided barn. He appeared to be talking to himself.

'He must have seen someone in there,' Nicola said with pointed nonchalance. *Don't ask*, her tone implied. Magic was important to her. The spell of belief obliged her to defend its self-anointed ministers. These weren't just oddball chums. They represented a faith.

So I said nothing when we returned to a house covered in damp towels and three children in the living room fighting over the television remote.

If questions about my own sanity came up, I kept them to myself.

CHAPTER TWELVE: A STACKED DECK OF TAROT CARDS

I never thought of my mother as a strong woman. She was physically weakened by a double mastectomy when cancer was diagnosed two years after my younger sister was born, back in the day when they treated tumours with mustard gas. She had two serious heart attacks, one when I was in grade school and another about two decades later. She was a soft person with a pleasant smile who had a small collection of rare books acquired over years of clerking in a specialty bookstore in New York. As far as I know, she never read them.

Her pleasures were the local newspaper, which she read cover to cover daily, *The Lawrence Welk Show* and the operettas of Gilbert and Sullivan. She never worked after she married, never drove a car and had no hobbies or interests beyond her children. But she survived her illnesses, overcame a difficult, fatherless childhood living in poverty with a fearful mother and five siblings, marched with my sister and me against the Vietnam War, and outlived her husband by ten years. She even found a boyfriend at the nursing home when she was eighty-five. She was, in retrospect, much stronger than I realised.

I've always liked strong women.

A flurry of phone calls and emails with Nicola brought us back together.

'When you left after New Year's, I told my friends, "I'm never going to hear from him again",' she said. 'I wouldn't have blamed you. It was all a bit crazy, wasn't it?'

Yes, it was. She was connected at the spiritual hip to two of the oddest individuals I'd ever encountered – and considering I'd spent half my life in show business, that was saying a lot. What did that say about her?

A few attempts at reconnecting with Margaret brought no response. Sam would answer the phone and chat with me about his latest music gigs or the school play he was going to star in. But he never asked, 'Do you want to talk to Mom?' I didn't ask either.

I'd fallen deeper into trouble there, if that were possible, by sending flowers for our anniversary. The florist delivered them – with the message 'Love always' – a week early, giving an unintended implication of finality instead of 'honouring this day'. I tried to explain by email but it went unanswered.

I was haunted by the spectre of having made the biggest mistake of my life. I've always been impulsive. Was separating from Margaret reckless? Was it self-sabotage? Was it survival? What was I doing? What had I done?

I imagined my divided self in front of two doors. Behind one was Margaret; the other opened to Nicola – or no one in particular. I examined the qualities in each: one was solid, secure and heavy. The other was weightless, risky, lighter.

I remembered something the actor John Goodman once told me, early in both our careers. 'I'm not afraid of failing,' he'd said. 'Because if I fall, I always fall forward.'

I decided not to decide. I would keep both doors open by not walking through either of them. I would let time decide. But time was not on my side.

Margaret opened a credit-card bill that had all the charges from my trip to London. It obviously looked to her like I'd suddenly gone 'whoopee!' living the high life, decking myself out from Saville Row, buying rounds for the pub. And, by the way, *who do you know in London?* A few days later, I received a letter from an attorney, freezing our bank accounts and filing for divorce. The door home was now slammed shut.

The Reptile Room had over a hundred snakes and lizards, along with a tortoise the size of a sports car. The tortoise was housed in a storage room on Stage 24 but it had eaten through a wall overnight and was discovered the next morning buried under cartons of fruit in the adjacent cubicle where they stored catering supplies. Animal wrangler Jules Sylvester coaxed him onto a furniture blanket and four men carried the monster runaway back to the set of Uncle Monty's inner sanctum.

Glaswegian comedian Billy Connelly, in the role of Uncle Monty, stood on the porch of a full-scale Arts and Crafts-style house with a six-foot Burmese python draped around his neck as the EPK crew interviewed him. The studio had been throwing visitors at me all week – most with little advanced notice – but Billy handled them as adroitly as the snake that kept nuzzling his cheek.

'It's like having a scarf that likes you,' he quipped for the EPK camera.

Connelly was a huge star in Britain, a BAFTA nominee as Best Actor for his performance in *Mrs Brown*, a sold-out draw in UK concert halls for his music and comedy act but relatively unknown in America. He was playing a world-renowned herpetologist and the orphans' new guardian who wants to protect them from Count Olaf. But like all the oblivious adults in this seditious series, he won't listen to the children's warnings and falls victim to Olaf in one of his many disguises.

Billy hung out with the crew between scenes and enjoyed chatting with anyone who wasn't too busy. He was enormously entertaining and I grew comfortable in his company. I mentioned I had a 'girlfriend' (it was a strange word) in the UK and how difficult it was being in a long-distance 'relationship' (another strange word).

'It's not like flying to another planet, man,' he said, his brogue dropping consonants and rounding vowels. 'Why don't you go see her at the weekend?'

Margaret, probably on advice from her reptilian attorney, drained $17,000 from our joint bank account. Since I was still sending every pay cheque home to her, I was broke. A $700 (£385) plane ticket to London for a weekend wasn't something I could afford. But it was a flight I couldn't afford not to take.

The plane was late, so Nicola was on time to pick me up at Heathrow. We went straight to her flat and straight to bed. We hardly left the bed that weekend, though the only sleep I recall getting was during the first act of a play for which she'd bought us tickets, *Stones in His Pockets*, at the Duchess Theatre in the West End.

Sunday morning, we went to a café for breakfast and she bought newspapers. The *Times* had run a version of her story on Ladakh, which she read aloud in melodious Queen's English. That afternoon, we took the Tube to Blackfriars and walked across the Millennium Footbridge – the Wobbly Bridge (no longer wobbling after reconstruction two years earlier) – to the Tate Modern Art Gallery. The south side of the river was a carnival of humanity. A tide of tweed coats and frothy hats swooshing by T-shirted couples in romantic embrace, boats of all sizes, rowing, sailing, motoring past a giant Ferris wheel, customers queuing for tickets at Shakespeare's Globe, music blaring from restaurants and pubs. We pitched coins in the hats of buskers, break-dancers and jugglers along the boardwalk, crossed back over the bridge, then walked the length of London to her flat.

At night, she got out her deck of Tarot cards and told both our fortunes: she drew Death & Transformation, which she interpreted as 'finally burying' her old life and 'getting on with the new'. I drew the Burning Bush, which was passion. She leaned across a lit candle between us – the edges of her blouse dangling dangerously above the flame. *You're gonna burn your…!* Her arms draped my shoulders and we toppled to the floor, all concerns for fire safety gone up in a smoky kiss.

I slept on the flight back to LA and awoke feeling it had just been a dream.

CHAPTER THIRTEEN: THE ENCHANTED COTTAGE

Laurel Canyon.

More than a famous street, it's an acid flashback for people of a certain generation, a 3D paisley poster, an Aquarian phantasmagoria. I'd shared a house there with my flower child sister at the height of its hippie notoriety. It had been legendary long before that.

In the early 1900s, silent-movie cowboy star Tom Mix built a log cabin at the corner of Lookout Mountain, half a mile from the Canyon Lodge, an oasis where Wyatt Earp allegedly shot a beer mug from the raised hand of a rowdy customer. A few years later, Harry Houdini built an estate, reputedly rife with secret rooms, across the street from Mix.

In 1968, Mix's cabin became home to legendary musician Frank Zappa. When LA's music scene exploded in the 1970s, Joni Mitchell, Carol King, Crosby, Stills, Nash, the Doors, the Mamas and the Papas, even the Rolling Stones had houses in Laurel Canyon. Close your eyes and their music still wafted through the winding streets and eucalyptus trees. The Canyon was a state of mind. It was where I was happiest in this sprawling city of status seekers.

The Tower, even with Nicola's live plants and smiling Buddha, had become a cell block with a view. So I packed my clothes, the plants, a few books and the Buddha and moved to a small house on a dirt road off Kirkwood Drive above the Canyon Store.

The house was a 1940s wood-frame whose two stories sloped

uphill. It was furnished with a hotchpotch of items rescued from charity shops. One ratty couch was partially blocking a six-by-eight entryway and a small dining table was stuffed in a corner of the downstairs bedroom. But the house had light, it had a private garden patio and it came with a cat named Dash. I'd sublet from a special effects sound mixer working in Toronto. He didn't know how long he'd be gone and I didn't how long I'd be staying, so, as people in the movie business do, we left it open-ended.

With my bonus from *Hotel Rwanda*, I bought a car, a three-year old, first-generation Toyota Prius. It was a declaration that I now lived here. Again.

Production had begun on *Hotel Rwanda* and my trip to London meant I'd missed a breakfast meeting Monday with the heads of Lionsgate publicity and the public relations agency Premier. I met with them later that week. We agreed on the obvious: it could not be a 'tragedy' movie. It was a movie about heroism.

Position it any way you want, a movie about the murder of a million people in Africa, starring black actors not named Denzel, wasn't box-office catnip. Later that week, I met with veteran marketing guru Arthur Manson to discuss alternative titles.

'You say "Rwanda", you say genocide, ugly, painful. You say "Africa", people aren't interested. "Hotel"... maybe.'

My personal life was starting to interfere with my work. I avoided scheduling set visits in the early morning so I could stay up late talking to Nicola, eight time zones away. My concentration was fuzzy because angst over finances and despondency about my divorce skulked behind every window in my psyche.

A series of emails from Margaret's pit-bull attorney, suggesting I give her *everything* – including three quarters of my earnings for the rest of my working life – was just an opening salvo but it showed a willingness to detonate any future friendship we might have.

How had it come to this?

She'd been my best friend for almost twenty years. We'd built a life together. We were each other's confidants and companions. Part-time companions. Marriage must mean something more than time spent together. But time spent together must mean something. To her, being married meant there was a wall around the castle and all that mattered is that you both had a key to get in. *Ah, you're here. What a nice surprise.* To me, your partner is the castle and the castle has wheels. In that way, Margaret had left me long before I left her.

Still, it was the friendship I would miss. *Was* missing.

Living in Hollywood exposes one to shiny objects that can be mistaken for symbols of power. At my level – repeat along with me – there is no power, only access. To an outsider, these can appear to be the same thing. To an outsider you'd like to impress, well, you use what tools are in your toolbox.

Because my life needed more complication and expense, I invited Nicola for what I hoped would be the Date of the Century: the Academy Awards ceremonies, followed by a romantic stay at the Hollywood Argyle Hotel, a stylish deco landmark on the Sunset Strip. It already felt like weeks, not days, since I'd seen her. The Oscars were a month away. She needed the prep time.

'I'll have to buy a dress. Maybe I can sell a story. Can we get into any parties?'

Meanwhile, she was planning a trip to Connemara, Ireland to research background on Peter O'Toole and perhaps even track him down there before their arranged lunch next week.

Nicola called from Connemara at around 3 a.m., her time. She didn't find Peter – who hadn't been seen there in years – though she did find an entire island full of O'Tooles. She also found a bloke named Paddy who'd taken a fancy to her, shown her around and made a play for her in the empty lobby of her bed and breakfast.

I was jealous. Was it because I thought she might say 'oh, why not?' alone in a secluded lodge with an Irishman in heat? More likely it was the vulnerability of embracing monogamy on faith with a woman I hardly knew. Alright, I'd sort of done that with Margaret but she was a different kind of person. Nicola was a wild child. We got in a pointless fight.

'Would you rather I didn't tell you things?'

No. I'd rather know.

'Good because I don't want to feel like I have to censor myself so you can handle it.'

And I want to be free to react however I feel like reacting!

'Then I can react however I feel like reacting to your reactions!'

It was not our finest telephone moment.

However, most of our conversations – before and after her Irish explorations – were warm and lovely. We talked for hours, about everything and nothing. I was besotted by her. I was in lust with her. Was I falling in love? Was I already in love? If so, might I not have thrown a dart at a thousand names and come up with 999 that were less of a challenge?

Love is trust. Trust in love.

Fuck you, John Lennon.

My sons flew to LA for the four-day Presidents' Day holiday. Their embraces were a balm for all that ailed me. I cooked spaghetti at my Laurel Canyon shack and played them a CD by Nick Cave. They played me music tracks they'd recently recorded. Casey said his latest dream was to open a recording studio in New Mexico. Why New Mexico? 'There's a lot of open space and not many people.'

They'd grown up on the *Lemony Snicket* books and the film sets made the stories come alive. An alternate universe to most kids, it was a moment that felt most normal for us. Visiting Dad on a movie set, just like always.

Sam wasn't saying much. He was still processing everything. I'd always been his safety net while Margaret poured her cossetting and worry into her disabled child. My leaving the family was a blow to both boys, and both were a little uncertain about how to relate to me in our new reality. Casey dealt with it as if our new reality wasn't much different from the old. His mom's voice was the only thing missing. For Sam, my new status – our new status – my new *home*, was more difficult to grasp. I tried talking with him about it but that only made him more uncomfortable. I dropped it.

Sam snapped out of his torpor when we picked up his new girlfriend, Olivia, from her uncle's house in Santa Monica. She was pretty as a blossom but guarded. His shift of attention to her was a huge relief to me, a sign that he was as healthy as any other self-centred adolescent. But Sam wore his heart on his sleeve. She was a teenage Ferrari who would leave him in the dust. One of many heartaches ahead from which I'd never be able to save him. He was my teenage self.

My time with them was too brief but it served its purpose. They were reassured I was still in their lives. I was restored by the reminder that I was still in theirs.

Nicola arrived on Thursday before Oscar weekend – with Psychic Masseuse. She'd told me her friend was coming but, not to worry, she'd be staying with a former client named Jeffrey, a successful interior designer who owned a fancy house in the Hollywood Hills.

We all met for dinner at the Beverly Hills Hotel, joined by Jeffrey's boyfriend and a couple of his other mates. Shortly after the first cocktail, Nicola broke the news that she'd got 'us' on the list for Elton John's post-Oscar Night party. By 'us' she meant herself and Psychic Masseuse. Would it be okay if she deserted me after the Awards ceremony and went off with her friend?

'No, that would not be okay!' I shouted in front of eight people at our table, loud enough to make neighbouring tables turn. Bye-bye, Mr Nice Guy. Hello, Hannibal Lecter. Everyone threw alarmed glances at Nicola. After dinner, the designer confided to PM that I 'truly frightened' him.

Oscar weekend was off to a bang-up start.

Alone together the next night, Nicola reported that she'd called Tim Rice, who'd guest-listed her for the Elton John extravaganza, and pleaded with him to add another guest.

'All for one and one for all,' she cheered in solidarity.

She had been assigned to write a 'getting ready for the Oscars' story for the *Daily Mail.* This was an *open sesame* to the orgy of pre-ceremony giveaways taking place all over Hollywood and Beverly Hills. She got a pair of Stuart Weitzman shoes and a designer handbag that she'd be allowed to keep if they showed up anywhere on the red carpet. She was loaned $20,000 worth of jewellery. She got her hair and make-up done by the best in the business at Chateau Marmont.

Somewhere in between all this swag gathering, she was supposed to write her story. However, while I was at work, she had generously lent my Canyon cottage to Psychic Masseuse for her massage business.

'I can write at a coffee shop,' she responded when I protested. 'And Jeffrey won't let her work at his house.'

Pick your fights, I told myself.

The next night was a doozy.

Nicola and PM had a dinner date with Tim Rice at the Four Seasons Hotel. For once, I was glad PM was tagging along. She took my car to pick up her friend around 8 p.m. I cooked myself a steak, finished dealing with email from *Sixty Minutes, Entertainment Weekly,* the *LA Times* and Margaret's bomb-thrower, turned on Turner Classic Movies and waited.

I knew Europeans were accustomed to late dinners. In LA, dinner started at seven and was usually over by nine. I anticipated they'd have a drink or two afterwards, long time no see, chat-chat-chat, isn't it all so exciting? But at 1 a.m., I started wondering where my housemate was. I called her.

'So sorry, my darling. We've been having champagne in Tim's room. We're just wrapping things up. I'll be home soon.'

She stumbled into the cottage at 3 a.m. I was still awake. And steaming.

She was high on bubbly and started the conversation badly: leading off with Psychic Masseuse. Her friend 'hadn't seen Tim in ages' and 'we just forgot about the time'.

I'd had a night of contentious emails, a couple of drinks myself, a growing resentment toward her girlfriend and growing doubts about my own wisdom in inviting her here.

'Why did I have to call *you* at 1 a.m.?' I began. 'And it's two hours after you said you were on your way home!'

Now it was open warfare.

Nicola climbed onto the coffee table, looming above me as I sat on the living-room couch, shaking her small fists.

'My independence is the most important thing in the world to me!' she screamed, picking up an ashtray and heaving it vaguely in my direction. Dash the cat dashed under the sofa in the entryway.

Well, now at least I knew the rules. Instead of escalating the fight, I found her screed strangely calming.

'Enjoy your independence,' I said. 'I'm going to bed.'

She stayed up, finished my bottle of wine and fell asleep in the living room.

I caught myself chuckling as my head hit the pillow. Let's get through this weekend and I'll never have to see her again.

Nicola spent the afternoon of the Big Event being photographed by the *Daily Mail*, outfitted in a gorgeous silk dress, bejewelled, coiffed and made-up to perfection.

'How's the story coming?' I asked.

'Oh, they gave me an extra day.' As if that explained what she'd been doing the past week. A driver picked us up and took us to the Hollywood Boulevard drop-off for arriving attendees.

Tonight was Nicola's red-carpet night and she was going to make the most of it. We were standing at the entrance to the press processional, surveying the scene, when Will and Jada Pinkett Smith's limo pulled up. Will sprang out of the car, with an energy only he can project, and mine was the first familiar face he saw.

'Hey, man!' He threw his arms around me. I got a nice kiss from Jada and introduced them both to my companion. A tip to guys who want to impress a date: arrange for Will Smith to give you a bear hug in front of the Kodak Theatre on Oscar night. My date, however, was preoccupied.

Will and Jada were led away to Joan Rivers, and Nicola and I began walking toward the theatre entrance. Despite ushers urging us forward, Nicola insisted on circling back, time after time, soaking in the full rush of adrenaline – and hoping to get her borrowed designer handbag on TV so she could keep it. It was funny at first, then slightly annoying, then embarrassing as the same usher asked us for a third time to 'please move toward the theatre!'

The awards ceremonies are probably better watched on television. Once the lights go out and you can no longer see the celebrities yakking with each other in the front rows of the orchestra section, the tech category speeches become a little monotonous and the commercial breaks seem endless. During one break, Nicola got up to go to the bathroom and didn't get back before they locked the doors.

When she returned to her seat, she was flushed and breathless.

'I got locked out and decided to have a ciggie on the balcony,' she reported. 'The man next to me asked to borrow my lighter. It was Johnny Depp! He was there with his wife and Sean Penn. I may *never* give up smoking!'

The ceremonies ended, *Lord of the Rings* swept and we met our hire car to pick up Psychic Masseuse at the cottage. Nicola and I were both on a high and PM got a laugh out of her retelling the smoking-break story.

Elton John's party in West Hollywood was not an intimate

affair. It was a benefit for his AIDS foundation and there must have been a thousand people wandering the floor of the Pearl Nightclub. We walked around, doing a bit of celebrity spotting: Ben Kingsley, Sting, the Osbournes, Patrick Swayze. We found our host, Tim Rice, sitting at the front of the stage with a publicist I dimly remembered from Disney. Introductions were made and we took seats beside him, waiting for the show.

I'll confess here, if it hasn't already become evident, parties are not my thing. Despite the showbiz crowd, I was as out of my element here as Nicola was on the red carpet. But music was my thing and we enjoyed an opening set by soulful Joss Stone, followed by Elton himself. The music portion of the evening ended, Tim stayed awhile to circulate, then said goodbye to Nicola, PM and me and left to meet his driver. It was about 11 p.m.

That was when the negotiations started.

How about if I tell our driver to pick us up at midnight?

'That's not fair,' PM complained. 'You two have already had a full night but my night's just starting.'

I had to be at Paramount by 7 a.m. to meet an *Architectural Digest* photographer who was shooting our sets before we began the day's filming and Nicola still had a story to write that was due in London before close of business tomorrow.

'Why do we have to decide on a time now? Let's just stay until we feel like leaving?' Nicola bartered.

For me, and about half the original crowd, the party was already over. All I wanted to do at that point was get my gorgeous girlfriend back to our overpriced hotel room, shag her senseless and get six hours' sleep.

'If we're still here at two o'clock, I'm gonna go ballistic.'

All PM heard was 'two o'clock'.

'Fine,' she said, linking arms with her bestie. And off they went.

It was 1 a.m. and I hadn't seen either of the women I came with for two hours. I found them on the smokers' patio in a circle of five young guys wearing blazers and no socks.

'Oh, we were looking for you,' PM lied.

I tapped my watch.

'Just one more drink. Please,' Nicola begged.

I went to the bar but it was closed. When I came back, they'd disappeared. I called our driver to come get us. Or, at least, me.

I did another once-around and easily found them. There were only a few dozen hard-core revellers left. Security was patrolling the floor, clearing them out.

PM was incensed that we were leaving 'so soon'.

Back at the Argyle, Nicola and I got out of our party clothes, talked out our differences and had half-hearted sex. She was pissed off. I was pissed off. She was pissed off that I was pissed off.

'This isn't going to be a long-term relationship,' she said, putting on a robe.

Amen to that.

She opened her laptop and wrote while I got a three-hour nap.

The *Mail* had picked up the tab for another night at the hotel and Nicola was doing the final edits on her story when I returned from the studio that evening.

We were barely speaking to each other. She sent off her article at around 7 p.m. – 3 a.m. in the UK, which meant the earliest it would be published was two days after the Oscars.

She was worried it might no longer be timely enough to run. I had no sympathy.

At least PM was on a plane home that night. She'd made clear her fears about 'leaving you alone with *him*'. It meant nothing to me. We went to the restaurant in the hotel for an early last supper.

'I think I'm going to Santa Fe tomorrow,' Nicola announced after we were seated.

'I think I'm going to sleep at my house tonight,' I said.

About halfway through our meal, couples started appearing in fancy dress from the 1940s. Some sort of theme party, we assumed. Then a ten-piece band climbed onto the stage, tuned up and began to play. Suddenly all the zoot-suited men and pleat-skirted women rose in a wave and started jiving, Lindy hopping, whirling and twirling to the infectious horns, pounding piano and crashing drums. Ecstasy erupting in music and motion.

Whatever dance moves I had were as close to these as the waddle of a penguin to the flight of an eagle but nobody with a pulse could sit through this. I got up from our table, extended my hand and we started to swing.

Contact. Breakthrough. Attitude turning to crazy laughter. Not a word getting in the way. Tired as we both were, we made long sweet love that night. Another wordless connection. Maybe if we never spoke again we could make this work.

Nicola decided to extend her stay with me. The extent of this extension was yet to be determined. One day, while I was at the studio, she managed to shove the entryway sofa into the living room and carry the downstairs table on her head to that now-vacant spot, making an office for herself. Some might call that 'moving in'. Others, 'creating a base of operations'.

CHAPTER FOURTEEN: DOUBLE DUTY

Meryl Streep joined our cast at the end of the week. She was playing phobic Aunt Josephine, another of the hapless orphans' hopeless guardians, who lived in a house that teetered at the edge of a cliff. A spinster obsessed with proper grammar, she cringed at a dangling participle but was oblivious to the dangers of an approaching hurricane, as well as the diabolical intentions of Count Olaf, who woos her disguised as a sweet-talking old salt.

Most actors carry fame like it was a steamer trunk. With Meryl Streep, it's an overnight bag on wheels. She's Katharine Hepburn with an authentic laugh. She's a serious actress who doesn't take herself seriously. She's friendly, she's funny, she's accessible.

Okay, maybe not *that* accessible.

She has Roy.

'Anything you need her to do, tell me and I'll see if she's willing to do it.'

Roy was a six-foot-four-inch former female impersonator who did Meryl's hair and make-up. He was fit, fashionable, sixty-something and Ms Streep's personal guard dog, with a toothy grin that flashed *Don't Even Think About It* at anyone who got too close.

You didn't want to get on Roy's bad side.

My other job was requiring an increasing amount of my attention.

I'd sent syndicated UK journalist Garth Pearce to the set

of *Hotel Rwanda* – nobody had come up with a better title – in Johannesburg. Garth was an old pro and his stories were published throughout the English-speaking world, so he was an important element in our international publicity campaign.

Nicola and I were at dinner, celebrating her fortieth birthday with her only friends in Los Angeles, Drew and Estelle. We'd just popped the champagne when my phone rang. It was producer Alex Ho, calling from South Africa.

Rwanda star Sophie Okonedo was not only refusing to talk with our visiting journalist, she refused to report to work if he was there. She'd caught him 'lurking' in the lobby of the hotel where the film's stars were staying.

Garth had made the first of his two-day scheduled set visits on a day when Sophie wasn't working, so the locally hired unit publicist suggested he might find her at the hotel. He sent Garth there – unaccompanied and with no forewarning to the actress. Besides the total inappropriateness of that, what to his wondering eyes did appear but Ms Okonedo and Nick Nolte, arms around each other, exiting the elevator together – from which our journalist might conclude… you get the picture. Sophie freaked out.

'Fix it,' Alex said.

A week later, I ran afoul of Roy.

'You didn't tell me the behind-the-scenes crew were coming today,' he said, smiling through gritted teeth.

I'd sent a schedule but the days had changed, I explained. The EPK team had been pretty much showing up when the scenes matched their needs, regardless of shifting dates. Okay, maybe I should've sent another memo. Meryl was only halfway through her work on the movie and there were many more visitors who needed Roy's, er, her approval.

'Sorry about that. Won't happen again.'

He never forgave me.

In early April, filming moved to Downey Studios. The wrap date, which had shifted from 23 March to 21 April was now set at 14 May.

From the mid-1930s until about ten years ago, the city of Downey, in southeast Los Angeles County, was the centre of aerospace manufacturing, most of which was dominated by Rockwell International, producer of systems for the Apollo space program. Rockwell went out of business and their grounds were purchased by a group of venture capitalists who turned the high-ceilinged rocket-ship factory into a film sound stage.

The stage was a 275,000-square-foot tin shed that we were assured had been cleared of asbestos. It was musty, dirty and decrepit. But there was ample space for the production's ambitious 'lake build' – four sets we needed to construct around water. Our construction department dug out the stage floor and filled it with 2.5 million gallons.

The best that could be said about Downey Studios was that it was a far enough drive from Paramount that studio employees and guests wouldn't be dropping by every five minutes. The worst, well, an *LA Times* exposé about the health hazards of working there would help shut down the facility a few years later.

The hazards of Downey had less immediate impact on my health than shacking up with Nicola.

A Maori healing was purported to cure everything from

infertility to psychosis. I was unsure if Nicola had a specific target when she urged me to experience one from a travelling band of practitioners passing through Topanga Canyon.

I should've run when I heard the first screams coming from behind a screened section of the auditorium. When it came my turn, I joined a room of people lying on mats with healers digging their heels into various portions of prone anatomies. The head honcho, Papa Joe, assigned a young, stocky New Zealander to treat me.

'This is going to hurt,' he warned – just before the lights went out.

'You went completely grey!' Nicola exclaimed as she led me from the room. 'Papa Joe said you were very brave. He also told me the guy who treated you was called the Baby-Faced Assassin. I couldn't believe how loud you were screaming.'

She said all this while trying, unsuccessfully, to stifle giggles.

I was limping for a week.

Nicola flew off to visit her mother in Cape Town and Sam flew to me for spring break. I was relieved to get off the roller-coaster of whatever-you-might-call-it my lover and I were establishing together. Never a dull moment had left me longing for some dull moments. Sam's arrival also prompted a temporary ceasefire from assault by Margaret's attorney.

Sam loved the freedom of LA, where he had friends and family. I think he also liked having his dad all to himself. I hadn't realised how oppressive things had become at home.

'Mom lays down rules because she's fighting with Casey and I have to follow them even though I didn't do anything,' he complained. 'He's depressed. She's depressed. I feel guilty that I'm the only one enjoying my life.'

My time with Sam raced by. I took him to the sets at Downey Studios one day and his aunt took care of him on other days when I was at work. Alex Ho cooked dinner at his house one evening and showed us some cut footage from *Hotel Rwanda*. Later in the week, Sam and I saw the movie *The United States of Leland*, starring *Rwanda* lead actor Don Cheadle. He chose it to help me with my 'research', he said.

He was in my world but it was also his. He loved the movies. He was, however, changing his mind about wanting to be an actor.

'I'll probably study acting in college but I want to keep a band going when I move to New York,' he said. 'I'm thinking maybe I'll give it until I'm twenty-six to be a musician. If that doesn't work out, I'll be an actor.'

It's always good to have a practical fallback, I chided.

'Don't you think I can do it?'

I delighted in the indignance of that comeback.

I spoke with Nicola almost every night after Sam had gone to bed. Morning, her time.

Sam overheard us one night when I thought he was asleep.

'Was that your girlfriend you were talking to?' he asked.

'Just a friend,' I answered.

Sam flew home, Nicola was back in London and I flew to meet her for the UK premiere of *Troy*. From there, I thought it would be a swell idea to fly to Nice for the *Hotel Rwanda* Cannes International Film Festival party, hosted by the South African film commission. We would just go there for a night of partying. *Sans* hotel. Perhaps ending with a romantic stroll on the Croisette at sunrise.

It was a crazy dolce-vita thing to do. How jet-set of us, I preened.

It was a disaster.

The party was filled with South Africa's anodyne elite and neither *Rwanda*'s producer nor director nor any of the stars were in attendance. The music was background to shuffle your feet by. There was nothing to do but enjoy the free drinks. Nicola went to the bar and came back with only a drink for herself. We got in a fight.

We moved to the Soho House where a group from Revolution Films – the company Anita worked with – were gathered. Anita, voice of reason, wasn't there. We closed that party and wandered off to someone's yacht with some of the Revolutionaries. They left after a couple of hours, leaving us with the boat's owner, who kept trying polite ways to say he'd like to go to sleep. But Nicola didn't want the party to end, so she kept talking. Sometime before dawn, she paused for breath and the boat owner made his escape. She still wouldn't leave until the morning air warmed enough for her to relinquish a borrowed blanket. This concluded our Festival festivities. No sunrise stroll; no croissants on the Croisette. We took a cab to the airport and sat in stony silence on the flight back to London.

Differences. You have to have differences. Without differences you have no storyline. Harry meets Sally and they instantly bond over the complexities of ordering lunch? Doesn't work. But how different is too different?

Maybe differences make less difference than the ability to accommodate differences. *Go ahead, take an hour to order a sandwich.* I'll wait. Spending so much time away from Margaret may have masked our differences. Spending time with

Nicola was exposing them, consequently forcing us to deal with them. We all want companionship and we all want autonomy. Maybe the process of intimacy is conflict. Maybe we were learning that from each other. But how different is too different?

Unfortunate Events was winding down and I was anticipating the end of a six-month period of relative stability. My divorce was still slow-drip water torture and the sound mixer from whom I'd been subletting was coming back.

Not wanting to leave things in limbo after the fiasco in France, Nicola flew out to be with me. Together, we said goodbye to the enchanted cottage and she helped move my belongings – and a few of her left-behinds – to the former office of my late friend, arranger-composer Peter Matz. It was a bungalow with a bathroom and no kitchen.

Laurel Canyon had provided the illusion of a home. This set-up only emphasised my transience. My here-now-gone-tomorrow girlfriend had become my only port in the storm. Or was she the storm? Either way, it was getting harder to say goodbye to her. Our battles had shown our strengths and weaknesses as a couple. Alone together, we were great – laughing, talking all night, working side by side. We just had to avoid parties and I had to avoid any criticism of her psychic sidekicks who were now renting her flat for a pittance.

'That way, I can stay there when I go back,' she said to justify the arrangement.

The flat share allowed her to keep one foot in and one foot out of our relationship. That was okay with me. I was still in no position to consider our future. Things were fine between us in the present. I would hold on to that. I needed something to hold on to.

The last week at Downey, I evaded Roy to introduce Nicola to Meryl, who welcomed us into her trailer. I understood why she needed a six-foot-four-inch roadblock. She chatted away during what should have been her rest time until I finally had to throw us out.

Despite her bodyguard-cum-hairdresser, Meryl was a delight to be around and a wonder to watch. She joked with the crew between takes, sat doing crossword puzzles between scenes, and, when the cameras rolled, made you forget there was an actress inhabiting paranoid grammarian Aunt Josephine.

Aunt Josephine ended her time with us hiding in the Curdled Cave of Lake Lachrymose, the water around her pulsing with mechanical leeches. The set interwove nightmare and nature in an ominous water park. Pumps churned out choppy wavelets as a gimbal rocked the little rescue rowboat and leeches splashed around them. Meryl was gleeful as a kid in a mud fight. For those few days, we almost forgot what a scummy, toxic dump Downey Studios was. For those few days, it was Disneyland.

By the end of the week, Nicola was back in England.

CHAPTER FIFTEEN: COWBOYS AND NERDS

The science fiction genre found its gold standard in 1977 with *Star Wars.* In the next two years, studio vaults were opened to make *Star Trek: The Motion Picture* and Disney's most expensive movie to date, *The Black Hole.* The appeal of these space adventures was that they were interplanetary westerns, giving audiences a recognisable structure on which to hang their Stetson hats while transporting them to places 'where no man has gone before'. The sci-fi-western portmanteau went a step too far in 1999 when Warner Bros. adapted the 1960s TV classic *Wild Wild West,* which lost a ton of money and temporarily blew the genre out of the saddle.

In the Hollywood of 2004, a period dominated by contemporary comedy and drama, making a sci-fi-western from a failed television series with no stars, anti-hero leads who spoke an invented slang, on a budget that had to squeeze all the bells and whistles from practical effects rather than costlier visual effects was counter-intuitive in every way. But Universal Studios was willing to go where others weren't, primarily to corral one of the hottest talents in the business.

Joss Whedon had created *Buffy the Vampire Slayer,* a moderately successful movie that became a long-running hit TV series. The table-turning feminist perspective, the hip, contemporary voice and crackling dialogue soon made him one of the most sought-after screenwriters and script doctors in town.

Firefly was a post-*Buffy* series Whedon created for Fox in 2002. It was about nine interplanetary outlaws rebelling against a totalitarian government that crushed independence movements across the galaxy. It lasted a single season. But in reruns and a DVD box set it began gathering loyal new legions. Now, Joss was going to reunite the original cast in his feature directorial debut. He'd call it *Serenity*, after the rebel's spacecraft.

'I'm not done with this yet,' Whedon said. 'I want to get back on a ship with these guys again.' So, Universal gave him a modest $25 million and sixty-one days to blast off and return – hopefully with the first chapter of a film franchise.

I was a fan of the series. The job didn't pay much but I could support my family while my credit cards were adding zeros. All the filming would take place around Los Angeles and I needed to feel rooted. LA was treating me kindly. I had a job. I had a used Prius. I had a roof over my head.

I still needed a map of the world to find my girlfriend.

Nicola was about to board a plane to Paris, on her way to meet Paul Rusesabagina, the real-life hero of *Hotel Rwanda*.

They called him the African Schindler and his actions were no less courageous than the German industrialist who protected Jews during the Holocaust. Rwanda's inter-ethnic vengeance lasted a hundred days and saw the slaughter of nearly a million people. As manager of the Hôtel des Mille Collines in the capital city Kigali, he kept Hutu death squads at bay for seventy-six days while sheltering 1,268 terrified Tutsis inside the luxury resort.

Paul had not been back to his home country since the genocide. Nicola was going to accompany him and write a story about his return for *The Telegraph*. This was not a safe assignment. The new president of Rwanda was a Tutsi who was resentful of Paul, an ethnic Hutu. Rusesabagina had no illusions that he'd be greeted with ticker-tape parades. But he had the movie coming out, it had been ten years since he'd been home and it was time to revisit.

Travelling with a Western journalist would create a façade of protection but it wouldn't guarantee anything. Ethnic animosities that had triggered the slaughter were still prevalent. The violence had subsided in most of the country but revenge killings were not infrequent, and civil war still raged along the borders.

There were other hazards. As in much of sub-Saharan Africa, sanitation was a concern. There'd been a SARS epidemic only a year earlier, though it was reportedly contained. Westerners were advised not to travel at night, especially outside Kigali where road conditions were horrendous. Though auto safety within the capital was improving, it had been ranked as one of the worst in the world only eight years ago.

I'd set Nicola up on this story. I was worried, even if she wasn't.

CHAPTER SIXTEEN: TRUST IN THE UNIVERSE

I never met a dame yet that didn't know if she was good-looking or not without being told, and there's some of them that give themselves credit for more than they've got.

– Stanley Kowalski

In the minds of men, gorgeous women can always find a way to get their way.

It can be as graceful as a ballet, as gentle as a kiss, or as forceful as a jujitsu move that turns resistance on itself to flip an opponent face down on the floor.

But no man can understand the journey a woman takes from exposure to empowerment.

Nicola was an attention-hungry middle child, shuffled off to boarding school at age eleven. Her father's death a year later made her a special case in school, admired and pitied, resented by classmates for privileged treatment, unsure if her promotion to choir leader or lead in a school play was based on merit or sympathy. As a result, she both shone and withered in the spotlight. She began to prefer the safety of shadows. It became easier to give away her power than to claim it. Her strength would remain secret, sheltered, untapped.

Then she grew breasts and her boyish face became beautiful. Men swarmed like the biblical plagues. Male friends became psychotically proprietary. She walked around thinking there must be mustard stains on her shirt.

Boys make presumptions; your uncle makes a pass. The world presents you with images that make you feel inadequate. Men want the girl on the billboard. But that's not who you are. You try on disguises until you can figure it out. Nothing fits. You grow a shell. But life is no fun under a shell, so you take a chance. If you're lucky, the first time is affirming. If not, there must be something wrong with you. You look for a safe place to hide. It turns out to be smothering, so you escape. And try again – until you find sanctuary or embrace your strength.

Nicola never found sanctuary.

Her strength was her trust in the universe – a pretty dodgy security system to most. Her strength was never allowing fear to stop her from an adventure.

Nicola survived Rwanda and was back in London. It had been an intense experience.

She'd seen the pile of bones made into a monument to the Hutu victims.

A taxi driver gave her a tour of the city, pointing out genocide landmarks. When she told her driver about being there with Paul, he went cold.

'We think he is a liar,' the driver said. Rwanda was still an angry place with suspicious people. There were rumours – unsubstantiated but persistent – alleging he had profited off his heroism, taking money from those he protected.

Nicola spent the bulk of her time getting to know Paul's version of the story, getting to know Paul and his wife, and absorbing the details of the hotel where he'd made his stand.

She dined alone most nights in the fourth-floor restaurant

of the Mille Collines, from which she could see the Church of the Holy Family where hundreds of people sought refuge and were massacred. She saw the hotel cellar with its stocks of food and wine. From the food stocks, Paul had parcelled rations to keep 1,200 refugees alive and with the supply of spirits he bribed military officials. She swam in the pool that had been the main source of water during the siege.

One night, alone at the restaurant, a man asked to join her for dinner and she accepted. She told him about her 'boyfriend in Los Angeles' and he asked why the boyfriend wasn't with her on this dangerous trip.

'I told him I was "pathologically independent",' she said, laughing at herself.

She admitted being ashamed of not having the courage to venture outside Kigali. Her dinner partner suggested that was 'self-preservation'. Nicola attributed it to an intuitive sense that the dead regarded her as an interloper, a tragedy tourist to whom they could be most inhospitable. On advice from Ghostbuster, she abstained from drinking during the week she was there.

Her return flight included a layover in Addis Ababa where she 'went on a ten-hour binge with a wild woman'.

She had planned to come straight to me after a forty-eight-hour stop in London. But Nicola plans and God doubles over. She phoned to tell me she was staying in France to do a story about Lourdes, the shrine to St Bernadette where 6 million Catholics and curious – miracle seekers and volunteer caregivers – pilgrimage annually.

'I love that place' – she'd been there before – 'and the *Times* bought my pitch. I think it's just what I need after Rwanda. I can write both stories from LA.'

'I miss you,' I told her. 'But I can wait another week. Come back with a great story.'

I didn't have to add, 'Keep in touch.' I knew she would.

On her second night at Lourdes, she phoned in tears. One of the head nuns had accused her of being a spy and saboteur, intent on writing a damning piece that would discredit the faith and make a mockery of all their good works. It struck Nicola so deeply because it was such a false reading. The nun made Nicola's reporting from inside the hospital unbearable and ultimately impossible.

But she found a better story outside the infirmaries, on the grounds where young volunteers brought the *maladies* to the shrine, in the streets of the town where wheelchairs outnumbered automobiles, and in the bars at night where teenage girls in tube tops drank at tables beside white-haired men in clerical collars.

Lourdes was a place that appealed to her heart and her hedonism.

'We pray hard and we play hard,' one of the priests told her. 'These kids will be up close to dawn, ready to clean bedpans and dress bedsores. They'll be looking after the sick all day, taking them to mass. At night, they need to let go.'

A young Welsh volunteer told her his mates called Lourdes 'St Bernadette's Dating Agency'. One of the doctors put the miracles in more ecclesiastical terms.

'Youth from all backgrounds come here and change from children to mature adults in the space of a week. Now, that is a miracle.'

Nicola called me every night after her research at one of the bars. I was in her thoughts at the end of every day. And I was content to share space at the top of her priority list, alongside her independence.

On her last night in Lourdes, I received a call that reminded me she was an impossible girlfriend.

'I just need to ground myself,' she said. 'I can't wait to see you, but I can't bear the thought of getting on another plane so soon.'

I'm not good at hiding disappointment.

'I just need a week,' she continued. 'Or, I don't know. Maybe an extra weekend. There's a concert the first weekend in August. I might want to go to that. My friend Iper is playing with the Wailers.'

Isn't Iper the ex-lover who wanted you to be his 'baby mama'?

'He's more like my brother. Anyway, I haven't decided yet. It's a long drive.'

And where would you stay?

'Probably with one of the Wailers.'

Dead silence.

'I'm joking. I miss you terribly and I have so much to tell you. Please don't sound like that.'

The sound of one hand clapping.

Producer David Lester was a man who'd learned the business from the bottom up and never forgot where he came from. If a fast move was required from one camera set-up to another, Lester would lead the charge in moving chairs, lights and equipment for the turnaround. He relished getting his hands dirty.

He hated what I did for a living. He was all about the business of getting a movie made. Publicity was a speed bump along his purpose-driven highway.

He was a short, bearded, no-nonsense guy with intention in every stride. They didn't make them like David V. Lester anymore. But the business had changed. He was talking about retiring.

'I'm just sick of the bullshit,' he declared.

After three weeks at local locations – deserts, open roads, a quarry, a modern high school – the movie moved to soundstages on the Universal lot and all our jobs calmed down. Except maybe David's.

We can do a practical effect. I don't wanna pay for VFX.

Do we need to dress that corner of the set? Will we ever see it?

What the fuck do you mean 'he doesn't like his pants'?

I hung around base camp and schmoozed with the actors, showed my face on set so Joss remembered I was there and got approvals for my few allotted press visits. Those were all weeks away.

Publicity's most important break on this movie was coming soon.

Attached is Universal's itinerary and info sheet for Comic-Con this Sunday.

Notes:

- *Panel participants should be aware there will be no hair & make-up personnel at the convention centre.*
- *Everyone will provide his/her own transportation to the Van Nuys airport. If you're driving to San Diego, you may park in any of the visitor spots.*

- *Please allow time for a punctual arrival since we're running on a tight schedule.*
  In case of emergency, my phone number is...

At around 6 p.m. on Friday, I was driving home from the studio to pack for the weekend when my phone rang. It was Nicola. I couldn't hear her opening greeting – or maybe there wasn't one.

She proceeded to scream at me for the next ten minutes, excoriating me for being so negative about her 'friends', for trying to control her, for not trusting her, for being so negative about her friends (she mentioned that more than once), and somewhere in there was something about me being 'a dog person' and her being 'a cat person'. I would've asked for an explanation on that one but she screamed over any attempts to get a word in. She'd been spending the week with Psychic Masseuse and Ghostbuster. I didn't need further explanation.

'Are you done?'

'No! You never take responsibility for anything... *screech, screech, etc.*'

I hung up on her.

When I got home, I wrote a long email breaking up with her. I'd had it. My life would be immeasurably simpler without her, Psychic Masseuse and Ghostbuster in it.

I wrote with calculated indifference. You go your way and I'll go mine. So long, it's been good to know ya. I felt mostly relief, as if I'd slammed the cage door barely ahead of a pursuing lion.

And since I was already online, I signed up for a dating-site trial membership and made dinner plans for Saturday night with someone who lived in San Diego.

So much for my monogamous relationship. On to Plan B.

Comic-Con is a four-day costume party in which thousands of nerds and nerdettes come together to be fantasy heroes and creatures summoned from comic books, movies and their inner child. We should all be so imaginative and liberated at least once a year.

There were Klingons and Spocks, Wonder Women and Supergirls, Batmen, Spidermen, Aquamen, Green Hornets, gladiators, Vikings, ladies in pink shorts and crop-top T-shirts promoting adult comics, an Elvis impersonator in a Storm Trooper uniform, and a bikini-clad lass in a glass box handling two live snakes to promote *Species 3*.

I led the featured speaker and his panel through the San Diego Convention Center to the side entrance of the main conference room. I couldn't help noticing how sexy Jewel Staite looked in tight jeans and a spaghetti-strap blouse. She caught me staring and winked. A new universe of possibilities opened.

The packed auditorium leaped to its feet as Joss and the *Firefly/Serenity* cast approached their chairs on stage. The queue at the microphone in the centre aisle stretched to the last rows of seats and replenished its numbers throughout the hour of Q&A. Joss received most of the questions and answered with appreciation for even the most oddball inquiry. There wasn't a hint of condescension in his repertoire. These were his people and he was one of them. I gained a lot of admiration for him that afternoon.

That evening, I took my internet date for a casual meal and ended the night with a stroll through the downtown Gaslight District. She was a sweet, attractive, well-read mother of two young children who worked in a law firm. I walked her to her car where we both said we'd had a 'nice' time. But there were no sparks.

Back in my hotel room alone, I turned my phone back on. Nicola had called seven times. I didn't call back.

My mulishness continued through Monday. Nicola's phone calls tapered off but didn't let up. I was aching for her. But why? She was unreliable, irrational and geographically unavailable. She had little interest in movies, she knew nothing about music before 1980 and her taste in friends was... well, I liked Anita and Katherine. She had spiritual beliefs that were wacky, no concept of punctuality and a pathological aversion to commitments.

What made me think she was committed to our relationship?

Fifteen phone calls suggested she wanted something more than to get in another boyfriend bashing.

One of Nicola's better traits was that when we argued, she would never let it go unresolved. She was tenacious about battling through to resolution. Among the worst things about Nicola was that she thought all our problems were my fault. She would never say, 'Oops, my bad.' It was always something about me that needed fixing. I was sure she'd got that from PM who would build her up one minute, then tell her in the next she was broken and only her psychic guidance could make the needed repairs.

But being in a relationship forces you to examine your own behaviour – once you've exhausted all defences for it. I was awakening to the uncomfortable realisation I was a less-than-perfect partner. I was mistrustful. I was controlling. Rather, I was feeling out of control – on many levels. I was angry – and angry about the fact I hadn't let myself be angry in eighteen years because it would chase Margaret into a cave from which she would emerge three days later to counter an argument I'd long forgotten.

And once in a while, Nicola would look in the mirror of us and see a reflection of her own maturing.

'You're teaching me how to love,' she wrote in one email.

In moments like these I trusted my feelings. I could let go of control and allow my heart to freefall.

My phone rang. I answered.

'I'm sorry,' she said.

Nicola was back in LA, back in my arms.

There'd been something affirming for me in letting her go. I knew I didn't need her, knew I wanted her and knew I was running from this relationship as fast as she was. Possibly faster.

In the past month, she'd been in Paris, Cape Town, Kigali, Lourdes and London, spent time with her two fractious families – the real one and psychic one – and, in her first week here, flew to San Francisco for a night to interview an environmentalist for a piece in *The Ecologist*. Chaos was merely windblown detritus she closed her eyes and strolled through.

I threw her into my own maelstrom of lunches, dinners and screenings. She joined a junket interview on set with Joss and Chiwetel Ejiofor. It was a foreign world speaking a foreign language, but she was used to those.

At night, we danced wildly in our office apartment, bumping into furniture, falling in a heap on the sofa where she would speak to me in French. My comprehension was better than I let on. And what she said was lovely.

On the final day of filming, I said my farewells around the *Serenity* set. Joss gave me a courteous 'nice working with you' and Jewel gave me a warm hug.

I sought out David Lester in his office.

'Thanks for all your help on this one,' he said. I shook his hand, knowing I'd done little more than stay out of his hair. 'I think we've made a helluva movie.'

Serenity would be David V. Lester's last movie, in a career that went back to the original *Star Wars*.

Nicola helped me pack and drove me to the airport the day after wrap. I was flying to Baltimore to start my next job. She would close the composer's office, put my few belongings in storage, then fly east to see me in two weeks.

But as usual, plans would change.

PART TWO: WAR AND PEACE

CHAPTER SEVENTEEN: SYRIANA

On 11 September 2001, I was working in Los Angeles on *Men in Black II*. A phone call from Margaret woke me at around 6 a.m.

'Turn on your television.' Her voice was a pitch below panic.

I turned it on in time to see the second plane hit.

I listened to the radio news in a trance as I drove to the Sony Pictures lot. Due to pending Screen Actors and Writers Guild strikes, ours was the only picture filming at Sony and one of the only movies filming in Los Angeles. An apocalyptic vacuum had sucked in the golf carts, Mercedes traffic and all sound.

I walked to Stage 12 where television sets with jerry-rigged antennas were turned to the news. No one was working.

'The world has changed forever,' director Barry Sonnenfeld proclaimed.

Robert Baer was a CIA operative, working mainly in the Middle East for twenty-one years before retiring in 1997. In 2002, he published a memoir entitled *See No Evil*, in which he suggests America's unpreparedness for the 9/11 attacks resulted from the disuse and misuse of American intelligence agents. The book describes his political education in Washington bureaucracy where career advancement is a greater imperative than service, corruption greases the wheels of government and breaking rank is the sole unforgivable sin.

Movies about politics are complicated. Movies about international politics are more complicated. Movies about petro-politics are impossibly complicated. But the links between them fascinated two high-profile Hollywood filmmakers.

Baer's book was purchased by Section Eight, a production company owned by Steven Soderbergh and George Clooney. The task of making cinematic sense of it was handed to Academy Award-winning screenwriter Stephen Gaghan, who would also be given the director's chair on this one.

Gaghan had written Soderbergh's Best Picture Oscar nominee *Traffic*, a multi-layered investigation into the dark world of drug trafficking and the futility of the so-called war on drugs. While he was researching that movie, the Justice Department approved the largest corporate merger in history, between Exxon and Mobil. It was a time when the anti-narcotics and anti-terrorism investigative units were both under the auspices of the Drug Enforcement Administration. The misdirection of terrorism units toward the drug war became clear when, two months prior to the release of *Traffic*, the USS *Cole* was blown up in Yemen.

At some point between his research and the film's release, Gaghan had an epiphany.

'I started thinking maybe the biggest addiction in our country was cheap oil.'

Syriana had been in production for two weeks before I joined the team in Washington. Warner Bros. held my place knowing it was a movie I desperately wanted to work on for its political messaging. The challenge for publicity would be guarding the media borders while positioning the film's message in a time when its relevance was being buffeted by breaking news on a daily basis. Escalating protests over the Iraq invasion, leaked photos of torture at Abu Ghraib and the 2004 presidential race, which was turning into a referendum on the war, made D.C. a thorny place to shoot a political thriller about a secret American agenda in the Middle East. The script – in an early, perhaps slightly sanitised, version – had to be submitted to the Justice Department for permission to film in the Capital. The security contingent assigned to the filming was as much monitoring the movie as guarding it.

While Nicola was in LA writing her Lourdes and Rwanda stories, another issue of social import distracted her from deadlines. A shaggy-haired Texan named Rupert, who'd written a book about the Bushmen, invited her to an Amnesty International fundraiser for the African First People hosted by singer-songwriter Jackson Browne. The Bushmen were being robbed of their traditional lands by governments in South Africa and Botswana and a delegation had been brought to the US to plead their case in Washington. The American organisers planned to take a contingent of Bushmen emissaries from LA to Washington, via the Hopi and Navajo reservations in Arizona.

'What do you mean you want to drive the Bushmen to an Indian reservation?'

'Two of them are my friends.' And if further explanation was needed: 'They're very small. It's not like they're going to crush the springs on your precious car.'

'It's called "the suspension" and… hold on, how many are you planning on taking?'

'Only four.'

That meant five.

'When are you coming to Baltimore?'

'It's just a few extra days. I probably won't go for the whole two-week trip.'

Probably?

But I didn't ask that. Instead I asked myself why it took me into the red zone.

Her unpredictability was becoming the most predictable thing about her. I was used to being away from my partner for months at a time. If all I wanted was predictability, I'd have stayed in my marriage. But was anarchy the only alternative?

What kept me from stamping my feet and throwing my toys out of the pram was a growing assurance that she wanted my affection as much as I wanted hers. If I could let go of expectations and trust what I felt when we were together, I could enjoy the bumpy ride.

So instead of picking a fight over 'probably'...

'Don't wreck the car,' I told her.

Was my indecisive, experience-junkie girlfriend, crusader for lost causes, consumer of spiritual smorgasbord, making me a better person?

Probably.

Nicola left the Navajo Trail in time to meet me in Baltimore for an End of Week Four party on Friday night. Crew parties may seem like an extravagance but they're often as necessary as lunch breaks. The collective experience needs to be constantly reinforced. Factions will grumble about working conditions in isolated pods at the hotel bar where entropy occurs organically. There is nothing that unifies a crew like free drinks and food.

Nicola wore a beaded V-neck, full-length brown cotton dress that clung to every curve. She was luminous. I was glowing in the light of her. My attention span for a party was approximately the running time of a feature film, but we stayed at this one for almost four hours, then followed some of the diehards to an after-party at a blues bar called Full Moon. The doorman looked at Nicola, then looked at me and pronounced, 'She's a goddess.' Indeed, she swept through the room like a queen on a palanquin but with my hand in hers.

In the morning, she told me she had to go to Washington where an assembly of Native American tribes were gathering for the soon-to-open American Indian Museum. She planned to meet her friend Zena, a South African *sangoma* (witch doctor).

She'd be back in time for dinner, when we'd be joined by two special guests who were coming to Baltimore for the Labor Day weekend.

Nicola was nervous about meeting Casey and Sam.

'Maybe they're not ready. Maybe they blame me for breaking up your marriage. What should I wear? I think we should meet at a restaurant. I don't think they should see that I'm staying with you. What do they know about us? Should I shake their hands? What have you told them about me?'

We agreed to meet at a restaurant on the harbour. But the boys and I had been to the science museum, watched a surround-sound IMAX movie called *Sacred Planet* and run out of things to do. And Nicola, as usual, was running late.

I phoned from the lobby of my corporate apartment.

'We're coming up.'

I opened the door and Nicola stood in the middle of the room with wet hair, a frozen smile and her hand extended.

Sam strode up and wrapped his arms around her.

We walked to the harbour restaurant, Sam and me ahead, Nicola and Casey behind. Nicola clung to Casey's arm with a vice grip, steering him away from anything and anyone he might bump into. The boardwalk was packed with pedestrians but they were the least of her worries. She was suddenly aware of kerbs he might trip over, baby-buggy wheels his cane might get caught in, dog leashes he could get entangled in, lamp posts, rubbish bins…

'She's great, Dad,' Sam declared as we walked. He judged people by how they were with his brother.

'I'd never been with a blind person before,' Nicola said after I'd taken the boys back to their hotel room. 'I was terrified.'

Our getting-to-know-the-girlfriend weekend flew by without incident. Nicola said she'd put a 'psychic bubble' around Casey so no harm would befall him. The bubble apparently only worked in her presence.

I took the boys to the airport on Monday and watched as two security men at the metal detector ignored Casey passing through unescorted – without his cane – and he slammed his head on the side of the machine. Only when I rushed to my son's aid, as the bump above his eye began to swell and redden, did either guard take notice.

'Sir, you really can't be here.'

I ran to the airline desk and got a pass to go through the detector, cutting to the front of the queue and growling at the implacable guards. I caught up with Casey and his brother at their boarding gate.

'Are you alright?' I asked with too much urgency.

'Dad.' He gritted his teeth. 'I get enough of this overprotective stuff from Mom. I don't appreciate getting it from you too.'

On George Clooney's first scheduled day of work, I was standing outside the Maryland State Capitol in Annapolis when I spotted Waldo Sanchez, the star's hairdresser and close friend. I'd worked with them both on *The Perfect Storm.*

'Where's the boss?' I asked after an exchange of greetings.

'Right behind you.'

I turned to see a pudgy figure with a receding hairline and a salt-and-pepper beard in a cheap suit.

George grinned at me. 'Geez, I guess they let anybody in here.'

Stole my line. You certainly look like a guy who could blend in anywhere.

'Yeah, it's great being anonymous,' he said with a straight face. 'I can walk into any restaurant in town and not get a table.'

His bodyguard, an ebullient Italian named Giovanni, cast his eyes skyward.

'When I met Bob [Baer], he was overweight, so I thought I should add some bulk,' George explained. 'The next time I saw him, he'd been on a diet, slimmed down, he looked great. The bastard.'

Even with an added thirty pounds, a beard and a shaved-back hairline, it didn't take long for the public to figure out who he was. Warner Bros. wanted to keep Clooney's new look a secret but that proved difficult when he kept posing for photos with everyone who asked.

Nicola spent her days in D.C. with her friend Zena and the tribes camped in front of the American Indian Museum for a six-day celebration of its opening. At night, we'd dine in one of the restaurants along the Baltimore harbour or she'd cook in our small apartment. It all felt very life-work balanced. That equilibrium would be short-lived.

This coming weekend, she wanted to be in two places. Inconveniently, they were at opposite ends of North America.

I'd invited her to the *Hotel Rwanda* premiere at the Toronto International Film Festival. Her new friends from the Hopi reservation had invited her to the San Gabriel Mountains in Southern California for an event called The Gathering, a powwow of spiritualists and healers who came together annually to fight over which ego-maniacal messiah was going to lead the charge toward world transformation.

It didn't require a clairvoyant to predict which event she'd choose.

We had no plans for when we'd see each other next. From The Gathering, she 'might stay in LA awhile', then fly to London.

'I think I'll skip the next location,' she said.

She hated the place in Morocco where we would be filming for the next month. It reminded her of something she'd rather not be reminded of.

Another crew party was scheduled for our last Saturday in Baltimore but I had important business elsewhere.

I made a five-hour drive to Ithaca to stay at our house with Sam, while Margaret flew off to Oregon with Casey to show him the piano-tuning school he'd be attending next year. She and Casey had been fighting more than usual and in a terse email to me, she said that maybe seeing his independent future would 'improve his attitude'. She'd caught Casey drinking with some friends in his loft bedroom and had cleared the house of alcohol. She'd also hidden the pipe rack in my office where I kept my grass.

'Mom never did anything bad when she was a teenager,' Sam told me. 'So she just doesn't realise it's all normal.'

Sam wanted normal. Especially with us. He wanted us to do all the things we used to do on the weekend. We had breakfast at the State Street Diner. We played catch on the lawn. It was beautiful and painful seeing my son so dedicated to making things feel normal. For me. For himself. For us. No Casey. No Mom. No Nicola.

He'd told me once when he was very young, 'Mom has Casey and I have you.' He always had both of us, of course, but now their home wasn't my home anymore. He was grappling with letting me go and trusting it wasn't forever.

I took him for a two-hour driving lesson in my old Volvo station wagon. He was a quick learner, focused, patient with himself when he made mistakes.

The Volvo and I transported Sam, his band and their equipment to a downtown café where The Fuzz Brothers – the new name of their band – had a gig. Sam was electric on stage, throwing himself into each song, connecting with his audience.

The show ended around 9 p.m. and most of the crowd filed out, having seen the band they'd come to see, but Sam wanted to support the next group. I watched him work the room before the following act started. Kids stayed because he was staying.

Instead of going out with his friends downtown, he said he wanted to come home with me and watch a movie. We sometimes used to sneak one in after his brother and mother were asleep. Our little secret. We watched *Bend It Like Beckham*. Sweet, if unexceptional. We cuddled on the couch, just like we used to.

After Sam went to bed, I sat in the music room with Etta James and a bottle of Cabernet I'd picked up in town. I tried to imagine what it felt like for him, living in that house with my ghost. Aside from my record collection, it had been purged of me.

The subtext of our movie was fathers and sons: Bob Baer and his son, the attorney Bennett Holiday and his father, the young Muslim boy who becomes radicalised after his father is beaten by police, the oil market analyst whose life changes when his son dies, the idealistic heir to the Emir betrayed by his father.

There is no greater love than what I feel for you, Etta sang.

Tell it to him, Etta. Tell him he'll always have me.

CHAPTER EIGHTEEN: TERROR ALERT

On 16 May 2003, terrorists hit five targets in Casablanca in which forty-five people were killed.

In March 2004, Spain suffered the worst terrorist attack in its history, a train bombing which killed 191 people. The attack was initially blamed on Basque separatists. A month later, evidence indicated the attack was in retaliation for Spain's joining the coalition fighting the Iraq war.

Both the Spanish and Moroccan attacks were executed by the same group, the Moroccan Islamic Combatant Group (MICG). They were serious. They were dangerous. They were still around.

One of the targets of the Casablanca bombings was the Hôtel Farah, two blocks down the Avenue des Far from the Sheraton where *Syriana* cast and crew would be housed for the next month. Despite the risks, the producers of *Syriana* had decided a realistic movie about the Muslim world couldn't be shot in a non-Muslim country.

'Locations inform what we do as actors,' Clooney said. 'We're immersed in a passionate belief system here. Anyone who thinks you can bomb that ideal out of a country needs to travel more.'

The production invested $1.5 million on security in addition to having the Royal Guard on loan from the king. *Syriana* would be the first American movie to film here since the bombings.

The road to Morocco was a long one – eight hours from Dulles Airport to Paris, a three-hour layover at de Gaulle and three more hours to Casablanca. It was an overnight flight, so everyone's time clocks were off. To reset those, the production threw a party.

Where is the ideal place to throw a Welcome to Casablanca party?

Rick's Café, of course.

With a domed ceiling at the centre of a palm-dotted open floor, a teak bar and alabaster deco arches supporting two tiers of balcony, it wasn't a replica of the gin joint Bogart presided over but a resplendent homage, complete with fez-topped waiters and a piano man named Issam (pronounced I-Sam). Its American owner, Kathy Kriger, who went by the name Madame Rick, had abandoned her career in the diplomatic service a few years ago and found a 1930s mansion at the edge of the old Medina that could fulfil an enterprising dream.

'The aftermath of September eleventh made up my mind to do this,' she explained. 'I wanted to remind people there's more to American values than invading foreign countries.'

Our writer-director Steve Gaghan arrived with producers Jennifer Fox and Michael Nozik. I introduced them to the madam and she found us a quiet table in the back.

It was good to see Gaghan outside work. I hadn't spoken with him much in Baltimore and the only non-business interaction we'd had was a brief conversation at the last party. Tall and thin with steel-blue eyes and shaggy brown hair, his easy-going countenance was deceptive.

Raised in an upper-crust Kentucky family, he got booted out of his expensive prep school a week before graduation for driving a go-cart through the corridors. He'd written *Traffic* partly from his own experience as a former drug addict. In creating his screenplays, he researched endlessly, then sequestered himself until there was a satisfactory draft. But he was never satisfied. This intensity, combined with an off-the-charts intellect, little sleep and possibly some residue chemical imbalance could send him from charming to spikey at the flip of a switch.

Nozik started talking about a scene we'd shot in D.C. with Jeffrey Wright as investigative attorney Bennett Holiday. He comes to collect his alcoholic father, passed out in the corner of a bar, after the bartender discovers a card that reads, 'If you find this card, call my son.'

'That was my grandfather,' Gaghan said. 'He was an old-school, chain-smoking, hard-drinking journalist and he used to carry a card in his wallet that said the exact same thing, with my father's phone number.'

His father had died when he was fifteen and I offered my observation about the father–son themes in this movie.

'That's all I write about – or fathers and daughters,' the charming Stephen acknowledged.

'Don't put that in the press notes,' Spikey Stephen added.

I left the party around midnight, walking back to the Sheraton Hotel past the old medina, along narrow streets where men sat in plastic chairs outside dimly lit storefronts sipping syrupy tar from demitasse cups and puffing on hookahs.

Casablanca is not a pretty city. It has neither the charm of Marrakech nor the classic splendour of Fez. But it is bathed in noir. It feels deliciously treacherous, day or night. Night-time masks the poverty in central Casablanca. The police are out. Criminal elements hide. During the day, the slums become more porous and their denizens join the commercial centres of the city. Pickpocketing, purse snatching, muggings are all part of the fabric of life where extreme wealth and desperation exist in each other's shadow.

I phoned Nicola in LA. She missed me. I missed her. I told her about the party at Rick's. She told me about Richard.

After suffering two suffocating four-year relationships from her late teens to her late twenties, Nicola met Richard at a yoga session off Portobello Road. He was everything she could have dreamed of: slim, handsome, spiritual and born to a class of which her mother would approve. Their attraction was instant.

Richard was a romantic and thought of Morocco as the most romantic place in the world. They flew to Marrakech, where they spent a couple of days wandering the old medina, then rented a car and drove south toward the walled city of Taroudant, over the Atlas Mountains, crisscrossing the Sahara. Both were explorers of land and life, shunning the main roads in favour of dirt tracks to nowhere, sleeping in the car in the middle of the desert, dancing under the stars.

Richard was spontaneous and reckless and free. Once, when they were driving, he threw his passport out the car window, shouting, 'I'm never going home!' Nicola had to go look for it. Another time, he stopped the car, stripped naked and went skipping across the scorching sand. He would make up poems that were mostly gibberish but would recite them in such elegant Elizabethan as to make them sound like undiscovered works of the Bard.

When they got to Casablanca, he sank into inexplicable despondency. Nicola tried to blame it on the ugliness of the city, ghosts of the transatlantic slave trade, even an unhappy past life there. Richard spent the night weeping and wouldn't leave the hotel room. She eventually coaxed him into the sunlight, packed him in the car and started back to Marrakech. He brightened with each mile they put between themselves and Casablanca and both vowed never to return to the gloom of this city.

They continued seeing each other in London and travelled the country from Wales to the Hebrides. His depressions appeared sporadically but the highs were so rewarding, she stayed loyal through the down times. One rainy weekend, they drove north, with no destination, and found themselves in an isolated part of the Scottish Highlands where they rented a cabin. That night he tried to kill her.

It started with the invented poetry, as they sat staring into the fireplace. His eyes grew wide as flames threw shadows across his face and the recital became more frenetic, no longer even partly in English. Frightened, she begged him to go for a drive with her. He grabbed her keys. Then he grabbed her throat.

She fought free and ran to the road where she flagged one of the few cars passing. At a tavern in town, she called emergency services. They took Richard away. When she phoned his mother, all the poor woman could say was, 'I'm so sorry. I was afraid something like this might happen.' Nicola had to sign the papers committing him to a state hospital.

She told the story as if it had happened to someone else. She'd been someone else then. In the decade that had passed since Richard, she'd never trusted her heart to anyone, she said. Until now.

'I love you too.'

I felt the power in the words I'd been holding back.

They may have scared her.

'Mmmm,' she purred.

We changed the subject.

Paris-based production designer Dan Weil would be using Casablanca for two cities that would've been even more hazardous to film in: Tehran and Beirut.

'Casablanca is a good match for the older parts of Beirut because of its French architecture,' Weil said, motioning to the building where we were shooting. 'Tehran is more complicated because it looks more like a Soviet Bloc city, less ornate, more industrial. We wouldn't have got permission to film in either of those places and even if we did, they wouldn't have allowed us to do some of the things we're doing here.'

I'd arrived on set with behind-the-scenes cameraman Steve Wacks who had just flown in from Los Angeles. Steve was a great guy to work with, smooth and unobtrusive, and even better dinner company after work. He was an amateur sommelier and a bargain-seeking gourmand with a deceptive sense of humour and a deft touch on the piano if there happened to be one around. Vic Davis was producing. We'd worked together numerous times and he was one of the best interviewers in the business.

The new stills photographer, Glen Wilson, would also be good company at work and after hours. I'd had dinner with him our first night here. A lanky, six-foot-tall, light-skinned black man with a Clark Gable moustache, he was more a fine artist with an interest in portraits and documentary photography than a movie stills guy. He was relatively new to the movie game, but he had a good eye and a good understanding of the job ahead.

Professional, companionable, collaborative, it was a solid team. Perhaps the best I'd had all year. All I had to do was win the support they needed from the actors and director to get the job done.

We were filming at our hotel the next day. The main scene took place in an elevator. It was the only scene Clooney and Matt Damon – as oil analyst Bryan Woodman – had together in the entire movie. Steve Wacks shouldered his video camera behind our stills photographer, who positioned himself for coverage between boom and A-camera. Assistant director Simon Warnock ushered them away before the first take.

Alexander Siddig, a lean, elegant Sudanese, raised in England, was playing the reformist leader Prince Nasir who hires Damon's character as his advisor. This was the second day of his first starring role in a major film. He'd arrived yesterday, with no sleep, to deliver a speech in Arabic – a language he didn't speak – to a crowd of 150 Arabic-speaking extras. Exhausted at the end of his workday, he entered the hotel lobby to go to his room and collapse. He rushed to the elevator behind two men who had just entered as the doors were closing. Sid pushed the button in time to catch them. A burly man inside stopped him with an extended hand and an apologetic smile.

'It's alright, Gio,' Clooney said to his bodyguard. And Siddig got into the lift.

'George had no idea who I was but he was magnanimous enough to let me in and I was too shy to introduce myself,' Sid told me later. 'The next day's scene involved Prince Nasir getting in the same elevator with his bodyguards and letting George in at the last minute. He didn't make the connection until we began filming the scene and the irony unravelled. We had a good laugh over it.'

Video and stills caught a couple of candid moments of George, Matt and Sid laughing off set. Not much of a day for publicity.

Filming moved to the Old Quarter of Casablanca, doubling for Hezbollah territory in Beirut. There were actors with rifles on the rooftops and crowds of non-actors on the narrow street wondering what was going on. I was more concerned about paparazzi than assassins, but it became apparent no one in the crowd had the slightest idea who our Number One was – and anyone with the thought of kidnapping an American actor could see three men with semi-automatics who appeared to have beaten them to it. Why they kept doing it over every time someone yelled 'cut' may have been a mystery.

We got a brief EPK sound bite with Gaghan who told us this looked exactly like the Beirut neighbourhood where his car was stopped when he was doing his research. Just like the Bob Baer character, he was taken blindfolded to a meeting the real Baer had set up for him with the leader of Hezbollah. He felt safer there than in many other places where he was researching, he said.

Sometime after that interview, Simon Warnock kicked Wacks and Glen off the set. I never found out why.

CHAPTER NINETEEN: POLITICS

It was no surprise that Nicola was staying longer in LA than she originally said she would. There was a birthday party, the possibility of a story in Nevada for *The Ecologist*, her friend Estelle was doing something exciting and the sun was rising in the east. This delayed her trip to London and the myriad things she had to catch up on at home. She'd softened her aversion to Casablanca since our conversation but the obstacles in getting her here were beginning to look insurmountable. It would require something more than just missing me.

I was talking to producer Jennifer Fox on set, telling her about my girlfriend the journalist, when she offered, 'She should come do a story on the movie that she could hold for release.' Unfortunately, she'd have to get an assignment first, which could take weeks. But it got me thinking.

After work one night, I was invited to join George, Waldo, Jennifer and cinematographer Bob Elswit for dinner in the hotel's Japanese restaurant. Once again, the topic was fathers and sons. And politics.

George had recently spent a week in Kentucky, fundraising for his father who was running for Congress. Nick Clooney was a local television personality and news columnist in his home state. In this election year, he'd decided to enter politics as a liberal Democrat in a conservative district. George was still steaming from a clash he'd had with his dad over compromising principles for political pragmatism. The issue was gay rights.

'After all the fights I've had with the press – *Hard Copy, Entertainment Tonight*, a lot of others – because they'd done something wrong and I put my career on the line to stand up to them, I've earned the right to criticise him for not standing up for what he believes in,' George began. 'There were times we'd go from living in a nice house one month to living in a trailer the next cuz my pop would say to some station owner, "You wanna lay off these twenty guys? Fine, I'm going too." And we'd be unemployed for a year. He taught me what it meant to be a liberal.

'So, now I see him cave to these idiots. Yeah, I'll fight with him. If I didn't fight all my fights, he'd be the first one telling me I was wimping out.'

He's 'pushing pushing pushing' Gaghan in the same way.

'Keep it real. Junk it up. Don't let the cameras be static.'

Movies or politics, he was all about 'keep it real'.

In filmmaking, as in life, he was also big on keep-it-family.

After dinner, Jennifer and Bob headed for the bar at the other end of the mezzanine. I followed George and Waldo to the elevator, where I popped the question.

'Warner's wants to hire someone to write a generic story for international publicity. I'd like my girlfriend to do it'

George gave it a moment's thought.

'Great. Get her down here.'

I called her from my room.

'Phone Mic Kramer at the studio tomorrow and book a flight. I'll send him an email tonight. You've got an assignment.'

That was a word every journalist understood as an imperative.

'I want you with me' would not have worked.

Nicola arrived late and we stayed up even later, so we missed the first half of the day's filming at a former French military compound in the old medina that Dan Weil's artists had transformed into a *madrassa*. There were 180 extras, mainly children dressed as students at the Islamic school.

We had lunch in the catering tent with actress Greta Scacchi and her husband Carlo. Carlo was a whippet of a man, barely Greta's height, with sallow cheeks and a five o'clock shadow. He looked as unlikely a match for a sultry movie star as one could imagine but they seemed to fit like puzzle pieces.

'He has a fiery Italian temper,' Greta confided to Nicola when the two had a moment.

It was the perfect introduction to Nicola's new assignment. She had an instant connection with one of stars and the four of us would become dinner companions over the next few nights while Greta was working here.

The next day, she met George.

We were filming in an open-air restaurant on a main street that was supposed to be a café in Tehran. It was an intimate dialogue scene between Bob Baer and his wife at a lunch table. Greta was nervous and Gaghan was frustrated. Steve Wacks got booted off set again.

While cameras were repositioning, Greta retreated to a holding area and Clooney came to where we were standing. I introduced the studio's embedded journalist and the three of us talked movies and politics. The scene was reset and George re-joined Greta in the café.

'I have to sit down,' Nicola told me. 'My knees are shaking.'

After another day's filming in which there was nothing much to report on, we had dinner alone at the hotel where Nicola admitted feeling lost and purposeless here.

Popping into a production in progress is like timing your leap onto a slow-moving train. There hadn't been any great scenes to watch, she hadn't done any interviews and the only person with whom she'd made a connection was Greta, who was on a plane home tonight. Meanwhile, I was surrounded by a hundred of my new best friends.

She had an assignment. She even had a badge that said Warner Bros. Publicity. She was part of the machine. She was a writer and writers know how to integrate into new environments. But this still felt to her like my environment. At the heart of her writings, her travels, her attachment to Psychic Masseuse and Ghostbuster, her efforts to be the peacemaker in her family was a craving for service. She wanted to feel like her presence on Earth served a purpose.

So far, she wasn't finding that on the road with me.

We arrived on set for the Big Explosion as the special-effects team rigged charges and stuntmen and women rehearsed. The scene was Bob Baer walking away from a kabob shop while the Amiri brothers, a pair of sleazy arms dealers, load their newly purchased missiles into a car. Baer gives a signal to a hidden cohort and the car blows up.

The explosion was loud, even with earplugs distributed by the PAs. Within minutes, people came rushing from their homes to see what was going on. Apparently, few had read the leaflets distributed by our locations department. There was genuine panic. It was May 2003 all over again.

Soon, press started arriving. But before dealing with them, I put Nicola together with our special-effects coordinator, Trevor Wood. It was her first interview and a good one. Later, we had a drink at the hotel with location manager Christian

McWilliams. He gave her some funny stories about calming down some of the panicked public.

She was working. She had a purpose.

She interviewed art director Laurent Ott who was very frank about Gaghan's whimsies driving them all crazy. '"I want Khomeini posters here. Where are the Khomeini posters? I want flags. I want this sign up on the kabob shop." But Tehran wouldn't have a sign like that. We spent a day painting the name [USS *Condoleezza Rice*] on the oil tanker and now we hear it's going to have to be removed in post.'

Probably not information that would make it into her commissioned story but the kind of gossip that makes one feel like an insider.

On our day off, we went shopping with Samia, the Arabic dialect coach. A professor of linguistics in the UK who also spent four years in medical school, studied law and was a devout Muslim woman writing a book about the misinterpretations of the Quran by religious fundamentalists, she was a strong, spiritual woman with whom Nicola would develop a friendship over the course of the movie.

Jennifer Fox was another impressive woman with whom Nicola had begun getting acquainted. President of Clooney and Soderbergh's production company, she filled a modelling role for Nicola: successful woman in a man's world. Jennifer also enjoyed a good party. A potential bond there.

Things were opening up and Nicola was not only finding workmates who gave her independence from me but getting interviews to add to her sense of usefulness.

I was delighted for her.

Until our last party in Casablanca.

The venue was straight out of the Arabian Nights, a tiled *riad* (palace) near the old medina where we were greeted by fire-eaters and dancing girls. Inside was an enormous swimming pool, a dance floor, a bountiful buffet and an open bar. The music was pounding and conversation was limited by the noise, but Nicola and I chatted with a few people, separately and together, before she excused herself to go to the bathroom. I waited, holding her drink. And waited. Forty-five minutes later, I spotted her on the dance floor. I walked up, handed her the drink and shouted above the music, 'You obviously want to be here by yourself. I'm leaving,' and headed toward the exit.

Ms Independence, who once threw an ashtray at my head for cramping her style, was now using bathroom breaks instead of ashtrays to assert her sovereignty. Why didn't I just put her drink on a table and go off to find my own entertainment? I felt churlish. I came back. It was a good thing because she hadn't heard a word I'd said. 'Stay just another few minutes and dance with me,' she pleaded. I thought that would be the mature thing to do.

We danced in a group with Simone, our vivacious production coordinator, and Louise from accounting, among others. Then, Nicola disappeared again. An hour later, I found her in the corner of one of the hookah rooms, smoking with three Moroccan men I didn't recognise.

She looked up at me, said her goodbyes to the mystery Moroccans and one of them pressed a scrap of paper with his phone number into her hand. She slipped it into her purse.

I suddenly felt like the carpet under my feet had caught fire. All I wanted was to get out of there. The red and orange tapestries, the swirling-patterned tiles, flickering lanterns, walls starting to close in. The dance music had become an assault on my ears. The mystery Moroccans? I didn't give a shit. It was the abandonment after I'd lingered so long at her urging. It was the anguish of something way more than it was, but I was incapable of intellectualising it. I just needed to get away from it.

'Why can't you just enjoy a party?' she shouted at my back as I raced ahead of her. By the time we got to the hotel, she was saying, 'We're fucked!' and I was shouting, 'We're over!' It was past 3 a.m.

In our room, she calmed down and wanted to talk. I fell on the bed and put a pillow over my head to drown out whatever she was saying.

Next morning, I took a long walk to the boardwalk where we'd filmed a scene between Clooney and British stage star Mark Strong a few days earlier. There wasn't much of a beach but the salt air helped clear my head.

Alright, let's figure out what happened last night. I wanted her to have her own identity with this travelling circus, didn't I? But I also wanted a partner who wanted to share this life with me. I admit here to a dim awareness of arguing to be right, not to find the truth. But the truth was she lied to me: *stay and dance with me!* Okay, 'lied' might be too strong a word. Still, *she* pushed the button that caused that explosion. I didn't react to nothing. Maybe I overreacted – a little. I shouldn't have bothered looking for her and should have just gone home by myself. Right. That'd show her. Shit-for-brains, you would've been up all night wondering if she'd been mugged in an alley. Is that parental? Is she a child?

It was around noon when I got back to the hotel and found Nicola in the lobby having a cup of coffee alone. She was hung-over. I was contrite. We only had one more day together here and neither of us wanted to say goodbye without resolving this. Credit sobriety or the absence of a techno soundtrack, the conversation was in a much lower register as we walked back to the beach. We only resolved that we had a problem with parties.

On Nicola's last night in Casablanca, we had dinner with Alex Siddig, Simone and her boss Sarah. Simone and Sarah, our production manager, had been working together for the past seven years. Simone, gregarious and animated; Sarah whip-smart with a biting wit.

Simone joked about the plethora of pages our mad maestro was churning out each night in lieu of sleep. Sarah told how an outraged Clooney had tripled the craft service budget after the explosion scene when we'd run out of food for the large crowd of extras. Siddig told us about his background, being caught in the Sudanese civil war as a boy, his British mother having to flee the country and send for him when the fighting stopped. How his uncle, the actor Malcolm McDowell, paid for his education and inspired him to try acting.

This was the kind of party I liked.

CHAPTER TWENTY: TWO WORLDS

The largest of seven emirates that compose the UAE, Dubai is a city state on the rise – literally. It boasts the world's tallest building, the Burj Khalifa, and the Dubai Mall, which is the largest shopping mall in the world. Skyscrapers seem to land overnight like alien starships in the middle of the business district.

It is also a state that exploits foreign labour, particularly Palestinian, Pakistani and Lebanese refugees, and jails reporters who try to document human-rights abuses.

Dubai's leader, Sheikh Zayed bin Sultan Al Nahyan, was in many ways a progressive monarch – one who might even have been a model for our movie's Prince Nasir. Sheikh Zayed created the nation of United Arab Emirates. He opened Middle Eastern minds to Western investments and consumer culture. He wanted a movie industry here.

Our filmmakers had no idea if he would approve filming once he'd read the script. But with minor changes, he opened Dubai to its first American production. He was smart in picking a controversial movie to start with – one that would make neighbouring oligarchies break out in a regional rash. If anyone were to question Dubai's commitment to free speech, all he had to do was gesture with one hand to our film – while keeping the other hand over the collective mouths of human-rights groups.

The production arrived during the holy month of Ramadan. It is mandatory for Muslims – unless they have medical dispensation – to fast all day, every day throughout the month. No eating or even drinking water between sunrise and sunset. Most shops are closed.

Out of respect to our local crew, tents were assembled around the set in which snacks and drinks were available to non-Muslims. No food or beverage was allowed outside, though some Westerners carried water bottles in their tool belts.

The average daily temperature was in the nineties, with heat intensified off bleached desert sands. The Muslim crew worked uncomplainingly.

Power lines stretched across the desert, framing a scene in which our two young principals, Mazhar Munir and Sonell Dadral, are among a half-dozen young men passing around a jar of home-made hooch, trying to get another of the boys to drink with them. The boy climbs a metal tower as they shout for him to come down for a swig. He will not and cannot. He's just sold one of his kidneys.

From one camera angle, the power poles stretch to infinity across an ocean of white. The turnaround reveals a modern metropolis in the distant background. Our characters, Wasim and Farooq, have recently lost their jobs in the oil fields as a result of a merger between our fictional conglomerates Connex and Killen – a scenario played out for real five years ago when Exxon and Mobile streamlined their Middle East operations, putting thousands of labourers out of work.

I got a ride from set to base camp with a young driver named Kamal. His family had migrated to Dubai forty years ago. He was born here twenty-five years ago. He was Palestinian and spoke very good English. The non-Muslim cast and crew would be breaking for lunch soon and several of them had already begun disregarding the memo about not taking food or drink outside the catering tents. One South African costume lady appeared to be flaunting it. I apologised to Kamal for the disrespect.

'It's hard but in Ramadan we are not supposed to harbour any negative thoughts, so…' He shrugged. 'My children are too young to fast so there is sometimes water and a little bit of food for them before the *iftar* (night-time meal). So, I think of these others like children who can't help themselves.'

He got one day a week off and drivers were on a rotating call to take the crew shopping or to the beach on Sunday.

What kind of work do you do when you're not driving a film crew around?

'Whatever I can. My father is a builder and sometimes he can find me work,' he said. 'He is lucky because he has a kind boss. Some people aren't so lucky, but they have to stay at the job anyway because if they leave, their boss will publish their picture and they will be sent away.'

If you were born here, aren't you a citizen?

'No one can become a citizen here. But I would like to leave. For three years now, I am sending an application for the lottery in the US to get my green card.'

Good luck with that, I said without irony. But I was struck by the cruel joke that the hopes of a Palestinian refugee lay across the Atlantic in a culture that, at best, distrusted him and, at worst, considered him the enemy.

My room at the Shangri La Hotel was ridiculous. A one-bedroom suite with a sitting room that was triple the size of any hotel room I'd stayed in. The bedroom featured a double king-sized bed in which you could easily lose your partner behind eight pillows and a duvet the length of a mainsail. The view of downtown at night looked like a set from *Blade Runner.*

I had it all to myself.

Nicola was in Norfolk, where her friend Anita had got her a two-day job doing interviews on Michael Winterbottom's *Tristram Shandy.*

The US election day was coming up and a bunch of the crew – maybe even Clooney – planned to gather in the bar to watch the early returns. Nicola had promised she would be here for that. I was driving to set, tuned to news on the local English-language radio station, when I called to confirm.

'You'll be here for Tuesday, right?'

'Darling, I'm giving a yoga lesson at a retreat this weekend and I may stay with my friends (PM and Ghostbuster) on Monday. They're so exhausted after a retreat and they asked if I could help with the kids...'

'You're like their slave! I don't know how you don't see it.'

'I don't know how this is going to work out between us if you keep being so critical of them.'

'I wasn't talking about them. I was talking about you!'

'That's even worse! They don't control me!'

'Right. Nobody controls you. World events stop for you. Days of the week freeze in place. The clock doesn't move...' My phone lost reception somewhere along the road. Which may have been just as well.

The end of the day found me in the gym, working out my frustrations. Clooney was there with one of his bodyguards, Gerry Flynn.

Stay in England, see if I care, I grunted to myself as Gerry spotted for me on the weight bench. *I'm having a fine time without you.* Grunt. Push.

'Slow down,' said Gerry. 'You get better results if you take it slow and easy.'

Executive producer Jeff Skoll was on set for the first day of our week-long shoot of the film's dramatic conclusion (spoiler alert), in which a caravan of SUVs carrying Prince Nasir, his family and Bryan Woodman are the targets of an American drone attack.

Skoll was the founder of eBay and had just launched his own film company, Participant Films. Participant's mandate was making films that 'inspire and compel social change'. I'd imagined him to be one of those head-in-the-clouds or nose-to-the-grindstone, inscrutable Silicon Valley types. I found him unassuming, engaged and eager to learn about the business. We chatted at length and he asked me what I'd been working on lately. I mentioned *Hotel Rwanda*.

'That movie was the model for the kind of films I want to do,' he said. We talked about the power of images and their lasting imprint. I asked if there was an image from this movie he saw as the poster.

'Look, we all know the poster is going to be George,' he said. 'But is there an image that makes me feel the power of this movie? Probably something with Prince Nasir. He's the visionary who's too much of a threat to be allowed to stay alive.'

It was exciting to talk with someone who was so passionate about movies as more than just entertainment – especially someone who had the money to make them. Like many other times lately, I found myself wishing Nicola could be part of the conversation. Her curiosity, her enthusiasm, the way she could draw people out added another dimension to every interesting encounter. Instead, she was babysitting the psychic kids and probably cleaning PM's kitchen. Well, I hope she finds that stimulating.

And that burst of petulance suddenly flashed like an X-ray of my selfish emotional core. Yes, I wanted her to be a part of everything I was experiencing on this movie. Was I expecting her to be a second skin? Opening the door to my life was becoming less a gift than a demand. How would I feel if she insisted I come along on Psychic Masseuse's retreats? Let's not go there.

I called her that night to report my epiphany and release her from any obligation to be with me for tomorrow's election.

'I had some insights over the weekend too,' she said. 'I'll be there around midnight tomorrow. Is that okay?'

Something was happening in the dynamic of us that was turning both our sights inward. The friction of self-examination makes the pearl. A few more insights from each of us and we might yet discover we were the perfect imperfect couple.

I had dinner in the hotel's rooftop restaurant with Alex Siddig and British-Iraqi actress, Badria Timimi, who plays his wife. Gaghan had been giving Sid a terrible time, criticising his performance without being able to convey what he wanted the actor to do. In the middle of our meal, the restaurant started buzzing and all the wait staff suddenly disappeared into the kitchen. When our waiter finally reappeared, we called him to our table and asked what was happening.

'Our president is dead,' he told us.

The death of Sheikh Zayed bin Sultan Al Nahyan sent shockwaves throughout the Gulf. Sheikh Zayed was more than the leader of his country, he was the Emirates' own George Washington. At wrap, I was called to a meeting. Present were the producers, the owner of the local service provider (Filmworks), a man from the nascent Dubai Film Commission and a woman from the airport authority who we were courting for permission to shoot there. Sombre looks of anticipation all around.

A solidly built, moustachioed man in uniform we knew as the Colonel entered the room. The Colonel was a ranking officer in Dubai's secret service and worked closely with line producer Georgia Kacandes in securing all our locations. Dark glasses covered his eyes but his stoic military composure was visibly sagging. It was obvious he felt the death of his president as a personal loss.

'He was our father,' the Colonel told us.

The funeral was tomorrow. Shops and businesses would shut down for the next three days. There would be eight days in which government and school buildings would be closed and an official mourning period of forty days.

'This should not affect your filming,' he said before leaving.

That was all the producers wanted to hear – though I noticed Georgia's sad gaze following him out the door.

Dubai was nine time zones from New York and polls opened on the East Coast at 7 a.m. Nicola's flight came in at around 11:30 p.m. We arrived at the hotel a little after midnight and went straight to the bar to join some of our crew watching exit-poll results. There were already disputes over voting irregularities in Republican-controlled Ohio.

'Fucking Florida all over again,' one of our guys commented.

The bar closed at 1 a.m. and I brought Nicola and her suitcase up to our suite on the thirty-ninth floor. I turned on the lights and she looked around.

'I feel like I'm in a James Bond movie,' she said.

The English-language radio station, like all the ones in Arabic, was running twenty-four-hour tributes to the Sheikh, so we turned it off knowing there would be regular text updates on the election from our post-production supervisor in the US.

It was sweltering, the hottest day yet. But the American crew were all standing in the sun, huddled around whoever was getting phone reception. All one had to do was read faces to get the news.

Clooney came back from filming and checked his Blackberry. His father had lost his Kentucky congressional race. 'Not only lost,' George clarified, 'but lost badly.'

Senator John Kerry wasn't losing badly but final projections were for Bush – unless Ohio was contested.

Clooney set his jaw and shook his head. Gaghan shot a why-hast-thou-forsaken-us look at the sky, then started doing zombie circles humming 'California Dreamin''. The mood turned from anger to bewilderment back to anger. Finally, the set radios called everyone back to work. But Clooney and Gaghan were having a meeting. The producers were called in.

An hour later, the director, producers and star left their meeting tent and headed to the picture cars in the desert. Everyone was wondering what just happened.

A few minutes later, the word spread. We had changed the ending of our movie. The Bush–Cheney re-election ensured ongoing war in the Middle East. To reflect the devastating impact of that, (spoiler alert) Bob Baer must die in the drone attack.

That night, in the bar, dozens of cast and crew gathered in front of two TVs and watched our slim hopes die as Kerry made his concession speech. Not a word about accounting for votes in Ohio, not a word about dirty tricks, not a hint of outrage.

'The senator from Illinois who made the keynote speech at the convention,' Clooney said, sending up a tiny note of optimism. 'Keep an eye on him. He could be the Democratic nominee one day.'

The special-effects department had captured a desert rat. They kept it in a cage on their truck and only a few of us were permitted to know about it – either by experiencing it first-hand or witnessing the shock of those who'd seen it up close. I'd worked with this team on *Gladiator*. On that movie, they kept a wild ferret. I saw it up close.

Nicola had interviewed SFX supervisor Trevor Wood in Casablanca and wanted some details about today's upcoming drone attack.

The special-effects department is often repository for the quirkiest characters on a movie crew. They are the motorheads, the tattoo junkies, the sci-fi buffs, the tinkerers, the Demolition Derby fans, the cut-ups. On set, they can be the guys working the most overtime hours, pre-rigging, testing, cleaning up after the gag has gone boom. They can also be the guys with too much free time, having little or nothing to do on a day when the lone effect is rigging a chair to collapse.

Today was slated to be a big effects day: the drone explosion and its aftermath. But having set the charges and positioned the smoke effects, SFX could stand down until the final scene. And there was some question we'd even get to the explosion before losing daylight.

Nicola finished talking with Trevor and one of his guys asked if she'd like to get a peek at the 'desert rat'.

'Never seen anything like it,' he said.

'We're not supposed to have this thing on the truck. What if she tells somebody?' asked another guy.

'You won't tell anybody, will ya?' asked a third.

Nicola agreed to keep their secret.

The first guy went to the back of the truck and returned with a cage. Something furry was moving around but she couldn't quite make out its features.

'Come a little closer.'

'Watch out for the claws.'

'Hey, Matt, did you fix the lock?'

Vooooooom!

The door shot open and the rat sprang out.

Nicola's scream pierced the desert.

The rat literally 'sprang' out because it was a cloth puppet on a spring launch.

The SFX team and conspiratorial bystanders roared until their sides ached.

'You've been initiated. Welcome to the crew,' Trevor told her.

She was finally one of the gang.

The Prince's caravan of cars had been stopped by a herd of goats and the family got out to walk among them as Nasir explained to Brian that Bedouins have the right of way. In the last scene of the day, the goats move away, the caravan continues and Bob Baer comes driving across the desert waving a white flag. Baer gets out of his car and all the Prince's guard have their guns trained on him. Resets were taking a long time because there were a lot of bodies and vehicles in motion.

Nicola and I stood chatting with Clooney's security chief,

Giovanni. Gio was delightful company, affable and disarmingly forthcoming.

'See those guys with guns pointed at him?' Gio indicated the extras playing the Prince's guard. 'They're all Iraqi.' Apparently, no one had done background checks, so Giovanni, in his charming way, spoke with them.

'One of them used to make sculptures of Saddam Hussein. His eyes still get teary when he talks about it. They all hate America for invading their country. But none of them knew who George was. So…' He shrugged.

Gaghan yelled, 'Cut,' and, after checking the gate, Simon Warnock pronounced, 'That's a wrap.'

The guards suddenly rushed George, surrounding him. Soon, wives and children appeared from over the dune behind us. There was a flurry of back-slapping, hand-shaking, hugging and taking photos with our star, who was tossing around the few words he'd learned in Arabic, laughing along with them.

Gio turned his palms up.

'Maybe some of their wives knew who he was,' he said.

CHAPTER TWENTY-ONE: GOING, GOING...

Nicola and I were on the cusp of celebrating her longest relationship in ten years. I was still in trauma from my last relationship but already headlong into this one. We were now working and travelling together. Despite the occasional meltdown by one or the other of us, it was going pretty well. We'd drive to set together around shooting call in time to have breakfast, have lunch together with some of the cast or crew with whom we'd become friendly and usually dine alone together before having a couple of drinks at the hotel bar with whomever was there. On set, we'd established a good working relationship. She was sanctioned press and I was there to help her get her story.

Couples on a film are a rarity. It's not unusual for partnered production personnel to be in the same business – he an art director, she a costume designer – but they're usually ships passing on different projects, at best making it home in time for dinner... so long as they're in the same city and one isn't working night and the other day. Couples in this business work together when they can because, ostensibly, they enjoy one another's company. Still, music is made by the spaces between notes, and allowing that space is vital in all but the most symbiotic relationships.

George had invited Greta to dinner on his last night in Dubai. Nicola was in the actress's hotel room doing an interview for the *Mail on Sunday* over mini-bar gin and tonics. George had said he'd call Greta to confirm a time.

I was supposed to have an *iftar* with Siddig, his brother who'd come to visit and a couple of the other Arab actors. At around 8:30 p.m., Nicola called and asked if George was in the second-floor seafood restaurant. He wasn't. He was around the corner in the bar, holding court with a dozen crew. I told her it didn't look like he'd be leaving anytime soon and invited them to join us.

Greta went back to her room after dinner. Clooney was still in the bar. Nicola led us in there. George only stayed a few more minutes and we didn't get a chance to talk with him.

In our room that night, Nicola tumbled into a pit of depression.

'Greta and I should have been in the bar with George and the crew, instead of having dinner with you,' she said.

She burst into tears.

What the...?

It didn't take a minute to realise it had nothing to do with Clooney.

When the tears dried, she proceeded to list her failures: she wasn't a mother and movie star like Greta; she wasn't a film producer like Jennifer Fox or her pal Anita; she wasn't anything like who she thought she *should* be. She should be *more* than who she was. She was 'pathetic'.

I reacted dumbly, holding her, mumbling reassurances. I had no idea what triggered this. But it wasn't my job to fix it. Just to hold her.

I'd coaxed my depressed darling to location at the Royal Mirage Hotel, a five-star resort on sixty-five acres of lush gardens, including a kilometre of beach and an enormous swimming pool encircled by palms. I insisted it was a key scene that, for professional reasons, she shouldn't miss. Actually, the scene – though key to the movie – was unusable in her publicity story. She knew the schedule as well as I did by this point but she came along anyway.

I had a meeting with the hotel's public-relations people and lost track of Nicola. I found her in one of the lounges talking with a man in a white dishdasha with a falcon on his arm. He was a sheikh from Abu Dhabi, out for a bit of sport with his bird. He looked disappointed to see me. He gave her his business card and, with polite farewells, took his falcon and left.

While still fingering his card, she told me he'd invited her to join him and some of his friends at an *Eid* to mark the end of Ramadan that night. She added, 'I'm sure it would be fine if you come too,' with no sincerity whatsoever.

The light bulb went on: the unattached Nicola might've had drinks with a famous actor or dinner with a sheik and his falcon. Instead, she felt obligated to be with me. The status downgrade of a loser. Anybody who's ever been in a committed relationship knows there's a price you pay for the reward you get. Anyone who thinks the only good relationships are the ones that come without sacrifices can look forward to a lifetime of disillusionment. The problem for Nicola and relationships was that she too easily gave herself and lost herself.

She took the sheikh's card and filed it in the Bermuda Triangle that was her handbag, never to be seen again.

Vic Davis and Steve Wacks flew home the next day. Matt Damon and Alexander Siddig also checked out, leaving only our two young Arab stars, Mazhar and Sonell, to film with over the next three days.

With his movie nearing the end, Gaghan's cooperation with the publicity department had vastly improved. He'd been coming to Nicola and me during breaks, offering comments here, anecdotes there. On our embedded journalist's final day in Dubai, he asked us to meet a friend of his in the city.

His tone was oddly imploring as he requested, 'I'd like you to hear what he has to say.' He gave us a name, bereft of biography, hoping we'd spark to it. We didn't.

At the arranged time, we walked to a small café in the business district where we met investigative reporter Jon Lee Anderson. He was passing through Dubai after covering the war in Afghanistan. He'd recently published an opus on *The Fall of Baghdad.* He had a lot to say and he talked non-stop, describing a catastrophe that was costly and unwinnable.

The Americans had committed a massacre in the Iraqi city of Fallujah less than two weeks ago, the extent of which had been minimised in the mainstream news. 'They used cluster bombs and white phosphorous grenades in heavily populated areas. It was shameful.' Details of the attack were just beginning to leak out, including a body count of at least 1,500 so-called *insurgents*.

He spoke of the transformation of the Middle East that the wars in Iraq and Afghanistan would bring about. 'This is only the beginning,' he warned. 'Both sides want instability.' Meaning al-Qaeda and America.

He talked about Israel and Palestine, the Israeli assassination of the founder of Hamas six months ago and what the death, last week, of Yasser Arafat would mean. 'He was a symbol of the guerrilla warrior on the international stage,' Anderson said, suggesting that would be a prototype for populist leaders in the region.

It was an informative, if not terribly uplifting, lunch. It reminded us where we were, what had been done in our name and how little news of that reaches the West. That was what Gaghan wanted us to understand: the reason he was making this movie.

On Nicola's last night in Dubai, we joined production coordinator Simone and her new boyfriend Baz, our A-camera focus puller, in the hotel's rooftop restaurant. They'd been keeping their affair under wraps but it was time for secrets to be revealed. Simone, waiflike, slate-black skin and a sparkling smile; Baz, a buoyant, chalky-white Kiwi with a goofy grin. No space for any emotion but love in the presence of these two. Nicola put her hand on my knee. Our world, for the moment, was right again.

At a corner table, another secret romance was being uncloaked. Our line producer Georgia Kacandes was a severe-looking woman, business-like and socially ill at ease. Tonight, in a flowered dress sitting across from a man she adored, there was a softness previously unseen. Leaning forward, staring lovingly across the table, dressed in a crisp, silk dishdasha, the Colonel smiled.

The world around us, for the moment, was at peace.

CHAPTER TWENTY-TWO: THE LOTTERY

Ability is of little account without opportunity.

– Napoleon Bonaparte

I'd worked on movies in African shanty towns, in urban back alleys, in prisons, in public housing neighbourhoods where you couldn't roll sound until the gunshots stopped. But our last day of filming *Syriana* brought me someplace more disturbing than any of those.

Rows of whitewashed crates rested on steel beams in the middle of the baking desert. When a chance breeze drifted by, it carried the stench of a nearby septic tank. The crates had doors, a few had windows and some had air-conditioning units but no sound of an active fan in any of them. This was a labour camp where hundreds of migrant workers, all men and boys, were housed while working on a construction site, the skeleton of which could be seen in the near distance.

Each crate had bunks for a dozen workers. We were filming inside one of them. It was a scene in which our two young Arab actors are watching an action movie on a fuzzy television, distracting themselves from hunger and hopelessness with images of superheroes and modern kitchens. Then one tells the other about an Islamic school where, 'They give you French fries… and lamb!'

The camp residents who didn't find work that day sat on boxes or stood around outside their barracks watching our crew. A quartet of them played a game using pebbles as marbles. Hot as it was by mid-morning, it was hard to imagine anyone still asleep inside the bunkhouses but, as the day progressed, a few stragglers emerged. There was little movement in the camp other than the movie crew doing its thing.

Ramadan was over and the crew were openly displaying food and drink. Most of them had respected the Ramadan rules. There was no disrespect intended now. But staring into the faces of the people around us, it wasn't easy to grab a tuna and cheese from the trays going around without feeling a little squirmy about openly eating it.

Waldo and I had brought our baseball gloves and tossed a ball back and forth to pass the time while filming went on inside the sweltering crate.

Catch, throw. Catch, throw. Time and place evaporating at a distance of a hundred feet. Catch, throw.

Slowly, shyly, by ones and twos, idle labourers came over to watch us fling a baseball like it was a live sporting event. In minutes, we were surrounded by onlookers following the trajectory of every arcing toss.

One of Waldo's throws bounced off my mitt into the aggregate of spectators. A teenage boy picked it up. He examined the ball, feeling the seams, the smoothness of the cowhide, transfixed by it. For a moment, I didn't think he was going to give it back. Then he placed it in the webbing of my outstretched glove as if it were an egg. His eyes stayed glued to this alien object, even when I said, 'Thank you.'

That was the image I would take away from this movie. Not the boy's face but how he caressed that baseball before handing it back to me.

As if a fuzzy picture on TV had materialised.

CHAPTER TWENTY-THREE: INTERLUDES

I'd never been in London this time of year but autumn greeted me like an old friend. It was crisp and blanketed in grey, the air sombre and full of reflection.

I loved everything about the city. The calliope of humanity: Africans, Indians, Pakistanis, East Enders, Eastern Europeans, Chinese tourists, villagers from the Shires. The old architecture, the new architecture, the Tube system, the parliamentary system, the quaint courtesies, the snobbery, the pubs, the parks, the markets, the museums. I loved the variety of newspapers, the seriousness of the BBC News, the silliness of the television shows, the reverence for the NHS. I loved Nicola's flat – the closest thing I had to a home.

Our first night in London, we had dinner at a pub in Shepherd's Bush with Anita. I loved Anita. Solid, serene and so in Nicola's corner. She'd been a guiding light through our relationship madness over the past year.

The next night we went to a gathering at the home of Katherine's mother, an artist. I loved Katherine. An artist in her own right, struggling to make a name in the fashion world. Witty and self-deprecating, fiercely loyal to Nicola.

My reach into her world was extending, her friends becoming my friends.

I don't remember who asked who or when or how – or if it was just something we both took as inevitable – but somewhere along the way, we'd made the decision to look for a home together in Los Angeles.

'We can't keep on with me living here,' she said.

Holiday lights sparkled across Manhattan and pavements were jammed with shoppers. It was fairytale season – the romantic backdrop of stories, songs and cinema in which everyone finds love and everything ends with a kiss. Arguably, the least glamorous part of this glittering metropolis was the Port Authority bus terminal. But it lit up when I saw Sam and Casey get off the Short Line coach from Ithaca.

My friends Marianne and Donald Berman, she a journalist, he an executive for Barbara Walters' talk show, *The View*, had loaned me their two-bedroom apartment in the West Village for the weekend.

Sam was here to see a couple of colleges. He was still a year and a half from graduating high school but he liked planning ahead. He'd grown so much in the past five months, maturing into a determined young man bursting to start his adult life in this city. We visited New York University, the New School for Social Research and Fordham. He said he also intended to apply to Juilliard.

Casey was happy for any excuse to get a break from Ithaca and coming here was a ceasefire from battles with his mother. He was content anywhere he could listen to an audiobook while Sam and I took the college tours.

As we walked, Sam confided he and Olivia had officially broken up. Rather, she officially broke up with him. 'We both cried,' he told me.

At night, we looked for places for Casey to hear live jazz, starting at Fat Cats and ending at the Village Vanguard. Back at the Bermans' we watched Donald's screener of *Fahrenheit 9/11* – Dad's idea of educational TV.

'I already knew most of that stuff,' said Casey.

'I want to start getting more politically active,' said Sam.

I dreamed of ways I could have them living with me in the coming year.

On our drive to Ithaca, Sam told me he'd had a good talk with his friend Ben about divorce. 'He told me I'm going through a rough time. But it'll get better. I think it's getting better already.' Was he that resilient or was I just eager to take the fig leaf? I certainly wanted to believe him.

Casey had fallen asleep to an audiobook in the back seat. Sam asked to drive and when we stopped, Casey woke up.

'Where are we?'

A gas station.

'Is Sam driving?'

Yes.

'Oh.' He fell back asleep.

He was going through a rough time.

I dropped the boys at home around dinnertime. I didn't go in to see Margaret. I'd see her the next day when the kids were in school. There was a country inn called La Tourelle a half-block from our house. It was the strangest feeling staying at a hotel so close to my home.

The next morning, I took a walk alone in the woods where Margaret and I used to walk the dogs together. There'd been a light overnight snow and the ground crackled under my shoes.

It was thirty seconds in my rental car to the mailbox I'd installed twelve years ago at the entrance to our long driveway. I drove through the pine forest from which trees toppled during the heavy winter snows, blocking passage to and from the house. This winter I wouldn't be around with my chainsaw.

Margaret greeted me at the door. She was rail thin. Her smile betrayed no emotion. Her but not her. She politely offered me a coffee and I politely declined.

I knew my invitation here was a gambit her attorney devised to disenfranchise me from the house. I also knew how difficult it must be for her living where it was still 'half Dad's house', in Casey's words. And this was another step down the road I'd set us on.

'Well, should we get down to business?' she asked pleasantly.

We went through our things – things that once brought pleasure acquiring together and were now joyless objects. The artwork we'd collected brought up memories.

'We bought this painting in Hawaii on *Black Widow*.'

'Ralph and Betty thought it was the ugliest thing they'd ever seen.'

'I still think it's great.'

'You should have it.'

'No, it should stay here.'

I picked a few pieces of furniture from the living room we rarely used and all the clutter and collections in my office and closets.

'Would you like a sandwich?' she asked when it was over.

'I think I should get on the road to Syracuse.' Where I had an appointment with my divorce attorney. An awkward hug at the door before I got in my car and drove away.

It was spineless of me not to stay and chat. But I didn't have anything to say. And I was probably afraid that whatever she might say could open my heart to her again.

CHAPTER TWENTY-FOUR: JARHEAD

The memoir *Jarhead* was less about the horrors of war than about its futility. Written by third-generation US Marine Anthony Swofford, it described the transmutation of testosterone-fuelled boys into fighting machines in preparation for the first Gulf War. It was a uniquely positioned anti-war story, depicting the dehumanisation of soldiers from the viewpoint of one who had entered the military gung-ho and come out changed not by his combat experience but by his preparation for combat. Most of the half-million soldiers sent to Iraq in August 1990 never saw battle action.

The book was purchased by husband-and-wife producers Douglas Wick and Lucy Fisher in galley form before becoming a *New York Times* bestseller. They commissioned a script from *Apollo 13* co-screenwriter William Broyles Jr, himself a former Marine. The script, like the book, had a pointedly anti-war slant.

Wick and Fisher sought a director capable of creating a classic. It's a short list. They hit the jackpot with Academy Award-winner Sam Mendes.

Thirty-nine-year-old Mendes was a theatre prodigy, directing major British stage productions while still in his early twenties. His first film, *American Beauty,* earned him the Oscar as Best Director. He followed that with the Depression-era crime drama *Road to Perdition*. It earned six Academy Award nominations and landed on numerous Best Ten lists.

Sam Mendes was inspired by characters and conditions,

relationships and their dark side. Those were the elements that drew him to *Jarhead.* He was not interested in making an anti-war movie.

Jarhead began filming at George Air Force Base in Victorville, California, a long-enough distance from LA that we were provided housing at a local Holiday Inn.

The base had shut down at the end of the Cold War, but the landing strip was still used for personnel in transit. That afternoon, real military planes carrying US troops bound for the new war in Iraq landed near the movie's 747, as our simulated soldiers retraced the steps up a boarding ramp that another generation of jarheads had taken almost fifteen years earlier. Some of the movie actors and military personnel drifted toward each other. Some of the soldiers stood watching the cameras roll on our cast. Our actors couldn't help noticing the trepidation in those young eyes. Their discomfort probably worked for the scene.

The first day of a film is Feel-Your-Way Day. No matter how many first days you've had, there's always an orientation. Senses keen as a racehorse and a thousand bits of information bombarding you, you start looking for familiar faces with whom you can find grounding, connection. The process goes on over days, weeks, as memory clicks in – *didn't we work together on…* – until you feel part of a unit.

I don't know the exact figures but let's make up something: according to the National Association of Theatre Owners, there were approximately 500 movies released in 2004. Cut that in half because many were non-union, cheap-o pictures that can't afford to hire a publicist during production. So, 250 films times a low-ball estimate of a hundred full-time crew equals 25,000 jobs. Let's say New York gets 5,000 of those and the UK and other English-speaking countries account for another 10,000. That leaves 10,000 people I might work with on any movie emanating from LA.

I spent the day rediscovering how small this film world was.

Our stills photographer was François Duhamel, with whom I'd become friends during our marathon collaboration on *Unfortunate Events*. I got warm hugs from our sound team, big bear Marvin Barnes and willowy Willie Burton, with whom I'd worked on four previous films. I ran into other old movie mates: first assistant director Alan B. Curtiss and second unit first AD Gary Romolo Fiorelli; cinematographer Roger Deakins and A-camera operator Scott Sakamoto; John 'Magic' Wright, whose feats of prestidigitation were as much a magnet as the snacks at his craft service table. Hugs and handshakes went on with a dozen more.

My orientation on this movie took no time. This was family, many of whom I'd grown up with in the business. By the end of our four months together, my film family would expand to include others on the production.

Perhaps 'family' needs to be defined here. I have cousins I may have seen a few times in childhood who are genetically considered family. The person with whom I worked on three movies, even if we haven't seen each other for a decade, is closer to me than these cousins. Filmmakers like to hire cast and crew with whom they've worked before and are most comfortable around, so each movie is a reunion.

Each movie is also a battle. A film crew is like any group that's operating in extremis. You get closer faster.

You talk with family like you don't talk with anyone else.

I had dinner one night with actor Dennis Haysbert, with whom I'd worked on *Major League*, his first starring role. He'd been through a divorce two years ago.

'What finally broke us up were the same problems that were there at the beginning.'

In the moment, I couldn't recall any problems Margaret and I had at the beginning. Maybe my ignorance of those was the problem. Maybe we framed our marriage on the canard of unconditional love and came too late to admitting problems.

Bitterness over our divorce was the problem now. I'd received another vile correspondence from her lawyer. How could I salvage a friendship with a vindictive woman who'd set her dog on me? What I'd hoped would be a civil proceeding between reasonable people was being poisoned by a hired assassin.

But Dennis had no advice on dealing with divorce attorneys.

'They're all the same,' he said, shaking his head.

I felt better about that.

My spiritualist-ecologist-journalist arrived in LA just in time for the *Hotel Rwanda* premiere at the Academy Theatre. Off the plane, get dressed, let's go.

It was a star-studded event with speeches by Harrison Ford and Angelina Jolie, followed by an introduction of the Rusesabaginas from writer-director Terry George and an award given to Paul by Amnesty International. The movie was wildly applauded by the VIP audience and feted at the after-party in a restaurant near the theatre. We hitched a limousine ride with producer Alex Ho and his girlfriend Chrissy to an after-after-party at the nightclub Pearl's, where Wyclef Jean gave a private concert at 2 a.m. Nicola and I didn't get to sleep until nearly dawn.

Welcome to Hollywood.

We awoke the next afternoon to begin a week-long search for somewhere to live. After looking at twenty-four houses and apartments that we either couldn't bear to live in or couldn't afford to live in, we found a one-bedroom with office space and a garage for storage in a restored Moroccan-style 1930s building on Beachwood Canyon, below the Hollywood sign and up the street from her friends Drew and Estelle. Rather than a credit check, we had to send the quirky landlord our astrological sun signs along with an essay on why we wanted to live there. Nicola wrote the essay. By mid-week, we were approved. We bought a bed off Craigslist and, on Sunday, combed the Rose Bowl Flea Market for a dresser and dining table.

On Monday, Nicola flew back to London. On Tuesday, she called to tell me how nervous she was about moving in with me.

There were elements of this I could understand – they all started with the letter 'C'. The biggest was, did she want to Commit to being my partner – at least on a trial basis? Others included, could she Commit to properly renting her London flat? We couldn't survive on what Psychic Masseuse was paying. Could she Commit to relocating in America? Life here would be a culture shock. She'd have to Commit to getting a green card.

Other elements were less easy to understand. My furniture, for instance.

I'd hired a moving company to pack and ship my things from Ithaca. I called to ask if Nicola preferred delivery before or after she returned to Los Angeles.

'Why do you have to ship it all at once?' my girlfriend/partner/shack-up/whatever demanded in a tone fringed with terror. 'Why can't you do it in stages?'

Because it would cost a fortune.

'Well, I need time to think about it. Hold them off.'

She also needed time to think about when she'd be coming back here.

'I have a lot of things to do. I can't make a decision yet.'

I was coming to realise my lovely whatever suffered from a condition that might be called Departure Disorder. If I changed the furniture delivery date, she might call to say she couldn't leave on the day we'd agreed and could I hold them off again. Her alluring complexity came in the same basket as her multiple complexes – which included indecision, depression and delusions that she was Wonder Woman on a mission to save the planet. I would have to embrace both the magical mystery tour of her and the deranged driver who occasionally commandeered the wheel, with satnav from the supernatural.

We agreed to talk about it over Christmas.

'I'm worried about Christmas too,' my girlfriend added. 'I think the boys should come sooner to give themselves time to get settled before we throw them in with the family.'

I was a little concerned about Christmas myself. Especially throwing them in with her family. Both her families. It would also be the boys' first Christmas without their mother. This holiday season was going to be challenging for all of us.

Perhaps it was the result of too many paternally imposed viewings of *It's a Wonderful Life* but my boys were sentimental about Christmas. What would the holiday feel like with me, Nicola and a bunch of strangers?

Nicola dreaded the holidays – for reasons dating to childhood – and was being driven nuts by both her families. We were staying at her mother's cottage where there were bunk beds for the boys. Mom was spending the week with her son Stephen, Nicola's Harrow-educated, staunchly proper brother, at a castle owned by a friend of his in the north. From what Nicola described of the family dynamics, it was best Mom and Steve weren't blended into this year's Christmas pudding.

On Christmas Eve day, we walked to sister Sheena and brother-in-law Marco's modest two-storey cottage, three fields away, adjacent to the formal gardens of the family mansion, Berrystead, which Mom had given to Stephen – along with 400 acres of farmland and five other houses – accelerating sibling rivalry to sound-barrier-breaking speeds.

My sons and Nicola's nephews, however, came together like they'd been lifelong chums. Sam, two years younger, connected with Ben, who had recently declared he wanted to study medicine. Felix, five years Casey's junior, connected with my eldest in a sweetly protective way. Caspar, the scholarly middle child, engaged both with the common language of music. The five of them disappeared to play video games after dinner. Sam came back into the dining room to announce, 'Dad, we all want to go see *A Series of Unfortunate Events*.' We took them in two cars to a theatre in nearby Milton Keynes. Felix sat beside Casey, whispering narration of what was happening on screen.

It went on like that for the rest of the week. All of them together all the time. To my great relief, my boys did not seem to be suffering Absent Mother Stress Disorder. They phoned to wish her a merry Christmas. It unburdened my heart to see that, as long as their parents were at the end of a phone line, they were solid and secure wherever they were.

We relocated to Nicola's flat in the city on the last day of the year. She'd made plans for the four of us to celebrate New Year's Eve with Psychic Masseuse and Ghostbuster.

Casey was quiet through most of the dinner and barely touched his meal. He'd been drinking coffee all afternoon to keep himself awake for the evening. It had given him a headache but he was determined to stick it out until midnight. The old year passed and he tolerated a bear hug from Ghostbuster and smooches from PM. We gave him the choice whether to join us for dancing or go back to Nicola's flat. He chose the latter without hesitation.

The last thing I wanted to do was leave Casey alone. The second-to-last thing was go dancing with Psychic Masseuse and Ghostbuster. But Casey convinced me he was okay. And Nicola convinced me it would be 'fun'. Sam was game to stay out late in London.

The car PM hired for the evening drove the five of us to a large warehouse at the end of a deserted street in an industrial part of the city. There were about a thousand people in a building with a capacity ten times that, making the atmosphere more cavernous than gala, but it left plenty of room on the dance floor. Nicola danced briefly with Sam while PM led me out for a marathon boogie and Ghostbuster went off to the bathroom for what seemed an inordinate length of time. I escaped PM to sit with Sam at the bar.

'I feel like a little kid, Dad. There's nobody here my age.'

He'd been excited about ordering an illicit pint when an undiscriminating bartender asked 'What'll it be?' but that was where the thrill of posing as an adult this evening appeared to end.

Sam and I sat watching the women dive into a Dionysian duet as it dawned on me we were at a rave. The inappropriateness of bringing my son here was discomforting on one level – though he seemed less bothered about being surrounded by ravers then he was about having no one to talk to. My own discomfort was operating on a different level. The problem here wasn't just about his age but about mine. I'd had my time in the drug-fuelled disco days but I was too old for this now. Was Nicola too young for me? There were fifteen years between us that we'd never entirely acknowledged. I had no desire to relive my youth here. But I didn't want to be the old fart who wrecks the party. *C'mon, lighten up*, I told myself. So I danced with PM again.

Nicola tried to get Sam back on the dance floor but he demurred. She tried to talk with him but it was a strain to hear anything over the music.

Ghostbuster returned with renewed vigour, handed off something to PM and she started toward the ladies' room, urging Nicola to follow her. Nicola shook her head. PM shrugged and went off without her. I rejoined my son at the bar and we watched together as Nicola danced with Ghostbuster – she danced and he convulsed – until PM came back. Ghostbuster twirled in blissful oblivion as my girlfriend and her friend had an animated talk off to one side. I couldn't hear any of it but at one point, Nicola gestured toward Sam, then stormed away. I could only lip-read but the word 'sixteen' was in there.

PM, eyes wide as a stalking animal, dragged me back onto the dance floor. I endured it, waiting for Nicola to come back. Waiting. Waiting. Shuffling my feet to the monotonous beat, scanning the room for my absconding aficionada. Waiting. I started to think Nicola's disappearance might be strategic, as in 'here's a chance for the two of you to get better acquainted'.

Thanks but I'd rather walk barefoot on hot coals. I tore myself away to find the girl who'd brought me to this dance so I could ask her why we were here.

'Stay and dance with me!' PM screamed.

I wove between dancers, drunks and the drug-addled, in pursuit of the woman who had deserted me at yet another party and, worse, left me in the clutches of the pickled paranormal. I found her, swaying solo in a crowd, before PM caught up with me.

'Sam's not having a good time and I'm not having a good time,' I yelled over the music. 'If you want to stay, stay. Sam and I will get a taxi to the flat.'

Ghostbuster appeared, grabbing Nicola's arm from behind.

'Ah, there you are!' He broke into his interpretative rhumba for the reluctant dead. PM joined in, waving me over to make it a foursome. I double-timed my steps across the warehouse and found Sam, still nursing his pint.

'Let's get out of here,' I said through gritted teeth.

Outside, I looked for a taxi. The street was deserted and there were none to be had. My frustration was building to a boil. 'Dad, relax,' my sixteen-year-old talked me off the ledge. 'It's just a bad party. It's not a big deal.' Did age mean maturity and youth the opposite? His maturity took me aback. All thoughts of my own discomfort fell away.

Nicola emerged from the club, spotted us in the street and rushed over. 'I'm sorry. I didn't know it would be like this.' She added, 'I know you needed to get away from them. *I* needed to get away from them!'

That took a moment to absorb. I'd almost resigned myself to the idea that uncritical acceptance of the demonic duo was something I'd have to drag along like Marley's chains through the entirety of our relationship. Was this the dawning of a new age? I dared not hope.

'The car isn't coming for us until 3 a.m. Can you bear it?'

'Sure,' Sam answered for both of us.

Nicola took one of our hands in each of hers and led us back into the dark night of the soul. We found PM and Ghostbuster at a table, slumped over their drinks.

PM brightened. 'Oh, we were wondering where you all went.'

Ghostbuster rose from his seat and, in a shouted whisper, invited me to join him in the men's room.

'No thanks.' I patted his shoulder.

PM started jabbering to Nicola in spirit-speak. Something about pagans and festivals. Nicola was processing something else entirely, her face impassive, PM's gestures becoming pantomime. I was witnessing a minor miracle. Her limitless indulgence of the cosmic couple had finally drawn a boundary.

Nicola abruptly got up to lose herself on the dance floor, spinning away into solitary abandon. Sam and I went off to find space at the bar.

'It's all fine, Dad.'

Yes, it is, son.

I put my arm around his shoulders and he put his arm around my waist as we stood trying to get the bartender's attention. Much good had come from a bad party.

Was this really the end of Psychic Masseuse?

Don't be silly. Things like this don't end so easily.

It would go on and on.

I just don't want to write about it anymore. So, PM's storyline ends here.

It would eventually end badly. But Nicola would be liberated.

I like to believe this night began the process. We'll leave it at that.

It was an oddly happy New Year.

CHAPTER TWENTY-FIVE: CARNAGE

El Centro is the centre of Nowhere. Alright, it's the centre of the Imperial Valley but that's the same thing. With a population of 40,000 – employed mainly by two major prisons and the US Border Patrol – El Centro isn't Fun City. It is hot. It is small. It is not charming. It would be the principal location for this movie.

The chain restaurant Applebee's was pretty much the only dining choice in El Centro for those not up for pizza or Kentucky Fried Chicken. It became the crew commissary. If all you wanted was a burger and good night's sleep, the fast-food joints were lined up on the drive back from set along Imperial Highway. After dinner, younger cast and crew might migrate to one of the pool bars off the main street – called Main Street.

There wasn't a hotel big enough to house us all, so cast and crew were scattered in motels on the outskirts of town. François and I were staying at the Comfort Inn, along with the supporting actors and a few of the technical department heads.

By this point, you should be disabused of the notion the film business is all glamour. There weren't a lot of perks at this location. Not even much shade. But there was greater camaraderie than on most film sets. We were invested in the project. The lack of pampering brought us closer as a unit – not unlike scenes we were filming in the Marine barracks. No one was sleeping in a tent, but the director and producers stayed at the same Holiday Inn as the majority of the crew. Off set, few choices of bars meant you could always find your mates at one or two regular watering holes. Few choices of restaurants made wine and cheese on François' balcony a bonding routine.

Most of the filming would take place on and around an abandoned landing strip, about forty-five minutes from the hotels. The ragged runway was our base camp and catering area. Production designer Dennis Gassner had built a tent city for the soldiers that spread across acres of cleared desert.

On the far side of the runway, his set decorators were working on dressing the Highway of Death.

...this was not a bunch of innocent people just trying to make their way back across the border to Iraq. This was a bunch of rapists, murderers and thugs who had raped and pillaged downtown Kuwait City and now were trying to get out of the country before they were caught.

– General Norman Schwarzkopf

The Highway of Death was downplayed and rationalised but it was the worst among many under-reported atrocities of Operation Desert Storm. The Defense Department's greatest lesson from the Vietnam War was 'don't let the press control the images'. They managed that with unprecedented success this time around.

The government's account was that all – or most – of the vehicles fleeing Kuwait City along Highway 80 to Basra were Iraqi military. *Killers. Rapists. Killer rapists.* But the public highway was also the main escape route for civilians – including 200,000 Palestinian refugees who had been evicted by the reinstated Kuwaiti authorities. On the night of 26 February 1991, they began evacuating – as the 3rd Marine Aircraft Wing began incinerating a mile-long stretch of the highway and everything on it.

One of the few instances of anti-war editorialising to which Sam Mendes might fairly be accused was the composition of the carnage along our set-designed Highway 80: a significant number of our corpses and vehicles were civilian.

Roger Deakins' camera doesn't dwell on the charred carcasses. But the shock of our Marine witnesses is expressed by Fergus, the sensitive jarhead played by Brian Geraghty: 'They were trying to get away.'

A movie can tell truths that neither newspapers nor television news are willing or able to convey. It can also call out a lie. You weren't going to see Vietnam-style atrocity footage from the conflict in the Middle East on the six o'clock news and even the most egregious examples might not make it to print. But this one would be in our movie. It was an inspiring, if sobering, couple days filming for all of us.

While I was in El Centro, Iraq, Nicola was preparing for a different kind of invasion: Casey was coming to stay with us for 'a while'. Maybe a long while. He had just turned eighteen and he and his mother had had it up to their chins with each other.

'I need you to talk to your son,' was the gist and length of most of my conversations with Margaret. The issue of Casey's marijuana smoking had come up again.

'Dad, I'm trying to follow Mom's rules,' he complained. 'I'm not smoking weed in *her* house. I'm not even smoking in my loft.'

He thought a reasonable compromise was climbing out the window of his loft and smoking on the roof of our detached garage. At 5 a.m.

'I was having trouble sleeping.'

He was of legal age to make his own decisions and his mother was granting his wish – or calling his bluff – to 'try living with Dad'.

I'd phoned Nicola to test the waters. How would she feel about sharing our tiny space, our first home together, her first real home in America, with a blind, temperamental teenager?

'It will be wonderful getting to know him,' she said. Not 'What's he going to do when you're away and I'm trying to work?' or even 'If his own mother can't live with him, how am I supposed to?' – though that question, as well as others, must have crossed her mind. 'The cupboard should be big enough for a single mattress and a chest of drawers,' she suggested. The cupboard was T-shaped with a long, low stretch at the back under a sawed-off staircase. It was currently stacked to the ceiling with boxes of books and bric-a-brac. While I was away, she somehow managed to stuff them all into our garage, clearing the space.

Nicola's test was a two-parter. She'd gone straight to the head of the class on Part One. Part Two was arriving next week.

I planned to pick up Casey at the airport and drive straight to our apartment where Nicola and I would spend the weekend with him. Then we would all decide whether he came with me to El Centro or spent a few days getting to know my girlfriend.

The decision was made for us by the girlfriend.

'I think you should spend some time alone with him,' she decided. 'I'm going to fly home for a couple of weeks.'

She had to prepare the London flat for new tenants and set up meetings with British newspapers and magazines. Why she couldn't have done those things before her move here would've been my only rhetorical question. Her enthusiasm for bringing

Casey to LA was, at least in part, so I wouldn't feel abandoned when she abandoned me. How our life would configure if Casey decided he wanted to live here was a question to be deferred.

When I was eighteen, I'd already been working for three years at the Los Angeles Music Center, first tearing tickets at the door, then answering phones at their switchboard. The latter paid above minimum wage and I was earning enough by the time I graduated high school to rent my own apartment. With an old car my parents had given me, I was fully independent.

Casey was escorted to the baggage area at LAX by a bevy of stewardesses and a pilot with whom he was discussing aeronautics. You could see him processing every detail, his mind adapting every flight instrument to bypass his impairment. Had he been sighted, he might've gone straight into the Air Force at this age.

He folded his cane, grabbed my elbow and allowed me to lead him to my car. We talked non-stop on the three-and-a-half-hour drive to El Centro.

He told me how difficult it was finding common ground with kids his age.

'They're not really into the things I'm interested in.'

He talked about his difficulties in socialising.

'I'm not very good at small talk.'

He talked about how he hates feeling 'obligated' to people who do him small favours, 'like driving me to a party or showing me to the bathroom'.

We talked life philosophies. Casey's could be summed up in three words: 'Ya gotta laugh.'

For a kid who's usually the silent type, he didn't let a lot of dead air transpire.

He slept most of the weekend and was still tired when he woke up. Margaret would have attributed that to his kidney condition. I attributed it to being eighteen.

I spent my waking hours thinking of how to help Casey make the adjustment to living here. He'd need something to do.

I'd received clearance from Sam Mendes to bring Casey to set – not mentioning his blindness. Eyesight didn't define Casey so why should I define him that way? Our first stop was John 'Magic' Wright's craft service table. Magic showed him where the sodas and pretzels were, so Casey could always find them. Having craft services as his base of operations provided a degree of independence.

We spent part of the morning with animal wrangler Jules Sylvester, who let Casey handle his collection of Iraqi rats, reptiles and arachnids. Casey loved animals. Maybe there was a job helping Jules? It wasn't a good day to bring this up. Ever smiling and patient, the sweat on the lanky Aussie's forehead wasn't from the desert heat. He had 3,000 incubating fly larvae that were due in front of the camera an hour ago.

I introduced Casey to our sound guys, Marvin and Willie, while they were waiting for the flies to hatch and the scene to begin. Willie showed Casey how to operate his mixing board while Marvin spoke into his boom mike to get a level. This was promising. Casey's acute hearing was a gift he might turn into a career. But along with the levers to adjust sound was a video monitor that allowed the sound mixer to watch how the scene was playing out so he could anticipate when to correct levels on different actors. Marvin suggested Casey might be better at post-production sound design, where skills are purely listening.

I had some business to do with our director but this didn't

appear to be a good day for it. With Marvin's suggestion shining like a star of hope, Casey and I went back to the hotel where I phoned Wiley Stateman at Digidesign.

Sound design is one of the post-production mysteries I know nothing about.

It has something to do with taking the recorded dialogue of a scene and enhancing or softening it to what's appropriate to the drama. Or maybe that's sweetening. I don't know.

It also had something to do with creating audio effects – bigging up explosions, screeching tires, doors creaking or the wind blowing.

But for all those you must match the sound to the picture. Casey couldn't see the picture. He could, however, operate his computer with modifications he knew how to make. And surely he could figure out how to big-up an explosion.

Wiley Stateman escorted us through the hi-tech headquarters of Digidesign where the banks of screens and mixing boards reminded me of NASA headquarters recreated in the movie *SpaceCamp*. Casey had attended space camp in a special program they had for the visually impaired. Maybe some of that experience would be useful here.

A seven-time Academy Award nominee, and Wolfgang Petersen's post-production audio engineer since his first American movie, *Shattered*, Wiley was a stand-up guy. At the end of the tour, he offered Casey an unpaid internship.

'Let's see what you can do,' he said.

Casey said he'd think about it. In the car, he told me the computer program they were using was too visual.

I took a day off work to go with Casey to the Guitar Center on Sunset Boulevard. It was one of his favourite hangouts in LA and he knew his way around every keyboard in their extensive display. I spoke with the manager and asked for a job application. The manager introduced himself to Casey and they chatted about the difference between the Yamaha and the Roland. Casey preferred the Roland. The manager said, for the price, he agreed. I was hopeful.

The next night, the manager called.

'I talked with my boss,' he began. 'He said all our sales people have to be able to write up orders. And there could be insurance issues. I'm sorry. I really liked Casey.'

Everyone liked Casey. But no one had a job for him.

Back on set in El Centro, Marvin was recovering from the flu and Willie had a long dialogue scene to prepare for. Neither had any time to spend with Casey today.

I introduced him to our director with whom I had to discuss an upcoming photo shoot. Mendes was kind and welcoming, registering no noticeable surprise at Casey's impairment.

'He's a fine young man,' he said, smiling, before returning to his monitors.

After lunch, Casey said he'd like to go back to the hotel.

'I want to do some more work on this song I'm composing.'

That night, he joined me on François' balcony. The Frenchman made him laugh. Back in our room we listened to music. I introduced him to Portishead and India Arie – both of whom Nicola had introduced to me.

I am ready for love, sang India. *Why are you hiding from me?*

He didn't find this one as inspiring as I did. He said he was tired and went to sleep on the couch. 'But you can play Portishead again while I'm sleeping.'

My dual focus should've been on my son and my job but nocturnal thoughts kept drifting to Nicola. Along with my longing for her was a concern: an independent, childless woman stepping into a parental role. Yes, she'd shown a protectiveness toward both my boys, but there'd never been a test of cohabitation and teenagers were a unique challenge. Yes, I was in love with her but my first obligation... no, obligation is the wrong word... my primary love was my boys. I once believed the core relationship – marriage or partnership – was foundational. You could make a lot of mistakes with child rearing but as long as the children had a paradigm of love at the bedrock of their family, they'd be okay. The paradigm had shifted. My thoughts shifted back to Casey.

Production moved to LA and my son politely declined all offers to go to the Universal Studios stages with me. He preferred to stay home composing on his electric piano and sitting on the back patio listening to the wild parrots.

I loved having him here. He loved sleeping in his cupboard under the sawed-off stairs. At the end of our three weeks together, he said he would 'think about' moving in with me. With *us.* A few days after he arrived back in Ithaca, I phoned him.

'I've been thinking. It's only a couple more months until I start piano-tuning school. Maybe I should just stay here until then.'

CHAPTER TWENTY-SIX: SOUTH OF THE BORDER

I'd been talking to Nicola daily and she'd always ask to talk with Casey. Her voice soothing, her interest in his thoughts and opinions genuine, she cheered him up.

Cheering me up wasn't as easy.

I couldn't really talk with her about the divorce. She was on Margaret's side.

'Give her whatever she wants. She's the mother of your children.'

I didn't want to tell her how much I missed her because I didn't want to sound like Casey wasn't sufficient company. She called faithfully at the end of every day. She wanted to stay connected to me. But did she want to be in the same place as me?

'I had lunch with an old colleague from the *Mail*,' she told me the night Casey flew home. 'I was telling her about my boyfriend in LA. She asked what I was doing in London. When I told her, she said, "You could do all that by phone. You need to fly right back to him." I'm booking my flight for next Saturday.' Her birthday was on Sunday.

'Could you make it earlier?' I asked. 'We're going to Mexico on Saturday.'

Nicola arrived on Friday. I was grateful for the reproach she'd been given by her old newspaper colleague but I didn't believe that was the route of her return. Was it an awakening? A what-the-hell, why not? Whatever it was renewed her investment in the carnival of my life and trusted me to hold steady in the swirling constellation of hers.

That night in bed, we kissed, we caressed, and I did what a responsible man does when it's time to move things along. I opened the drawer of my bedside table. I started to reach in. She held back my arm.

'We don't need that,' was all she said before covering my mouth with hers.

The second largest city in Baja, California – next to glamorous Tijuana – Mexicali is, bluntly, a pit. Located just below the eastern corner of the state of California, passing through Calexico – third on the list of Most Dangerous American Border Towns – Mexicali was once agricultural. Now it was mainly industrial, with piecework wages approximately one-sixth US minimum. It was a key thoroughfare for drug trafficking and one could hardly drive down a side street without seeing young women in high heels looking for new friends. Nicola and I were not going to be celebrating her birthday on the Riviera.

Birthdays are a Rorschach test. The way you interpret the ink blot tells a lot about your perception of the preceding twelve months. At their best, they are a time to be grateful; at their worst, they are a time to be grateful you've made it through another year. The most valuable gift you get is a pause for reflection.

Today, Nicola was turning forty-one. The celebration over her return to my orbit was temporary. We'd found some new insignificant boundaries to bicker about on the drive to Mexico. As, mile by mile, we helped each other out of the hole we'd started digging from the moment we left our Beachwood driveway, the only bit of information that broke to the surface was that her birthday, for reasons still unarticulated, was freaking her out.

Change is hard. She'd been through a lot of changes in the past few months. She'd finally removed the rose-tinted glasses through which she viewed her psychic family ('I still respect their work but I've lost respect for them'), her other friends were eight time zones away ('The only time I can call them is during the day, when they're too busy to talk.'), Drew and Estelle were moving to Berkeley and the only writing assignment she'd had was covering a junket for the TV show *Will & Grace*.

'I think I just want to skip my birthday.'

I'd reserved a table at the best Mexican restaurant I could find with two of my favourite people on the movie, line producer Sam Mercer and his fiancée Tegan Jones, who was directing the splinter unit.

'You go to dinner with your friends. I'll have something in the room.'

I didn't react. This was a process.

'I'm forty-one. I don't have a career. I don't even have a baby.'

Ahh. The rite of turning forty-plus-one had rung her biological clock chimes to remind her that, oops, she forgot to have children. The baby thing had been something we'd discussed, theoretically, from time to time, since our earliest days together. She'd made it clear she wanted one – when she wasn't worrying she might accidentally leave it in the supermarket. I was open to the possibility – when I wasn't thinking, *Do I want to take on a lifelong commitment with a woman who can't commit to a dinner?*

Then it started pouring out.

'I've accomplished nothing in my life. And now I'm just floating around with you! I'm not doing a story on this movie. You won't even let me interview Jamie Foxx and Jake Gyllenhaal!'

Uh, first you need an assignment, then I have to pass it by the studio...

'You are such a company man!'

I laughed.

She didn't.

The Mexican government had granted permission for our movie to shoot on a hundred-mile stretch of salt flats about sixty miles from the city. The salt flats were part of a wildlife protected area, a fragile ecosystem in which we were a foreign body – several hundred foreign bodies, along with a flotilla of vehicles and hardware. The production put in a temporary road system, brought in water, power, security and Musco lights for filming at night. It became its own military operation.

'Welcome to the suck,' Sam Mercer greeted us, using the term Marines use in referring to the Corps. 'You're not going to be able to see anything from here and Mendes doesn't want people around the cameras who don't need to be there. I've gotta stay here all day but you don't.'

We stuck around until midday. I introduced Nicola to Jamie Foxx's bodyguard, Rashon. He was a Shaolin martial arts master, an African drum virtuoso and a herbalist. He invited us into Jamie's trailer. He and Nicola had a common interest in herbal medicines – comparing African, which she knew something about, with Asian, which Rashon knew a lot about. Neither of which I know a thing about.

Jamie wrapped filming early and opened his trailer door to find us comfortably chatting.

'Can I talk to you a minute about something?' He gave a look for Rashon to leave and the assistant politely guided Nicola out with him.

An actor's trailer is his sanctuary and I wondered if he might want to chew me out for making myself too at home there.

'Listen, I did this movie last year about Tookie Williams – you know who he is?'

South Central LA was home turf to two of the most notorious gangs in the country, the Crips and the Bloods. Stanley 'Tookie' Williams was one of the founders of the Crips. In 1979, Williams was convicted of four murders by an all-white jury and sentenced to death. Twenty-five years later, he was exhausting the last of his appeals before execution.

What made Tookie's story stand apart from other gang-related convicts' was that, after spending six years in solitary confinement for fighting with other prisoners and guards, he had emerged a reformed man. He spent the next twenty years working for peace between the rival gangs, renounced his part in formation of the Crips, wrote eight books aimed at turning children from gangs and violence, wrote a memoir describing the misery of prison life and another book entitled *Blue Rage, Black Redemption*, on which the movie was based. Over the past decade, he'd been nominated six times for the Nobel Peace Prize and last year received a letter of commendation for community service from President George W. Bush.

'He's not going to win his next appeal and the only thing that'll be left to him is clemency,' Jamie said. 'I don't know if it'll do any good but I'd like to send a letter to the governor.'

He asked if I would draft the letter. I said I'd be happy to.

So, I had another assignment.

Meanwhile, Nicola was feeling like a spare part.

'Is everything okay?' she asked when I emerged from the trailer.

'There's something I'd like you to help me with.'

'I have a lot of work to do,' she protested.

'You'll want to make this a priority.'

Nicola spent the rest of the week researching and composing Jamie's letter, investing it with empathy and passion. At the end of the week, I handed it in.

'I might reword it a little but it looks great. Thanks.'

No need to tell him who wrote it. Nicola didn't need the credit. She needed the satisfaction of doing something that mattered. By the time we left Mexicali, she'd written a half-dozen pitches for other writing assignments and her sparkle had returned.

'There's an amazing drum gathering next month in central Mexico,' she said one morning. 'Five thousand drummers. It's a ritual to heal Mother Earth. I think I might go.'

I just smiled.

The drummers would have to heal the planet without Nicola because, having healed herself, new horizons began appearing in her working life.

Within days of getting back to Beachwood, she suddenly had assignment offers coming in. *The Mail* wanted her to file stories on Queen Latifah and William Shatner from interviews they'd set up in LA. *The Ecologist* wanted her to interview Native American activist Winona LaDuke in Minnesota. A call, out of the blue, came from a publisher in Memphis, Tennessee who'd read her story on Paul Rusesabagina in *The*

Week magazine – where it had been reprinted as Story of the Week – and wanted to talk with her about writing a book on another Rwandan 'hero', Bishop Somebodyorother. They were proposing flying her to Memphis to discuss it. If they came to an agreement, she would spend three to four weeks with the bishop in Rwanda.

How wonderfully transforming it is to feel wanted. She was sunnier, she was funnier, she was sexier. We went back to playing baby roulette.

I was finally confronting the fact I was head over heels for Nicola. Her lows could send me crashing and some of her highs flew above my capacity for whoopee, but I cherished what came in between – except for her need to run away every five minutes.

Nicola got an offer to go to Avalon on Catalina Island with a woman she'd met and some of her 'friends'.

Just a girl thing?

'There'll probably be some men there. You can come if you want to,' she added a non-invitation invitation.

I grumbled something cynical. She shot something back. The conversation spun downward from there through most of dinner, after which we retreated to separate workstations, her on email, me staring at my screen stewing in my thoughts: *Why am I always trying to include her in things when she seems most interested in going off on her own? Maybe I need to get a life. So what if she wants to go off for a weekend? So what? We only have weekends together if I'm working. Don't be an ass, it's a fucking weekend. Knowing her, it'll turn into a week. What is this feeling?*

'Who hurt you?' she abruptly interrupted.

A moment, please, while I gather. She meant, what woman had betrayed me and made me untrusting? I'd never thought about it.

I thought about it. The answer was: 'All of them.'

My prom date was secretly screwing her ex-boyfriend. My first serious girlfriend, Becky-from-Berkeley, left me for the guitar player who lived downstairs. Every girl I dated in high school dumped me for bad boys with better cars. My first wife, Ann, deserted me by dying. The only one who hadn't betrayed me, that I knew of, was Margaret. Though I could argue desertion there too.

'There's only maybe a thirty per cent chance of me going.' This was Nicola's attempt at reassurance. It didn't work.

The arrival of Sam for spring break lifted me out of the doldrums. Seeing him with Nicola, seeing her nurture him, drive him around LA, cook for him, put his needs, his happiness above everything swelled my heart.

His heart was over the moon: he and Olivia were back together. Better than ever. He sat me down for The Talk.

'Dad, Olivia and I have been talking,' Sam began with deliberation one morning while Nicola was still asleep. 'We both feel we're ready to have sex.'

He sipped his cup of coffee-milk and waited for my response.

'Make it a special moment, sweetheart,' I said.

He said he would.

The movie was almost over. We were going to skip the wrap party on Saturday and drive to San Francisco together. Olivia was waiting there, visiting her mother.

Nicola's interview with Winona LaDuke in Minnesota had

fallen through but her fallback for *The Ecologist* was a group of environmental activists called the Rainforest Action Network, based in North Beach. She spent the afternoon at their headquarters while Sam and I explored the streets of Berkeley and the UC campus. I regaled him with tales from my revolutionary days of higher education there.

'Cool, Dad, but I still think I want to go to college in New York,' he said.

We reconnected with Nicola for dinner at Fisherman's Wharf. She wanted to know how Sam's band was doing. 'We got, like, 150 people to our last show. And they kept asking for encores. It was the greatest feeling.' She wanted to know how things were going with Olivia. Sam had asked me to keep our talk 'just between us'.

'It's really good. We went out after my last play and she said we should get back together. It's been great but she graduates in June and, well, I don't know what'll happen after that. She'll probably meet some college guy.'

You shouldn't worry about that, Nicola told him. If you're meant to be together, you will be. You're an amazing boy and you'll find an amazing girl who's right for you.

I could've told him the same thing but it meant more coming from her.

After dinner, Nicola left to check the two of us into a tacky hotel in the Mission District. There was a twenty-four-hour porn palace across the street. The website hadn't shown that or the winos loitering on the surrounding sidewalks. She'd been looking for a hotel with 'character'.

I taxied with Sam to a fifth-floor walk-up studio apartment near the Presidio that Olivia's mother owned and was letting the teenage lovers use for a couple of days.

I lugged his heavy suitcase, stopping at every landing.

'So' – huff, puff, second floor – 'what do you think of Nicola?'

'She's fantastic, Dad. I'd like her to be my stepmom. I think you should marry her.'

Huff, puff, third floor.

'Well, she's pretty great but kind of nutty.'

'You need somebody a little crazy. You're a neurotic Jew. You worry too much. She's perfect for you.'

Neurotic Jew?

Huff, puff, almost to the fourth-floor landing. Stop for a second.

'Dad, lemme do that.'

'Wouldn't want you to strain yourself and risk the future of the family line.'

He said he didn't want me to hurt myself either.

'I've already had you and Casey. I'm too old to worry about it.'

'Well, Nicola's not too old.'

What did he just say?

I took a deep breath and made it up to his apartment without stopping.

CHAPTER TWENTY-SEVEN: WHAT NEXT?

Sharks gotta swim and production people have to keep working.

Jim Carrey's publicist, Marleah Leslie, called to offer me his next movie.

I was surprised.

'Jim liked you.'

That was the surprise.

Joel Schumacher was directing a mystery-thriller called *The Number 23*. It was filming all in LA.

'Sure. I loved working with you and Jim.'

In five months working with him, I didn't think he'd recognise me passing in an empty stairwell. But a request from a star is all the seduction most of us need.

So I committed to the film.

One of Nicola's most annoying and admirable attributes was making me – anybody, even strangers – relate actions to values. 'Do you want to support the pesticide industry? Then buy organic. Do you really think it's helpful to be so down on conservatives? Don't be so black and white. What's more important, spending fifteen minutes watching the sunset or being on time to a dinner? We don't have to be there at *exactly* 8 p.m.'

She had read the script for *The Number 23*.

'Do you really think this is a movie you want to spend your time on?'

Hmm.

Sam flew back to Ithaca from San Francisco, and Nicola and I drove along the coast route to LA, stopping in Santa Barbara for a romantic dinner at a jazz club. We lingered too long and didn't get home until nearly midnight.

One should never open email after a nice night out. But we both did.

A brusque ultimatum with an attachment from Margaret's attorney sat in my inbox like a time bomb. I opened it and quickly read the contents. I stormed off to the kitchen and uncorked a bottle of wine.

'What is it?'

Looks like I'm going to have to take Margaret to court.

'Let me see.'

Nicola read the new settlement proposal.

'From what you've told me, this doesn't look too bad.'

Well, of course it didn't look bad to Miss Give-Her-Everything. My temper was surfacing. I sat down with a glass of Merlot and took another look.

It actually didn't look that bad. It was basically everything I'd originally offered, with a longer alimony period than I wanted but without all the other contentious elements.

I read it twice.

The accompanying note from my attorney said he thought we could get a better deal in court. What I wanted more than a better deal was to avoid court. I didn't trust my attorney. I sent it to my accountant. He got back to me the next morning.

'This doesn't look too damaging,' he replied.

I had a divorce settlement I could live with.

I wrote back to my lawyer: I accept.

It was over.

The legal language for divorce in New York State was 'opting out'. My opting-out papers arrived a week after the email. I signed and sent them back. It would still take a month to finalise but my divorce was done. Repairing relations with Margaret would take a lot longer but Nicola would help with that too.

We celebrated over dinner at our favourite restaurant, Pace, in Laurel Canyon.

'To getting an 800-pound gorilla off my back,' I toasted.

'To the good years you and Margaret had together raising two incredible children,' she countered.

Nicola was flying to Memphis to meet with the publisher who wanted to commission a book on the Rwandan bishop. We had a sweet farewell at the airport, ending with her saying, 'I don't know if I want to go back to Rwanda,' and me saying, 'If it's good for your career, you should go,' swallowing all my fears about it.

As I watched her pass through airport security, I was overcome by a discomfiting sensation. I examined it – which was hard because it was an emotional pinball: bouncing off confusion to elation, falling back to disturbing, dipping close to frightening, then rocketing to heights that made the board light up.

I could have a child with this woman.

For that to happen, however, one or both of us would have to stop getting on airplanes.

Nicola returned to LA with reservations about the book.

'I liked the bishop and the publishers were nice. But I started to think about getting pregnant and spending a month in the north of Rwanda.' Not Kigali but the part of the country that was still in conflict. 'Is there any way you might be able to come with me?'

'Of course I will.' We would go before I started the Jim Carrey film.

A few days later, she got a call: they'd hired another writer.

Nicola was more relieved than upset.

'I don't think I was right for it anyway. It was a Christian publishing house and they would've wanted a lot of it to be about how God intervened.' Glad she sniffed the potential journalistic conflict in that. 'I think my only disappointment is that we won't be going to Africa together. Talking with them made me realise how much I miss it.'

Nicola was fond of saying her fairy godmothers must be working overtime. Mostly, she was referring to occasions when she stepped in a mineshaft just as the elevator was reaching ground level. But some of the time, her busy fairies found occasion to grant wishes.

As if her wistful longing had ascended to the heavens – or Burbank – I got a call from Warner Bros.

'Are you available for a job starting next month?' vice president of publicity Juli Goodwin asked. 'It's an Edward Zwick movie shooting in Africa.'

Do I have a couple days to think about it?

I had two things to think about: How do I tell Nicola in a way that won't have her claiming divine intervention?

Secondly...

Getting out of a movie you've committed to for another movie you'd rather do is very bad form. A commitment is a commitment. In the film business, at least in my end of it, you don't usually sign an agreement until after you've started work.

You make a verbal deal and it's sealed by your word. Same with the person who's hiring you. The First Commandment is 'Thou shalt not renege on a deal.'

I told Nicola about my dilemma.

'Are you crazy? You can't pass this up.'

I made a commitment.

'Company man!'

Within the forty-eight-hour decision period, I got an email: *The Number 23* was delayed. Instead of early December – with Christmas break – it would now not go until late January. Something about rewrites. I had an honourable out. I called Juli.

'I'd love to do *Blood Diamond*,' I told her.

'Great,' she said. 'Let me talk to Dawn. I know she'll be thrilled.'

Not as thrilled as my girlfriend, I thought.

PART THREE: DIAMONDS ARE FOREVER

CHAPTER TWENTY-EIGHT: BLOOD DIAMOND

I liked Edward Zwick instantly. Bearded, looking like a man who hadn't slept much and shifting in his chair, our interview in his office went longer than I expected. Ed was doing most of the talking.

'This is going to be a challenge for publicity,' he said. 'The diamond industry is going to hate this movie. They'll be on the attack and we need to fly under the radar.'

The diamond business had long been one of the most unregulated in world commerce. South African-based De Beers was the fat cat that had manipulated the gem market throughout the twentieth century, at one time controlling up to ninety per cent of the rough diamond trade. It was also one of South Africa's leading sources of revenue and, as such, even had the support of its venerated former president, Nelson Mandela.

So-called blood diamonds – or conflict diamonds – were the gem business's dirtiest secret. These were mined by slave labour in regions that used the proceeds to finance terrorism and insurrections in places like Sierra Leone, where this story was set. They allegedly accounted for only a small percentage of overall diamond mining but in a business where most of its product was kept off the shelves to maintain high prices, even a small percentage made a significant impact. So, companies like De Beers would buy gems with no questions about their origin just to control supply.

In December 2000, the United Nations passed a resolution calling for the certification of rough diamonds to ensure they were not mined in conflict zones. It wasn't until 2003 that the diamond cartels – reacting less to the UN than to bad publicity from human-rights groups – concocted a strategy to address the issue. The Kimberley Process Certification Scheme was named after the mineral-rich region in South Africa where the leading mining countries met to establish the agreement. It prohibited signatories from purchasing diamonds from countries that were at war. Enforcement provisions were weak, at best.

The film Ed described was set three years before Kimberley. The issues it would raise, including the use of child soldiers, slave labour and diamonds funding terrorism were still current. The diamond industry would not take kindly to a major motion picture, starring Leonardo DiCaprio, looking under its Certification Scheme carpet.

This movie was the kind of challenge every publicist dreams of.

We got up and shook hands.

He took me to meet his producing partner Marshall Herskovitz. A tall man with a generous smile and twinkling eyes, we met in the hallway and he merely said, 'Nice to have you on board.'

The next day's meeting with producer Paula Weinstein was a formality. I knew her from *The Perfect Storm*. We talked mainly about her godfather, the iconic singer, actor and civil-rights pioneer Paul Robeson. He'd been a friend of Weinstein's mother, a human-rights activist before the phrase was coined and a British television producer when women were rarely in such power positions. Paula and I got along just fine.

That afternoon, I made my deal with Warner Bros. It included an assignment for Nicola as the in-house writer for international publicity, as she had been on *Syriana*.

'It was meant to be,' Nicola said with understated assurance.

Among other things that were meant to be…

Noodling on the internet one day, I came across a drawing that reminded me of Nicola. It was the figure of a woman with tree roots for feet and arms like branches reaching to the sky. I took the concept to a jeweller in Beverly Hills and he produced a wearable work of art. I had no intention of placing it on a finger anytime soon. I hid the box in a desk drawer, deluding myself into a belief that my readiness – or lack of same – would be the dominant factor in a match of wills.

Nicola had recently attended the wedding of an old friend in Monaco.

'It was so beautiful,' she said. 'The ritual of two people making a promise in front of a crowd of friends and family transforms everyone, not just the couple getting married. Everyone who bears witness is sharing the vow to keep them together.'

Then, perhaps in a vision, she changed her mind – about the witnesses.

'I think I want to get married in Africa,' she blurted one night. 'I don't want a big church wedding. Just a guy in a loincloth, somewhere out in the bush.'

Taken off guard by this proclamation, I made the mistake of saying we didn't need to rush into anything just because we happened to be going to Africa.

'I don't even know if I want to marry you! Company man!'

I had the ring. I had the desire. But until I could figure out whether my head or my heart was giving me the right message, the guy in the loincloth would have to cool his heels.

Nicola was on a high. Her new LA psychic, a cherubic, middle-aged Latina named Angel, told her she would have two children and get married in April – when we'd be in South Africa. I didn't appreciate pressure from the spirit world.

A week later, she was depressed again – about not getting pregnant.

'It's God's way of saying I'd be a terrible mother.'

The alarm in my head was still ringing louder than wedding bells.

I'd flown to Portland, Oregon to help settle Casey into his new home across the state border in Vancouver, Washington. The modern complex was a maze of hundreds of apartments, a mile from the School of Piano Technology for the Blind. The two-lane rural highway between them was bordered on Casey's side by a cracked sidewalk which ran along a pine forest bisected by an auto-parts junkyard. He could take a bus to school but I knew he'd choose to walk unless the weather was too brutal. The school was on the opposite side of the highway. It meant crossing a road with a fifty-mile-per-hour speed limit and no stoplights unless you wanted to walk a hundred yards past the school to the edge of town, which I knew Casey would not.

'You have to call him every night to make sure he's okay,' Nicola insisted when I checked in. 'Or he has to call you.'

Good luck getting Casey to pick up his phone, let alone initiate calls on a regular basis. But I would try. I would also try to keep my worries to a minimum. The last thing Casey needed was Mom *and* Dad worrying about him. Dad's girlfriend assumed my role.

'He has to come here at least twice a month so I can feed him,' Nicola fretted.

Both boys were going to be with us over Thanksgiving.

The taxi that was supposed to take Casey to the airport didn't arrive, so he jumped on a bus – then another, then another. The last bus left him stranded in downtown Portland. Somehow, he made his way back to his apartment and phoned to tell us he'd missed his plane. Nicola went into action, rebooking his flight and finding a car company that would pick him up and escort him to the check-in desk.

An hour later, Sam called to say his plane from Ithaca had been delayed and he would probably miss his connection from Dallas to Burbank. Nicola took over, scrambling to find alternate flights to LAX or John Wayne Airport in Orange County.

'Thanks, Dad. I really appreciate it.'

We joined my sister and niece for a Thanksgiving dinner in Pacific Palisades at our cousin Jody's house where the extended family met Nicola for the first time. My sister, who had been close to Margaret, had got to know Nicola and casually hinted that she'd welcome her as a sister-in-law. Jody's husband, an earnest traditionalist, was cordial but told the boys – out of Nicola's earshot – 'Margaret is still part of the family and she's welcome here anytime.'

Family is a funny thing. When you're young, their approval means everything. When you're a young adult, their approval means nothing. At my age, it wasn't about approval. Bringing an outsider in was a statement. But what, exactly, was I stating?

Both my parents had passed more than a decade ago. I had my sister, my young niece, a handful of cousins with whom I was still in touch and one 84-year-old aunt – Jody's mother – who was also at the party.

'I like this one,' she whispered in my ear.

A few days after Christmas, we attended the wedding of Nicola's new friends, Jen and Andy. It was a beautiful, if unconventional, ceremony at a remote lodge in the hills of Ojai, California, featuring an 'energy' circle in which all attendees gathered to send positive vibes and offer testimonials to the bride and groom. Hours after the ceremony, followed by dinner at the marginal-friends' table, I was ready to leave – along with most of the guests who weren't staying at the wedding lodge. I stayed longer than I wanted; she had to leave before the last person standing. We argued about it on the way back to our B&B.

The next day, however, I awoke to a kiss and all she talked about at breakfast was the beautiful ceremony. No leftover edginess from last night's tiff. Only a champagne hangover and musings about how it would feel to be love-bombed in a circle of family and familiars. Our fights were becoming shorter.

We had a quiet New Year's Eve with Baz and Simone from *Syriana*. 'Quiet' meant no bickering. Baz barbequed, Simone was the DJ and we danced and drank until Nicola and I fell unconscious in their spare bedroom. We'd made it through another party together – more important still, a New Year's Eve – without war breaking out.

Nicola wanted to get 'unblocked' in 2006. Papa Joe and his band of Maori marauders were back in Topanga Canyon during January. I served as designated driver. She emerged from the experience a little sore but not crippled, wincing only slightly as she got in the car. Then she cried on the drive home – but not from the pain.

'It's part of the unblocking,' she managed to say, putting her hand on mine for reassurance.

The unblocking didn't result in a pregnancy. But it did unblock something in me. Maybe it was seeing how much she wanted to have a baby. Maybe it was how my sons, my sister, my 84-year-old aunt and everyone I knew had fallen in love with her.

I'd bought her a spa day as a Christmas present. This was the day she chose to redeem it. I told her I would cook dinner. She had understandable trepidations about that. The last time I cooked we dined on burned meatloaf and soggy broccoli. While she was away, I had two gourmet meals delivered and bought an expensive bottle of champagne.

I put candles on the patio table and kept her out of the kitchen. I didn't bring out the champagne because she knew I didn't like champagne and that would've been a tip-off. So I poured a nice white wine and we talked a bit about nothing in particular. I put on some music, went to the kitchen and came out with 'a little something I whipped up'. She went along with the gag. For dessert, I brought out the Dom Pérignon and a small box. I served the box on one knee.

Our eyes met through a rip in the fabric of time and a dam-burst of tears might have flooded the patio if we didn't look away. Her face beamed 'yes' in all the colours of the rainbow. Her arms encircled my head, holding until I had to come up for air. She put the ring on her finger.

'Hey, I'm supposed to do that,' I teased.

'Too late,' she said, smiling. 'I'm never going to take this off.'

There was no discussion of a date. But Africa was looming and somewhere on that continent a guy was dusting off his headdress and preparing to send his loincloth to the cleaners.

CHAPTER TWENTY-NINE: INTO THE JUNGLE

Some people shine a brighter light than others. It draws us to them.

Sometimes the light is enhanced by one's circumstances. Sometimes it cannot be dimmed by them.

There are also places like this. South Africa is one of them.

A driver picked me up in Durban and drove me to my apartment on the Wild Coast of KwaZulu-Natal. It was dusk and the main highway was lined with housekeepers and gardeners walking home. Dozens of people waited at a bus stop for 'black taxis' – white minivans crammed to overflow. My car turned off the highway, passing dozens more workers migrating toward the setting sun, as we entered the luxuriant, white suburb of Southport. Spider monkeys leaped from the spear-tipped, double gate to my complex, as the driver opened it with a card key. The car dropped me in front of a three-bedroom apartment with a full-length deck overlooking a wind-blown, white-sand beach. I was too taken by the beauty of my new circumstances to contemplate the ugly realities of economic apartheid.

'I bought a wedding dress today!' Nicola phoned in a flush. 'Anita and I found it in a second-hand store on Portobello Road. If I hadn't found it, well, we couldn't get married.'

What happened to the guy in the loincloth? Two words: Nicola's mother. Sheena had eloped, Steve was unmarried and probably a committed bachelor, so it fell to my betrothed to provide Mom a wedding march not her own. The twelfth-century church in Eversholt was a fairytale setting and Berrystead's five-acre garden would be spruced up for the reception.

We'd looked at the last page of the one-line schedule, checked that against a calendar, allowed two weeks for the movie to run over its targeted wrap and chose Saturday 8 July for our wedding in England.

Nicola hadn't relented on an African ceremony.

'We can have more than one wedding,' she said. 'In fact, I think we should renew our vows every year.'

She was approaching her nuptials with characteristic gusto: there was no such thing as overdoing a good thing.

The production offices were near the town of Port Edward, in a business park fronting the road to our main location. A mile of dirt drive led into the Mzamba Gorge, 500 acres of veldt surrounded by lush jungle, a swath of which had been cleared and muddied to build a mining camp.

A secretary showed me to my desk in the middle of the front office. Our executive producer, Kevin de la Noy, came out of his cubicle and greeted me with a firm handshake.

'Ah, here you are!' he announced to the room. 'You have your work cut out for you.'

Kevin was a rakish, rough-and-ready Brit, restless and born to lead. We'd worked together on *Ali*, in Mozambique. A large portion of this movie would also shoot there. He'd been Zwick's first call when this project was green-lit. He was a strategic genius, having managed logistics for the director on *The Last Samurai*. This movie would be an even bigger challenge with remote locations, multiple moves and equipment that included a Russian-made cargo plane and a fighting helicopter classified as a 'weapon of mass destruction'. Kevin liked nothing better than rolling up his sleeves and wrestling the impossible to the mat.

He introduced me to the office staff, all white South Africans: Janine, the production coordinator who gave me a start packet with forms for accounting; Joline, our hard-working housing coordinator who asked how I liked my apartment; Sue Ann, a wholesome beauty who handed me a stack of messages.

'So glad you're here,' Sue Ann sighed with relief. 'You'll have to tell me how you want me to handle these as they come in.'

A random sampling of the messages turned up the following: Danny Glover was starring in our movie. No, it was Djimon Hounsou. Glover had been set to reteam with Mel Gibson on a different South African film that had been postponed.

Our movie was shut down. No, that was the Mel Gibson/ Danny Glover one.

Our production was destroying the environment. One woman had left a half-dozen messages about this. Kevin assured me we had agents from the environmental commission on site and our contract with the landowner stipulated everything would be restored when we wrapped. He suggested I not return the serial complainer's calls.

'I'm sure she just wants money,' he said.

Poor Sue Ann would have to deal with her.

There were several people on the crew with whom I'd recently worked, including our brilliant script supervisor from *Jarhead*, Jayne-Ann Tenggren; production designer Dan Weil from *Syriana*; Ann Morgan, Jim Carrey's hairdresser from *A Series of Unfortunate Events*; Wade Allen, stuntman from *Troy* who would be Leo DiCaprio's fight trainer. There was also a contingent of old mates from *Gladiator*, including camera operator Klemens Becker, location manager Mark Sumner, and stills photographer Jaap Buitendijk.

Gladiator had been Jaap's first big movie. Then a gawky 28-year-old, now a confident veteran, I'd recommended him to Warner Bros. for *Harry Potter and the Chamber of Secrets*, which had prompted the studio to entrust him with other high-profile pictures leading to this one. We'd become good friends after *Gladiator*. I'd visited him in Scotland; he'd visited me in Ithaca. He had yet to meet Nicola.

'When am I going to meet this mystery woman of yours?' he said, grinning.

'You mean my fiancée?' The word came out more tentative than declarative.

Before leaving Los Angeles, Ed told me he'd been getting letters and phone calls from an organisation called the World Diamond Council, asking him to soften the message of his film. De Beers and its affiliates held four of the twenty-one places on the council. They'd also, apparently, got hold of the script. They weren't happy.

'Imagine what this film could do to our Christmas sales,' Jonathan Oppenheimer, director of De Beers, was reported to have said.

Our director forwarded me their latest communication.

The three-page letter began cordially enough with WDC's 'understanding' that the movie was focused on 'the now defunct rebel group' who funded its civil war in Sierra Leone with the sale of rough diamonds. The Council then laid out a ten-point dissertation on how and why the filmmakers should make clear the Kimberley Process had effectively dealt with what they now considered a dead issue.

... We believe ... this is a story that must be told – but it's not the whole story.

Point 2 gratuitously repeated the 'must be told' bit, adding that their organisation 'welcomes the production of the film' – while emphasising how African countries 'rely on diamond production for their economic development'. It continued with the pledge '... all the stakeholders in the Kimberley Process are determined that revenues from diamonds should never again be used to finance armed conflict and undermine the security of innocent civilians.'

Point 3 started getting a little more heavy-handed. It began with 'However' – never a good start – '... it would be a great pity if a movie as important as the one you are now producing told only part of the story.'

Points 4–7 are hardly worth mentioning. They basically re-emphasised how important diamond production is to African economies and how dedicated the Kimberley signatories were to getting the situation in hand. How, in fact, they'd pretty much solved the problem.

Point 8 was the killer. They asked Ed to provide '... some acknowledgment of the huge changes that have occurred in the diamond trade' since the advent of the Kimberley Accords. They suggested he give '... serious consideration to including a written broadcast [sic] message at the end of the film, and in accompanying promotional literature' endorsing that viewpoint. They very considerately even wrote their own blurb:

The conflict in Sierra Leone ended in January 2002. This was followed by free and democratic elections and today, virtually all global trade in rough diamonds is now conducted through the Kimberley Process... Sierra Leone is now using its diamond wealth to help build a secure future for all its people.

Zwick had every intention of crediting the WDC for its attempts at addressing the problem through Kimberley. He had no intention of suggesting they'd solved the problem. And that was what they wanted. Right now, the diamond empire was asking politely.

A lesson in public relations 101 – that won't come as a shock to anyone who's seen a mafia movie. First, it's nicely nicely. Then you find a horse's head in your bed. Then Luca Brasi comes gunning for you.

Your response can't go straight to... response. The opponent wants you to tip your hand, to play your cards too early. Your strength is in not responding. That means you must take a fair number of body blows and come through standing.

It's contrary to a filmmaker's most basic instincts not to want to punch somebody who attacks his/her baby. But unless serious damage is being done – like Mandela himself condemning the movie while we were making it – you save your punches until a few months before release. Then you attack with every combination you can muster – in this case, human-rights organisations. My job was to make sure the fight didn't break out while we were filming and to liaise with groups like Global Witness for the fight to come.

I knew little about the civil war in Sierra Leone. I knew nothing about Sierra Leone except for the fact that it had a civil war.

Less for my edification than for the movie's authenticity, Ed and the producers had hired an expert. His name was Sorious Samura. A big man with an easy smile, sad pouches under his eyes and the gift of gab, we had lunch during prep week and I got schooled.

You only have to watch his Emmy and BAFTA-winning documentary, *Cry Freetown*, to know Sorious is a kamikaze. He remained in Sierra Leone's capital when the rebel forces (the Revolutionary United Front – RUF) attacked, filming atrocities on both sides of the fighting while under fire from both directions.

'Ed has told me I should work with you to make sure you know things about my country,' Sorious began our discussion. 'Sierra Leone diamonds are some of the most desirable in the world. They have a size and colour that is almost unmatched anywhere else. The first fights in the civil war were over control of the diamond mines. During the war, all the buyers moved across the border to Liberia. Suddenly, a country that had very few mines of its own became a major exporter of diamonds.'

The conflict in Sierra Leone saw both sides enriching themselves from the diamond trade. 'The rebels sold diamonds to get weapons. The government leaders sold them to get rich. No one was doing anything for the people.'

Peace came in 2002 but, contrary to the WDC's proposed disclaimer, little else changed.

'The government is still corrupt. Now the RUF is a political party. They were given control of the diamond mines.' His mouth formed a half-smile and his eyes dropped to his plate. 'But at least there's not so much killing.'

He scooped up the last of his mashed potatoes and leaned back to see how much I'd taken in.

'Now I will tell you about the child soldiers,' he said, referring to the other controversial aspect of our movie. 'But first, let's get some pudding.'

He had been in Ethiopia last year, filming a new documentary called *Living with Hunger*. He'd shared the starvation diet of local villagers for five weeks. He never wanted to go hungry again.

I sorted the stack of messages on my desk into two piles. The largest, by far, was the pile of requests for Leonardo DiCaprio. I started returning calls and emails to the others.

Leo had not yet arrived but I'd had some initial contact with his publicist, a New York-based veteran by the name of Ken Sunshine. I had a lot of respect for Ken. He was as involved in his clients' altruistic endeavours as he was in managing their fame.

'Leo cares very much about this project,' he told me. 'But he can't spread himself too thin. His causes are the environment and wildlife preservation. There are a lot of important issues in this film – conflict diamonds, child soldiers – but he's not going to be a spokesman for those. It dilutes the impact of his other activities.'

Fair enough. I knew DiCaprio was among the few celebrities who did more than just lend his name to a foundation. I assured his publicist that we didn't want him speaking about our issues – especially conflict diamonds – during filming.

'Good, good. He doesn't do any press during production, so if you get any important requests, send them on to me or his assistant Jason and we'll deal with them.' So far, so easy. He added, 'We'll have to see about his EPK interview. He usually doesn't do them until he's seen a cut of the movie.'

There's just one thing I'd like him to do, Ken. We're going to have an embedded journalist writing a production story for Warner's International…

'Nobody told me about this. I'll have to get back to you on that.'

'What do you mean, Leo might not talk to me?'

Just get here. You'll have five whole months to charm him.

I was sleeping with the enemy.

CHAPTER THIRTY: DJIMON

There was only one black African actor currently working in film who could be called an international star. He had received an Academy Award nomination for his supporting role in Jim Sheridan's *In America*, a Golden Globe nomination as the lead in Steven Spielberg's *Amistad* and a Screen Actors Guild nod for *Gladiator*.

We were filming an African story in Africa. The main thread of our plot was an African father, Solomon Vandy, who finds a rare pink diamond and embarks on a desperate search for his kidnapped son. It was the most important role in the movie. 'The child is the gem,' was Ed's guiding mantra.

One might've thought my stack of phone messages and email requests would contain at least a few for Djimon Hounsou. It didn't.

This kind of snub wasn't new to him. Despite his acting accolades and unique position as the lone luminary of an entire race from this continent, he hadn't attained the recognition he deserved as a Hollywood star. On this movie, his agent negotiated everything, from name size on all advertising to trailer size at base camp, to be the equal of DiCaprio's. He wasn't competing with Leo. He and DiCaprio would become friends as filming progressed. He was just fed up with being dissed.

Djimon had changed since I worked with him on *Gladiator*. We'd had some meals and some good times together on that movie but his light-heartedness was gone.

Greeting me with a soft African handshake, he appeared wary, even of an old colleague. I tried to break the ice, asking about the woman to whom he'd been engaged then.

'I can't talk about her,' he flared. 'She was horrible. I think she was only after money.'

Oops. Sorry that didn't work out. I shifted to questions more generic.

'How's it going here so far?'

He hated South Africa.

'These people are racists,' he said. 'Even if they don't say anything, you can see it in their eyes.'

He caught himself saying too much, complaining too much, being too candid.

'It's good to see you.' His jaw slackened. 'Seven years is a long time. But seven is lucky, hey?'

He introduced me to his assistant, Polly, a sweet twenty-something white girl, pretty, not flashy, who spoke with a faint Texas accent.

'I'm going to look at a couple of houses for you today,' she told her boss.

'Good. I can't wait to get out of that hotel.'

He said the production had given him 'inferior accommodations'. They'd rented him a house that had problems with plumbing or heating or both. It might've happened to anyone. But he wasn't just anyone. In his mind, he shouldn't have to fight for the consideration a white man of his stature was accorded. They'd temporarily put him up at the Wild Coast Sun, a tacky casino where most of the crew were staying. It was the only big hotel in the area.

'Are you staying there?'

I downplayed the magnificence of my apartment.

'Good for you,' he said, with an affirming nod. He had a keen sense of fairness and there was no envy at my being treated *fairly*.

He asked about my family, who he'd met on *Gladiator*. I told him about my change in marital status since we'd last seen each other.

His lips spread into a warm, familiar smile.

'You're engaged!' he exclaimed. 'I can't wait to meet your lady.'

Everyone was looking forward to meeting Nicola and there would be plenty of opportunity. We would be together on practically the entire movie, living and working side by side.

Be careful what you wish for?

Our flight from Los Angeles had included a layover in England where we arranged to meet Nicola's mom for lunch. The prospect of meeting my future mother-in-law wouldn't have fazed me, except for the way in which Nicola introduced it.

'She can be intimidating,' Mary Williams Graydon Summers' daughter prepped me. 'Watch your table manners. She might not get your humour. Don't be too forthcoming or get too personal. She appreciates discretion. For God's sake, don't talk about money. It's so American. You're huggy. She won't feel comfortable with hugs from someone she's just met, so don't hug her. She loves the Royals so don't insult the Queen. Just be yourself and you'll be fine.'

Mrs Summers was an imposing woman, nearly six feet tall with a great mane of silver hair. She took my hand and offered me a cheek.

We've all heard the tropes about mother-daughter mirror imaging: if you want to know what a woman will be like in thirty years, look at her mother. Mary was regal but not unapproachable. She liked a glass of wine with lunch. She had that delightful British agility at keeping a conversational ball rolling. As she spoke, I caught glimpses of the rebellious debutant who fell in love with a handsome South African and married beneath her station. So far, the apple wasn't falling far from the tree.

There were obvious distinctions between the two. Mary oozed sophistication. Nicola grew up faking it through childhood dinners at the Savoy with her wealthy grandparents, but she shared her father's disinclination toward pretence. If Nicola was going to grow into Mary, grounded by her father's humility, I could live happily ever after with that. But there was more to my fiancée than fancy table manners, conversational ability and enjoying a glass of wine or three. Meeting her mother revealed how little I knew about the woman I intended to marry. There was a restlessness in Nicola I didn't see in her mother. What was that about? What did marriage mean to each of us? We had love. Why marriage? I questioned whether we knew each other well enough after two years to take this lifelong leap. I answered that marriage is about finding someone you want to learn about and learn from. Or is that serial monogamy?

After dizzying myself with those quandaries while Nicola and her mother caught up over lamb roast, my fiancée absented herself from the table, giving Mary and me a moment alone. Emerging from a haze of misgivings, I located my good soldier and bade him to do the expected thing.

'You know I've asked Nicola to marry me,' I sputtered. 'I'd like your blessing.'

There was only a brief pause before her response.

'Are you absolutely sure you know what you're getting yourself into?' Deadpan.

Then she smiled.

I smiled.

But she'd made me blink.

Alluvial diamond mining is a poor man's process of finding surface gems. It doesn't require heavy equipment burrowing deep underground. It's a bunch of people with shovels and pans, wading in mud and waist-deep water.

This was the land we'd been accused of destroying to build our set. It was a mess. Artistically arranged to appear so. But a mess, nonetheless. We'd savaged acres of wilderness to top soil, then piped in thousands of gallons of water to fill pits and make a soupy surface.

We hardly needed it. February is summer in South Africa but it's also the rainy season in KwaZulu-Natal. It had rained the night before and a grey cloud hung over our set on the first day of filming. The sky remained consistent and cinematographer Eduardo Serra (*Girl with a Pearl Earring*) shot wide to utilize the natural filter, adding to the gloom of the scene. Mud was everywhere and half the South African crew were walking around barefoot. The front page of tomorrow's call sheet would add a note requiring 'appropriate footwear at all times'. The danger of nematodes, parasites that enter your body through your feet, lurked in the wet earth.

The day began with the dramatic entrance of our African first AD, Isaac Mavimbela, leading 150 mineworkers to the set. Emerging from the jungle in a *toyi-toyi* trot, they chanted a Zulu battle song as they wound their way in double columns down a hill path to the diamond pits. Throughout the day

– and ensuing days – when the spirits of his performers flagged from boredom or exhaustion, as they waded in the muck and hid from the rain, he'd rally them with another refrain, boosting the energy of the entire production.

We'd cut a narrow road into the jungle where the grips built a platform for the big crane we'd be using all day. There was no space for a second camera and very little room for crew. Producer Paula Weinstein and I hiked to a hill above the set where we could watch the action. Paula spotted our armourer Simon Atherton. He fell in with us.

'Simon, what's your biggest concern on this picture?' she asked.

He gave it a moment's thought before answering, 'Losing a gun. If we lose a single weapon, the government will shut us down.'

Explosions ripped through the mining camp as filming moved closer to the river. There, Solomon is cornered by Captain Poison (British actor David Harewood) just before a paramilitary attack with a Russian Hind helicopter. Kevin had somehow convinced the South African government to rent this to us despite its classification as a WMD. Our props department could overthrow a small African country.

We were shifting to a split day-night schedule and our make-up department head, Sallie Jaye, threw a turn-around party at her rented house. I went with Jaap and we both left after a couple of hours. I was home too early to reset my body clock for night work, so I spent the next few hours on the phone with my fiancée.

She'd been at her mom's making wedding arrangements.

'It's never too soon,' her mother had told her. They'd recently been interviewing organists. 'Like Michelin-star restaurants, the best ones are booked a year in advance.'

The contrast of our days couldn't be more extreme. Me here, her in London; me hanging out at the mine pits, her shopping for shoes on Marylebone High Street. I listened while she told me about menu options for the reception. She listened to me describe a chase scene through the jungle.

'I'd rather be there,' she said. 'But it's going to feel a little strange at first.'

I woke up too early and got to the office before most of the staff. Our housing coordinator, Joline, was standing outside having a smoke. I joined her.

You look tired.

'I spent all day yesterday trying to find housing for three vultures,' she said. 'I finally found them a big cage but it wasn't easy.'

How'd you do it?

'Just called everyone in the area who had anything to do with animals. The elephant and the leopard should be a breeze by comparison.'

Yeah, things might seem a little strange at first.

'You won't recognize Maputo,' Kevin said as he called me to his office. 'It's not just the Chinese money that's been pouring in. It's a completely different set-up from *Ali.*'

Ali had been the first big movie to film in Mozambique. *Blood Diamond* would be the third. In between, a Nicole Kidman–Sean Penn film, *The Interpreter*, had shot there for a few weeks. *Ali* was crewed almost entirely by a seasoned South African company, with only the most menial jobs going to Mozambicans. Now there was an indigenous production company in charge.

'I'd like to send you there for a day or two to get a jump on things. I think you'll need an assistant who speaks Portuguese.'

The Maputo International Airport is fronted by Bairro Hulene, a shanty town built around the city's main garbage dump. More than half the residents of Maputo lived here. It is a mile-wide scar that welcomes visitors to Mozambique's capital city.

A production driver took me to an industrial park near the city centre that was our headquarters on *Ali* and would be again on this movie. Nothing appeared to have changed in five years, from the shabbily uniformed guards at the chain-link gate, to the buildings' peeling paint, to dry patches of lawn and a parking area where cars were being washed by hand. I stood for a moment suspended in memories: the out-of-body feeling of a twenty-four-hour filming day that ended in a tunnel under the stadium as the sun came up, a near riot of 30,000 unpaid extras, a walk with Will through slums where a group of kids spontaneously lifted him on their shoulders and paraded him through the village. *Ali* had been a difficult production – with director Michael Mann driving his crew hard – but a rich experience.

A man was waving to me from the car wash. He beamed broadly and fluttered his rag in my direction. His shirt was torn and one leg of his trousers was pinned under a stump. He grabbed his crutch and hobbled toward me.

'You know me?' he asked.

Of course I did.

'Louis! How are you?'

'Fine, fine. Happy see you.'

Louis had been my Buddha throughout the chaotic filming of *Ali*. If I had a crap day, Louis's smile would turn my mood.

If I made a mistake, his infinite bliss would set it right. If my trust was betrayed, the sight of Louis taking his washrag to a hubcap made it impossible to cling to a petty grievance. How could I not remember Louis? How could anyone who'd ever met him forget him?

He lost his leg to a landmine when he was a child, he'd told me. He spoke five languages – three tribal plus Portuguese. His command of English was enough for basic conversation. With Louis, you didn't need much conversation. His spirit spoke volumes. I'd visited his village and met his extended family. He became my friend. And he became my heart connection to this beautiful, tragic and resilient country.

The production office staff was now mostly black and mixed-race Portuguese. On *Ali* the pecking order was strictly colonialist and some of the departments – particularly transportation – had been overtly racist. One of the secretaries led me to another part of the building where our two production managers had their desks. Nick Laws and João Ribeiro greeted me expectantly. Pleasantries exchanged, we got straight to business.

João was a native Mozambican of Portuguese descent. He'd worked on *Ali*, though I didn't remember meeting him. His title then was 'consulting producer', which probably meant he was a fixer and maybe hired some of the low-level crew. He was now an executive with the media conglomerate SOICO, whose holdings included the largest television and radio stations in the country and who were the local suppliers for this film.

'This is an important movie for Mozambique,' he began. 'SOICO can be very helpful in getting publicity for *Blood Diamond*. We should have a press conference. The head of SOICO is a very influential man. He might even be able to get President Guebuza to participate. Perhaps even Mr Mandela, who is currently living here.'

We prefer to keep a low profile while we're here, I said. I did not tell him Nelson Mandela was the last person on earth we wanted at a press conference.

Nick Laws suppressed a smile. João scowled.

'We have some logistical challenges on this movie,' Nick switched topics. 'You probably know that Mozambique suffered fifteen years of civil war. Our staging of the Battle for Freetown will make a lot of noise and probably scare a lot of people. SOICO is working with us to alert the citizens of Maputo that the gunfire and explosions are only part of a movie and there's nothing to be frightened of.'

The production would be testing explosions a week prior to our arrival to give the neighbourhood an audible sampling. He suggested taking me to the downtown location where we'd be filming the scene for ten days.

The streets in central Maputo didn't have to be dressed down to resemble war-torn Freetown. Our art department would alter a few signs and add a façade to a building that would be hit by a rocket launcher.

We toured the site of our test explosion and Nick explained the production's plan to reassure residents. A soft spoken, slightly built Englishman in his mid-forties, Nick had been in Mozambique in 1990 when the civil war was still raging. He'd finished his first movie in Africa, Bob Rafelson's *Mountains of the Moon,* and was bitten by *mal d'Afrique* – the peculiar disease in which the continent gets under your skin and won't let go. He met a South African woman and moved with her to a remote farm in the Eastern Cape. They had pilots' licences and a small plane in which the family could commute to Port Elizabeth or Cape Town if they needed supplies or contact with civilization.

On our walk back to Nick's car, we passed through a small square where a stunningly beautiful teenage girl sat, long legs tucked under her dirty cotton dress, holding a basket of bananas. A policeman, who'd been chatting her up, walked away as we approached. Nick over-paid for two bananas and she flashed a dazzling smile.

'If she'd had the good fortune to be born in Paris, she would have been a fashion model,' he said, handing me a banana as we continued.

This was a lesson Africa teaches: it's not the Great White Hand reaching into deep pockets that transforms lives. It's the understanding that on this plundered and pillaged continent, your future is limited by the resources within your reach. If Nick had bought her a little kiosk with a comfortable chair to replace the dirty piece of cloth she was sitting on, she would still be a banana peddler. But access to seeds might have made her a farmer, a sewing machine might have made her a seamstress, an education might have made her a teacher.

Nick had recently worked on *The Constant Gardener,* which shot in remote parts of Kenya. He helped set up a fund to finance basic projects – bridges, wells, roads – that would improve lives there after the movie had pulled up stakes. He floated the possibility of doing something like that on this movie.

At our meeting next day, João said, 'I have someone I think would be a good assistant for you. She's in your office now.'

He was supposed to have lined up several candidates, so I had to assume this one was a spy he wanted to plant in the publicity department.

Teresa was a willowy woman in her late twenties who could barely contain her nervousness. She had a degree in media and communication and had worked in television in Portugal where she'd lived for the past five years. She met João through a mutual friend who asked if he could find a job for her on this movie. We spoke for about thirty minutes. I liked her. If she was going to be working for me and spying for João, I'd deal with it.

Nicola flew to South Africa shortly after I returned from Maputo. Driving through KwaZulu-Natal, she saw the streams of people walking the highway toward their villages.

'I always wondered why I found the streets of London so lonely after coming back from Africa,' she mused.

She swooned over our accommodations. On our deck, she breathed in the intoxicating air of a part of this country she'd never experienced.

'I'm home!' she shouted into the surf.

Jaap met Nicola and turned on the charm.

'You're even more lovely than he said you were,' he told her.

He had a girlfriend, Emma, with whom he had a daughter. He was thinking about asking her to marry him when they came to visit next month.

'You absolutely should,' Nicola told him. 'Even if she says, "It doesn't matter," trust me, it does.'

While in London, Nicola had filed 'the Banns' that English law requires be 'posted' before a marriage licence can be issued. She was marching us steadily toward the aisle.

'Just don't buy her a diamond ring,' she admonished Jaap.
'Too late. I already have.'

CHAPTER THIRTY-ONE: DANGER

The diamond disinformation campaign was plodding along in pursuit of a watered-down message and/or an end-card disclaimer for the movie.

I took a call at the office from a woman who said she worked for the government in Sierra Leone. She invited the filmmakers, the cast and me to visit the country, meet the President and fly in his private helicopter to view some of the diamond mines. I suspected the mines we'd be shown were sparkling examples of good labour conditions and clean operations. I reluctantly declined the invitation.

I got a call on my production mobile from a woman in Israel who had written a couple of books on diamond 'branding' and purported to be contacting me to offer her expertise. Shortly into the conversation, it became clear she was more interested in grilling me about the movie than telling me about the industry in Israel, which is one of the major centres for buyers and cutters of raw diamonds. She offered to set me up by phone with a representative from De Beers with whom I could 'debate' the issues. I asked her to refer any further questions to me by email. Later, I called our production office to remind them not to give out my private phone number. They said they hadn't.

I spoke with Ed about these and other related inquiries over lunch at our base camp. 'They're coming after us and they'll keep coming – through Alan Horn (Warner's CEO), through me. Now they're trying to go through you. This movie isn't about De Beers.'

If any confirmation were needed that he wasn't being paranoid, our South African producer, Gillian Gorfil arrived in Port Edward and I invited her to dinner at our apartment. Nicola cooked.

Gillian was an impressive woman – a tall, impeccably turned out blonde in her forties, divorced with a teenage daughter. *Blood Diamond* was based on an original story she'd optioned from a writer named C. Gaby Mitchell. She paid another writer, Charles Leavitt, to develop it into a screenplay. Zwick and Herskovitz had then done extensive rewrites.

'De Beers has every draft of the script,' she confirmed. 'They're trying to finesse me over to their side, calling to invite me to dinners, offering free safaris for the cast. I told them I wouldn't dream of accepting but they keep calling.'

Gillian knew she would be on the frontlines long after we were gone.

'I'll tell you honestly, I'm pretty nervous about it.'

It had been a tough week for production. We'd lost a half-day to rain, and the additional mud slowed equipment movement the next day.

Leo twisted his knee when his character, Danny Archer, runs from the mercenary invasion of the mining camp. 'I'm fine,' he told a worried Ed Zwick as our medic wrapped an Ace bandage. He made it through the scene but the schedule was juggled to allow time for his leg to strengthen.

Later in the week, the special-effects team were setting charges for a scene in which a squadron of mercenaries attack the mining camp with missiles from the Hind helicopter. All other crew and stuntmen were relegated to the periphery of the set for safety. Nicola was interviewing Sorious Samura, who was telling her how realistic our mining operation looked, when we heard an explosion.

We couldn't see anything other than a scattering of people running toward the smoke. Second unit director Paul Jennings received a radio transmission. He ran off in the direction of the commotion.

I asked one of Paul's assistants what was going on.

'One of our effects guys was rigging an explosive device. It went off.'

Edward V. was twenty-two years old and had little movie experience. He had applied for a job with our props department but they were fully staffed. The special-effects department were hiring. Edward went through safety training along with the rest of the department. The charge he was laying blew his hand off. Five people around him were also wounded. The camera helicopter that was to be filming the scene was used to fly the injured to the nearest hospital. The crew were shaken. They wouldn't need another memo to remind them there were multiple risks on this production. We think we live in a movie set where real life doesn't touch us – until we're reminded that it does. Work resumed when the helicopter returned, everyone feeling a little vulnerable; me taking a step closer to Nicola.

Mary Summers flew to the Wild Coast from her second home in Cape Town the same day our female star, Jennifer Connelly, arrived. The first time on set for them both was in a refugee camp that production had created on a dusty patch of bushland. Hundreds of extras, including many amputees, had been recruited as background. There was no such thing as a glamorous set on this movie but this was probably our least glamorous. Jennifer wore khakis and boots. Mom was dressed in a casual frock befitting a proper Englishwoman, a floppy hat to shield the sun and a plain linen scarf to cover her mouth when the wind kicked up.

Nicola introduced her to Ed and some of the crew while I spent the day with Michael Huggins from the World Food Program, which had lent us its logo for the scene. This was a welcome break for him, having just come from the real thing in Ethiopia.

'Add another million people and this is what it looks like,' he said.

With transport vehicles adding dust clouds to the dryness and discomfort, Mary stood uncomplainingly by her daughter's side or stood contentedly alone when Nicola left to interview Mike Huggins. There was no place to sit, and if you didn't move around you'd be coated in red earth. With a stiff upper lip and a sturdy back, she did the Queen proud.

Toward the end of our workday, a crowd of raggedy villagers gathered at the periphery of our location. When first AD Nilo Otero called, 'That's a wrap,' we watched them descend on the camp and begin hauling away lumber and wire.

'It saves us having to pay for deconstruction, and better it goes to some use than to a landfill,' Kevin de la Noy explained.

'Extraordinary,' Mrs Summers proclaimed.

Nicola's forty-second birthday celebration was dinner at our local beachfront restaurant with Mary, Jaap and his partner Emma, who'd just arrived with their baby daughter. It was a fairly abstemious affair by Graydon-Summers standards, as wine was ordered by the glass, not the bottle. The waiters came out with a cake and sang 'Happy Birthday'. Nicola asked them to sing the post-apartheid South African national anthem, 'Nkosi Sikelel' iAfrika' (God Bless Africa). Every customer – mostly white Afrikaners – stood and joined in. The black waiters then segued into the pre-1994 national anthem in Afrikaans: 'Die Stem van Suid-Afrika' ('The Call of South Africa'). We were witnessing the emergence of a new nation, only eleven years after the miracle of Mandela.

There was little chance this night of celebration would end at dessert. Jaap and Emma were game for a party, and Mary said she'd look after their daughter. We drove in separate cars to a shoreline joint called Riptides in Port Edward where a crew bash was being hosted by Leo's assistant Jason and Djimon's assistant Polly. Leo had flown off to a private party in Cape Town but Djimon was there, as was our director.

Ed joined us at our table. He needed to get his head out of the movie. The conversation came around to love and marriage and the pitfalls of life on location. His wife, Liberty, had laid down the law: he'd been away too much and this movie had brought her tolerance to a breaking point. If he didn't stop making epic films with long travel schedules, their relationship was in jeopardy. His teenage son Jesse was sharing this adventure with him but Liberty and their daughter would only be joining them for a brief visit.

'She doesn't like travelling with me,' he said. 'She's designed her own life working on environmental issues. Part of the problem is she wants to move out of LA. That's where my business is. I don't know. Is twenty-three years of history enough reason to stay married?'

Both Nicola and Emma were too quick to say, 'No.'

The ink barely dry from my divorce, I felt a hypocrite rooting for Ed's marriage. But to my ears it was a solicitation for support, maybe even a little optimism from two couples who were just beginning love's volatile voyage. Nicola and Emma had no clear idea of the madness they were signing up for in marriages to movie guys. I think he was saying, 'I've had twenty-three years of practice trying to hold on to these two conflicting passions and I still want to believe it's possible.'

'Hang in there,' the irony of my marital downfall echoed.

A few days later, I joined Kevin, Nick Laws and South African production manager Alan Shearer for dinner. It was ostensibly to discuss strategy for our explosion test day in Maputo but it was really just a guys' night out. Kevin needed the camaraderie. His wife had left him.

A man of resolve, not accustomed to showing emotion, Kevin was raw. As we talked, it became apparent the marriage had fallen apart some time ago. He was struggling now to arrange the pieces.

'It got to the point where she didn't want to go anywhere with me,' he said. 'We had an invitation for a weekend, for the whole family, aboard Michael Ovitz's 173-foot yacht in Monte Carlo. She wasn't interested in going.'

His pain was doubled by guilt. He knew he might've been a better husband. But he'd been a good provider and a good father.

'I could've taken a studio job any number of times...' his voice trailed off.

At a time like this, it's the first question you ask yourself: might it not have happened if I'd had a desk job? Might I still have a family to come home to if I wasn't on the road so much? But there are always factors other than travel. You can't pin the whole blame on working in the movies.

Alan had taken a different route.

'I tried to stick with local jobs when my kids were young,' he said. 'But eventually those dry up. I wound up taking a civilian job for three very depressing years. I made great money. Ran a Mercedes dealership. But I could feel myself dying a little bit every day.'

Nick was the luckiest one.

'My wife and kids have gone with me on almost every movie I've worked on,' he said shyly. 'It's always more difficult with children. We do a combination of home schooling and using tutors. I think the six months we spent together in one of the poorest parts of Kenya (on *The Constant Gardner*) was a better education for them than they could've had in any classroom.'

We all drank too much that evening and took taxis back to our respective residences.

Kevin got a few hours' sleep, then went out driving. Just driving.

'It clears my head,' he said the next morning. 'I do some of my best thinking when I'm driving.'

I think we were all a little worried about this.

Mom flew back to Cape Town and Jaap, Emma, and their daughter moved in with us. In a private moment on the beach, Jaap proposed marriage. Emma said yes.

Nicola cooked a celebratory dinner, I lit a fire and chose a romantic music mix from my iPod. We raised glasses and I proposed a toast to 'a long and happy life together'. Despite the occasion, this was not a group to let that sentiment go unchallenged.

'To a deepening of our love for each other,' Emma amended.

Here was an opportunity to discuss what marriage meant with two lovers who had also decided to take the plunge. Maybe it was my iPod playlist but I was feeling as old-school sappy as a family comedy on black-and-white television. I was feeling happiness – slightly wine-induced – for two couples, in this room, who were preparing to sanctify their love for one another. Finally, the conversation I needed to define the promise of 'forever'.

Emma wasn't having it.

'It's a formality,' she said. 'Love is all that matters. For as long as it binds us.'

I found myself defending something that had failed me. Emma and I had both been divorced. Was I a fool not to share her jaundiced view of love's lifespan? Marriage is a gamble. But there's no pay-off without chips on the table. Blame my parents but I was conditioned to believe in it.

'I think marriage is like a grocery item with an expiry date,' Nicola declared. 'Sometimes it just goes off.'

That snapped me right out of my romantic bubble.

Then, like an interventionist god, Bruce Springsteen sprang from the portable speaker.

'Listen,' I silenced the gathering.

We said we'd walk together baby come what may
That come the twilight, should we lose our way…

'Who is this?' asked Jaap.

Pearls before swine.

It wasn't one of The Boss's better-known songs but it was one that had stuck with me. He was singing about love that lasts because two people work at it. Love that lasts because each person accepts the inconstant pace of individual growth. Love lasts when people understand that love needs patience and nurturing.

I'll wait for you
And should I fall behind
Wait for me

'Could you pass the wine,' Jaap asked Nicola.

'Shh!'

I wanted them all to hear – to feel – the truth in this. You don't walk in lockstep with another person. You allow one to sprint while the other lags. But you don't let the distance grow so wide that the other is out of reach.

Emma whispered something to Jaap, Jaap said something to Emma, Nicola leaned in to hear what they were saying. They spoke quietly – so as not to interrupt my reverie. Mine and mine alone. No one was really listening.

Should we lose each other in the shadow of the evening trees
I'll wait for you
And should I fall behind
Wait for me

Let them have their expiring marriages. Like a punctured tyre, I could feel the lyrics slowly leaking meaning as I pulled off the road of blissful union into a ditch of doubt.

Then, the last guitar notes faded, Nicola moved closer, linked her arm in mine and put her head on my shoulder. 'I love you,' she whispered in a tease. You sentimental goofball, she was saying. I was listening, she was saying. Help me believe.

Marriage doesn't have an expiry date. It goes bad if you leave it out and unused.

Later that week we emailed 'save the date' announcements to friends and family, which included a photo Jaap took of us with the Wild Coast as backdrop. Our pending nuptials were now on a fast track. We'd figure out what the ever-after journey meant as we went along.

Jaap came down with tick-bite fever and could barely lift his aching bones from bed to drive Emma and their daughter to the airport in Durban.

We had planned to drive with him to Maputo in a caravan led by Kevin – which included Jayne-Ann Tenggren, Klemens Becker and his focus puller Bebe Dierken. Instead, he would spend two days resting, close the apartment, and fly there with the rest of the crew.

'I don't want to leave this place,' Nicola said over breakfast on our deck, the day before departure. 'It was feeling like our home.'

For me, home was wherever she was. But I'd miss this place too.

CHAPTER THIRTY-TWO: WHAT AFRICA TEACHES

To live anywhere in the world, you must
know how to live in Africa.

– Creina Alcock from Rian Malan's *My Traitor's Heart*

After an overnight stay at an elephant reserve and a wild ride following Kevin through Swaziland, we made it to the border crossing before it closed at 8 p.m. Traffic into Maputo slowed us enough to follow him to our final destination.

The Polana was a five-star colonial, built in 1922 and billed as the 'Grand Dame' of African hotels. I'd stayed there throughout the filming of *Ali*. It had been a favourite holiday spot for South Africans and Rhodesians during apartheid. After check-in, Klemens joined us for dinner on the veranda, the moon and stars putting on a light show, an Olympic-sized swimming pool shimmering beneath the alabaster deck where black waiters hovered to refill our drinks. Three whities in a gilded cage. An island of privilege in a sea of poverty.

Out of 177 countries on the United Nations Development Program Index measuring poverty around the world, Mozambique ranked number 170 – moving up from last place during the past decade. A recent influx of foreign money had boosted its overall economic standing but the privation of its citizens remained largely unchanged. Most of the 18 million residents still existed on subsistence farming, but drought and overuse of land had made even that hardscrabble life more fraught.

The brutal, decade-long war for independence and years of civil war had left many of its children orphaned and fending for themselves.

Our first two days' filming were in a small town about an hour north of Maputo that wars and floods had reduced to desperation. Marracuene's twenty-one-mile stretch of sandy beach was once a popular tourist spot – until Portugal laced the shore with landmines. Today, the broken pavement and ramshackle buildings were a movie set.

Our first scene saw a stream of refugees entering the town, Archer and Solomon cloistered among them. Jennifer's character, Maddy Bowen, meets them in a one-room school that production rented and dressed as the base for a refugee registration centre. Children composed a significant number of our extras on these days, as they had at the refugee camp in South Africa. Most had been contracted in advance by agencies working with orphanages and children's aid organisations, but there were also many who just showed up that morning, parentless and shivering from having spent the night on the streets.

It was a miserable place to film. But, of course, misery was what we were filming.

We watched fictional families huddled around the name board, scanning for loved ones. We stood outside with headphones, listening to a bit of dialogue between Leo and Jennifer inside the town's lone schoolhouse that was too cramped for us to access. There were no interviews to be had for Nicola because everyone was busy, or – like many of the artistic department heads: costume, production design, casting – they'd left early or decided not to make the drive here at all. Nicola was not comfortable being on a set watching other people work. As we walked to my car, she erupted in a mix of angst and annoyance.

'Why am I here? I'm losing all my contacts back in London. I can't get any traction on my life following you around.'

Yeah, this was a problem. We were in the unusually fortunate position of being able to share more of this life than most couples in the business. But one life isn't enough for two people. She felt she was disappearing.

I like to think one finds opportunity; it doesn't find you. Look for it high and low, in treetops, under rocks, it's there waiting to shake hands. Sometimes though – often enough for wishful thinkers to congratulate themselves – it strolls up, taps you on the shoulder and asks, 'Where have you been all my life?'

Over dinner that night, Nicola's fairies once again flew in for the rescue.

Lyndsay Cruz was a smart, personable, California blonde in her late twenties who first experienced Africa as the advance representative travelling with former US Secretary of the Treasury Paul O'Neill – just before he was fired from the Bush administration for warning about the coming financial crises. U2's Bono was also part of the expedition to explore the roots of poverty on the continent.

Through Bono's contacts, Lyndsay got a job with the international aid organisation Oxfam, recruiting celebrities to shine their light on African people whose visibility in the West was zero. Djimon was one of her celebrity recruits. She'd come here to discuss press coverage of a trip the two of them had made to Mali last year to meet with that nation's starving cotton farmers.

Lyndsay was excited to learn that our in-house writer shared her affinity for the forgotten people of this land. After dinner, we returned to the Polana where the two of them talked into the night about stories they could work on together: an interview with Djimon for the *Telegraph Magazine*, a trip in the fall to take *Sex in the City* star Kristin Davis on a tour of northern Mozambique to spotlight the predicament of women in that war-torn region.

Nicola was back in business.

On Monday morning, my re-energised fiancée contacted photographer Jillian Edelstein, with whom she'd previously teamed on a story about traditional healers for the *Sunday Times Magazine*. The two had discussed turning that into a book. Jillian was currently back in the Badimong Valley, site of their previous collaboration, in the former Orange Free State. Nicola booked a flight to Johannesburg.

Meanwhile, I was at a lull in which nothing of great import was happening in the publicity department. These periods of feeling like you're only around for the free lunch happen on most movies. The young and overeager try to find ways to justify their existence and make their jobs still appear relevant. They create problems in order to solve them, impressing no one except the doctor treating them for stress-related illness.

I worked a bit with Nick Laws to formulate a plan for a *Blood Diamond* charity. But mostly, I was just around for the free lunches.

Then, one day, I found myself shaking hands with my reason for being here.

Over the weekend an article appeared in the *Cape Town Argus*, written by a journalist who'd snuck onto our refugee camp set as part of a child amputee school group. It was a very positive piece, relating to the money the school had earned and the fun the students had being in a movie. Unfortunately, it also said we were doing a lot more for the kids than we were actually doing.

In addition to paying the school for the children's workday, Kevin wanted to pledge $2,500 to buy prosthesis for a few of them. He had to do battle with our accountant, Marge, who only wanted to budget $600. The newspaper reported we had donated $60,000. As nice – and rare – as it is to have the press exaggerate your good deeds, it created a problem: it confirmed to other worthy organisations that the Hollywood gravy train had rolled into town.

Among the people in Maputo who'd read the Argus story was Olivia Machel, daughter of Graça Machel, the nation's former First Lady and the only First Lady to have served two countries – the other being South Africa with her husband Nelson Rolihlahla Mandela – 'Madiba' to billions of adoring fans who called him by his clan name. International icon, defender of De Beers and potential disaster for our film.

'Like a most precious diamond honed deep beneath the surface of the earth, the Madiba who emerged from prison in January 1990 was virtually flawless,' fellow Nobel Peace Prize-winner, Bishop Desmond Tutu had said of him.

'The last thing we need is to have Nelson Mandela singing the praises of the diamond industry,' Academy Award-winning writer-producer-director Edward Zwick had said of him.

Gillian Gorfil and I met Olivia for drinks at the Avenida Hotel bar.

We braced ourselves for a discussion about her stepfather's objections to our movie but Olivia wanted to talk about the dire conditions of the country's education system and how

'Warner Bros. could help'. She was as charming as a person with a locked focus and singular agenda could be. She was informed and made a good pitch.

Once Gillian tactfully explained that the studio couldn't subsidise the government's inadequate education funding and the movie's purse strings couldn't be loosened through its heartstrings, the conversation changed direction.

'I have been an admirer of Leonardo DiCaprio ever since *Titanic*,' she said. 'I would love to meet him. Maybe he would like to meet my stepfather.'

Gillian, a liberal South African to whom Mandela was the Messiah, made what might have been a serious tactical error.

'I'm sure he'd love to meet Madiba,' she gushed. 'Let me talk to him.'

First, I reminded her, we needed to talk with Ed.

'If you fuck this up, you're banned from the set and all future contact with me and this movie!' our director seethed at our South African producer from his chair by the video monitors the next morning.

'And you' – meaning me – 'how could you let this happen?'

Well, it hasn't happened yet.

Ed drew a breath. If Leo found out he'd kiboshed a chance to meet the Great Man, it could affect their relationship.

'Look, I'd love to meet him myself,' he more calmly explained. 'But I can't be involved in a discussion about the diamond industry with Nelson Mandela. I want you two to figure out a strategy. Do not, I repeat, do not let Leo or Djimon get drawn into any kind of controversy about blood diamonds or the Kimberley Process or De Beers. This movie is not about De Beers!'

Gillian said she would convey that message to Leo and Djimon, and she and I would figure out how to manoeuvre around any such topics during our audience with the President.

The house where the Machel–Mandela family lived in Maputo was a spacious, ranch-style wood frame inside a fenced compound. The couple divided their time between this residence and one Mandela owned in Johannesburg.

Three black Land Rovers, Leo and his entourage, Djimon and his, and a third with Gillian, me and Jaap – who'd begged to come along as our photographer – pulled up at the high-gated entrance and announced our arrival through an intercom.

Olivia met us outside the house and escorted Leo, Djimon, Gillian and me inside. I asked permission for our photographer to join us. The entryway had a large framed portrait of Samora Machel, Graça's late husband, the first democratically elected president of liberated Mozambique. Our hostess led us into the living room where two cream-coloured sofas framed a square glass coffee table. Djimon and Leo were directed to the sofa where a vertical stack of pillows divided them. Gillian and I shared the couch opposite the actors.

Graça Machel entered with Madiba on her arm. We rose from our seats and my entire being vibrated. He was tall, maybe six foot three, and stood tall. There was nothing frail about him except his walk, but Graça's matching steps made his entrance processional rather than feeble. A powerful politician in her own right, she was formidable beneath a wary smile.

Madiba – close-cropped, cloud-white hair, in a silk shirt buttoned to the collar with an AIDS ribbon pinned below the top button – sat, with her assistance, between Leo and Djimon. Graça positioned the pillows behind his back and took a chair beside Djimon. The former president had limited range of motion and couldn't easily shift his body. The actors slid forward on the sofa so he could see them. Gillian and I were in his direct line of sight.

We awaited his profound opening pronouncement.

'I used to have hair like that.' Mandela laughed, pointing at my unkempt head of dark curls. We all laughed.

Gillian and I did most of the talking. Madiba asked Djimon about himself, and after that Djimon stayed respectfully silent. Leo hardly said a word until the subject of George Bush came up. He then launched into a lengthy invective about the American President's job performance. Madiba listened without assent.

'We got in a big fight the first time we met,' he said. 'When we were going to meet again, Condoleezza [Rice] was in the Middle East on some important state business but she cancelled the trip – cut it short – so she could come back and stop Bush and me fighting again.'

He laughed. His face lit up and fire returned to his cloudy eyes.

'It wasn't necessary [that Rice was there]. First you fight, then you must make peace. You can't always be fighting the most powerful country in the world. And the Americans think they're God anyway.'

His smile went flat. Then he laughed again. We laughed with him.

That was as political as our meeting got. After an hour of conversation that ranged from tourism in Mozambique to Oprah Winfrey, Graça made it clear our time was up. Jaap took individual photos of us shaking his hand. We followed him, Graça and her children to the entry hall where Leo and

Djimon's assistants and drivers were eagerly waiting. Madiba allowed time for photos with them all.

It is not uncommon in the hierarchy of a film production for a producer – or writer – who is outside the director's inner circle to be regarded as a nuisance. Gillian was courageous – or naïve – enough to ignore that. I'd be forever grateful that she did.

Jaap and I walked to the popular pizza restaurant, Mundo's, next door to the Avenida Hotel.

'That was amazing,' he said.

'Amazing,' I concurred.

The next day, Ed would say, 'I wish I could've been there.' But he was probably right in making the hard decision to stay away.

CHAPTER THIRTY-THREE: THE ROAD OF NO RETURN

A four-day Easter break at the end of the week was a timely antidote for a tense director and a crew exhausted from long days in difficult locations.

I was headed to a new location not on our production schedule. I'd promised to join my bride-to-be in a part of South Africa where I'd never been and had only the vaguest idea how to get to.

Oliver Tambo Airport in Johannesburg is a sprawl of chaos with long queues, poor signage, grumpy officials and no logic in its layout. My hotel was supposed to be five minutes from the airport, so I succumbed to a ride from the least aggressive cabbie I could find. The Airport Grand turned out to be nowhere near the airport and anything but grand. I would've liked to immediately hit the road for my ultimate destination but I'd taken a late flight out of Maputo and been warned about driving at night in Johannesburg, one of the most crime-ridden cities on the continent.

The layover gave me an opportunity to reunite with an old friend. Millard Arnold had played George Foreman's corner man on *Ali* but he was not an actor. He was a poet, an author, an artist, an attorney, a corporate executive, an anti-apartheid activist, a former official in the US State Department, a former journalist for the *Washington Post* and currently a partner in one of the biggest construction companies in South Africa. We'd met when I asked him to stop taking photos on the film set. He apologised and we started talking. It turned out he was also an exceptional photographer. I should've apologised. Instead we became friends.

Millard had just come off a plane himself but he picked me up at my hotel to take me to a 'decent' restaurant for dinner. He looked tired.

Where've you been?

'Bahrain,' he said with uncharacteristic heaviness.

He'd spent the past few days as legal emissary for his company, Murray & Roberts, dealing with the aftermath of a tragic accident. Dozens of their employees had been on a boat, celebrating the completion of Bahrain's World Trade Center towers, when the vessel capsized. He'd gone there to interview survivors and console the families of fifty-eight people who were lost at sea.

I offered an awkward commiseration. He reassured me there was nothing I could say.

'But tell me, how are you doing?'

Well, I'm working on this movie where, like most movies, people forget there's a real world in which real shit happens. How quickly the absurdity of delayed film schedules, underperforming extras and forgotten props comes into perspective.

But it was exactly that escape from reality my friend needed. It was what the parallel world of entertainment was created to provide for the real-life world of senseless suffering. So, I regaled him with the silliness of life in the movies. Light returned to his tired eyes.

'So, why are you here?'

I told him about my fiancée.

'You buried the lede!' the former journalist chided. 'I want to know all about her. When is the wedding?'

Well, I said, I think the first one is the day after tomorrow.

Nicola hadn't really planned this. Like so many things in her life, it came to her by process of serendipity and magical thinking. She didn't find her priest in a loincloth but she did know a priestess with whom she'd connected while researching her story on African healers for *The Times*. Her name was Monica and her address was Under the Cliff That Spills Fresh Water in the Valley of the Ancestors.

Monica had 'married' a couple Nicola knew from previous trips to Rustlers Farm. The couple, Gary and Andrea, suggested we should do the same. Nicola leaped at the opportunity to make her African wedding dream come true.

I was the last to be informed of these arrangements.

'Monica is amazing,' Nicola told me the night before I left Maputo. 'It's such a special gift that she wants to do this for us. Pick up a good whiskey at the airport.'

Why?

'Spirits for the spirits.'

Who was I to deny the ancestors a toot?

'Let all the spirits know it'll be an open bar. Anything else?'

'Yes. I can't wait to... show you the Valley.'

I can't wait to see you too.

The dirt track into Rustlers lay about twenty minutes past the two-lane highway that runs through Fouriesburg, an old Huguenot settlement. The town was a run-down remnant of the Boer Wars that had a ninety per cent black population, many of whom loitered along the main street in front of mostly white-owned businesses. I stopped at a gas station to get directions.

'Head on ten miles, you'll come to a road on your right. Don't take that one. Take the second one after that. Pass a couple farms and you should see a sign. Unless the hippies tore it down.'

The 'hippies' had invaded this enclave of *sterk* Afrikaners about twenty-six years ago in the person of a young Durban lawyer named Frik Grobbelaar. Weary of fighting the system, he traded his law books for farming tools and invested everything he had in a thousand acres of Free State land on which the current farmers were barely scratching out subsistence. He had a plan to use modern, sustainable agriculture techniques and make his farm a model for all of Africa. He renamed his holdings after the Basotho cattle thieves that used to roam the valley.

Frik didn't fare any better than his predecessors as a farmer. A drought that lasted most of the 1980s was partly responsible. But friends started coming around and Frik began building clay rondovals to accommodate them. More friends came and brought their friends. Someone suggested he turn it into a retreat. So he built a small restaurant and bar. An artist friend started making stone sculptures. Another painted murals and others contributed labour and imagination to gardens and water features. More housing was built for kindred spirits who wanted to live there. Others came and pitched tents. Somewhere along the way, musicians started turning up. In the 1990s, Rustlers Valley became South Africa's Woodstock with an annual festival that drew thousands of 'hippies' to this non-conformist oasis.

Then, in 1997, a fire destroyed everything but the original four rondovals. Frik's home, the restaurant, greenhouses, the other guest houses were rubble.

I drove through the sandstone gate and parked between an old pickup and a camper van. Nicola was waiting for me in the newly rebuilt restaurant, the Saucery. We walked the gardens as the evening sun streaked amber between peaks of the Maluti Mountains.

'It was Christmas, ten years ago, and I was in Cape Town, surrounded by white people,' she told me about her first trip to this place. 'It was so white, I was feeling claustrophobic. I wanted to be in black Africa. So I rented a car and started driving to Lesotho. I'd heard about Rustlers but I thought it was just a lodge where I could spend a night before driving across the border.

'I got here a day or two after New Year's just as the last car was leaving a big party. There were only a few residents that night and I listened to them all bad-mouthing someone named Frik, saying he was a dictator and things like that. He wasn't here. A day or two later, Frik's ex-wife, a gorgeous, neurotic, model-type, showed up and told me about a place called Badimong, the Valley of the Ancestors, that was just a few miles away.'

She volunteered to drive the ex and three other people to the Valley.

'I was blown away.'

A couple days later, Frik arrived.

'He was totally welcoming and said I could stay as long as I wanted. I stayed for two weeks, just wandering around, going down to the river to swim naked.' Reading my reaction, she added, 'There was no one else around. I've never felt more at peace anywhere.'

Did you and Frik have a little fling? I asked as casually as I could.

'No! He was just really nice. Maybe a little flirty but nothing happened.' She paused. 'There was one night when he got me stoned. I was looking at his face and it melted into an old Native American man. I think I was seeing a past life of his and that Frik was a real protector of the Earth. I thought that was kind of sexy. But I was really stoned. '

I was tired from my journey and wanted to take a nap but there was too much Nicola had to show me and too many people to meet.

A near-full moon lit the way over narrow bridges as she guided me through herb gardens, flower gardens and the permaculture garden that was the ongoing experiment in alternative agriculture Frik championed. We met Dale, the permaculture guru, and his petite, glassy-eyed girlfriend, Pixie, whose name was her description.

Permaculture, Dale told us, was a system of working with nature to create ecologically sustainable plant growth. It was an 'architecture', he said, that included water-resource management and waste disposal that went back into the earth.

'It's sort of like communal living, where everyone contributes whatever he or she has to support the group.'

Dale was one of the holdovers from the days when Rustlers was a commune.

'The fire was the best thing that could've happened,' Frik told us when we met him in the restaurant. 'It rid the place of all the freeloaders who were making camp here. Now it's a lodge. It's an enterprise.'

A big man, thick and hardy, Frik was pure Boer, with a family name that traced back to the Great Trek of the 1830s when wagon trains of Dutch-African farmers fought Zulu armies, then the British, to create the Orange Free State in these mountains and fields.

'I got the insurance money to rebuild and I got rid of the parasites. I lost every personal item I wasn't wearing but it was a purification.'

Frik spoke mainly to Nicola. My interjections were mostly ignored. No doubt in my mind he'd had a long-running fancy for my fiancée.

There were soon a couple dozen diners in the restaurant and Frik moved on to another table – Alpha dog sniffing out the pack, inviting challenge from friend and foe. One couldn't help admiring his breadth of knowledge and eagerness to stimulate debate, some of which could be heard over the din from across the room.

We were joined by Gary and Andrea, the witnesses for our upcoming assignation. Gary was about my age, with a long grey ponytail and a gentle disposition. Andrea was probably in her mid-thirties but looked younger. They'd met here. They lived half the year on an island in British Columbia and spent the other half in Lesotho, working alongside and educating farmers about modern methods of scratching a living from the ground.

Rustlers was a magnet for the idealistic and idiosyncratic and, whatever I thought of Frik, his vision was the attraction. It was an admirable gathering of live minds with strong opinions in the Saucery restaurant that night. The crowd was mixed-race, and politics appeared to be at the top of the menu.

As the evening drew on and dinner turned to drinks, we met two Indian brothers, Jay and Kumi Naidoo. Kumi was head of the NGO Make Poverty History; Jay was a former secretary general of the Congress of South African Trade Unions. Both had been prominent figures in the pre-1990s African National Congress. Frik re-joined us with the Indians and the three of them began debating details of African politics that quickly lost me. Nicola was fully engaged but my eyes were drooping.

'I'm tired,' I said. 'I'm going to our cabin to get some sleep.'

'Ok, I'll be there in five minutes.'

I walked to our rondoval. It was padlocked. Nicola had the key.

I went back. The key, please.

'Oh, just stay for another five minutes.'

Five turned into fifteen.

'If you're not ready to go, just give me the key.'

'Just another five minutes.'

Fifteen minutes later.

'Give me the damn key.'

Nicola slapped the key in my hand.

I was sound asleep by the time she came to bed.

The next morning, Gary joined me for breakfast.

'I gave her a good talking to,' he said.

That helped. But only slightly.

What was I doing? I knew this wedding didn't count to anyone but us. This was a grown-up game of make-believe. I'm a conventional guy. This was not a conventional thing to do. This was not a conventional relationship. Get me the fuck out of here!

'She might be just as nervous about this as you are,' Gary said.

CHAPTER THIRTY-FOUR: AN AFRICAN WEDDING

To enter Badimong, you must pay R10.80 (about a dollar) to a hobbling old man named Abraham – who then gives the money to the farmer who owns the Valley.

As we – Gary, Andrea, photographer Jillian, and the bride and groom wearing white shirts – walked toward an unmarked path into the wilderness, a woman sat, dark and brooding, under a tin roof by a fire pit. She glared at us and didn't respond to the traditional greeting, 'makhosi' (accompanied by a bow and clapping hands).

'We think she's a spy for the farmer,' said Jillian.

We hiked for about two kilometres, across streams and gullies, until we began to see huts tucked into the cliff face. Most of them were brightly painted – reds, purples, sun yellow – some with cement walls, others with walls of sticks. A turn off the path and a short climb over some boulders led the way to Monica's compound.

Passing the goat pen, where chickens ran free and *twasas* (apprentices) boiled clothing in cauldrons, rats as big as footballs sat sunning themselves on the rocks.

'They're dassies,' Andrea corrected. 'They're more like badgers.'

'The rats are all in Monica's house,' added Jillian. 'I won't go in there.'

But that was where the rest of us were headed.

Monica's house was a clay rondoval with a thatch roof. The curtain entrance was drawn shut and we waited outside at the instruction of one of the *twasas*, Thikhililana, a chirpy, slip of a woman whom everyone in our party seemed to know.

After a half-hour lingering beside the trickling fresh water dripping over a concavity in the cliff, a man emerged through Monica's doorway. He was wearing a fake leopard skin, off-the-shoulder tunic that came just above his bare knees. He held the curtain open for Monica, exchanged 'makhosi', retrieved his walking stick and trotted off.

Monica was short and round with a blazing smile and eyes that exuded force and madness. She hugged each of us as we handed over gifts – my whiskey, Nicola's flowers and a bottle of 'salt water from the Indian Ocean' that Andrea and Gary had brought for her. Thikhililana bundled the offerings and took them inside the hut.

All, except Jillian, followed Monica through the entrance where two older women wearing yellow capes with an embroidered red cross greeted us, then receded against a wall of the small main room. There was an elevated slab in one corner which served as an altar, four plastic chairs and cement shelves for a pantry.

The shelves were crawling with rats.

'They are my children,' Monica said, noting my unease at the rodent Cirque du Soleil running, jumping, tumbling over grain sacks, canisters and jars. Two of them popped out of a bread box and chased each other to the altar.

After an eternity of small talk that left me wondering if Monica had any inkling we'd come for more than just a catch-up visit, Andrea asked the question that was on my lips.

'Monica, do you know why we're here?'

'Tell me.'

Andrea explained that Nicola and I wanted her to bless our

partnership. This was protocol: someone other than the wedding couple was required to introduce the subject.

'Let me tell my children to start singing.'

I swear, I thought she was going to organise the rats into a choir. Instead, she gave instruction to one of the caped women who went outside to alert the camp. Monica was referring to her other children, the *twasas*. I was relieved. Moments later, a chant began to build and drums sounded.

Monica lit candles on the altar. Within seconds, all the rats on the shelves disappeared. She began praying, partly in English, partly in an African dialect. Nicola sat frozen, her eyes at half-mast, trying to dissolve into the soporific incantations. I was fixated on the altar. It had a vase of flowers that the rats had munched to their stems, a figurine of the Virgin Mary wrapped in plastic and an open beer can.

Our priestess put a lit candle in each of our hands, bringing our arms across each other and draping them with a leather, beaded bracelet. Then she gave a Christian blessing, in English, at the end of which she had us exchange candles. She continued the blessing in African as the chanting outside her hut grew louder and the drums picked up speed.

Monica took the candles from us and placed them back on the altar. She brought out a box of matches and began striking one after another, waving them above our heads. I heard my hair sizzle. Then her two assistants began singing the gospel tune, 'Somebody's Calling My Name', just those words, over and over again, as Monica broke into a rapid recitation of an African prayer and held her palms above our heads.

Suddenly, she shrieked. My spine straightened and Nicola dug her nails into my arm.

'Somebody's ca-al-ling, somebody's ca-al-ling, somebody's

calling my name…' The words and melody, the clapping, the singing, the drumming. 'Somebody's ca-al-ling…' Thump-thump-thump, thu-ump, thump. Nicola's eyes were shut tight. My eyes were the only body part I could move.

Monica reanimated. Slowly. Assisted by one of the yellow-capes, she knelt at the altar and fiddled with some potions. Yellow-Cape helped her to her feet and motioned us to stand. Monica produced an eagle feather, dipped it in the potion and sprinkled it in our faces, punctuating each spritz with something between a word and a shout.

Monica prayed again in African. The drumming ceased. Her prayer ended.

We felt one of her hands on each of our hearts and opened our eyes.

'Now you are married,' Monica announced without a flourish. We all burst into laughter and applause. Nicola and I, uninstructed, kissed to seal the deal.

As we exited Monica's hut, there were hugs and kisses all around. The sun glared and our eyes adjusted from the darkness. Time, shooed away like a pesky fly, returned to buzz around us. We had no concept of its length of passage. Minutes? Hours?

Monica squeezed Nicola's breasts.

'I feel a boy,' she said.

Gary presented me with a Lesotho shepherd's stick – a talking stick, he explained – that he'd carried up here.

'You're not allowed to hit each other with it. It's for talking things out.'

Andrea gave Nicola a large crystal in the shape of a heart.

Back at Rustlers, word of our ceremony had spread. There were a dozen guests in the Saucery when we returned. We accepted congratulations and Andrea proposed a toast.

'To sharing the joy of this day with new friends and old.'

Our new friends discretely left the restaurant soon after finishing their meals. We were alone at the bar with Frik. The conversation ranged from African politics to building plans for his new house.

'I'll turn the old one into a bunkhouse. Should be able to sleep six people.'

He was the same crusty bastard I'd met last night but something had shifted in his attitude toward me. Or maybe it was toward Nicola. Frik could've kept us up all night but Nicola pulled the plug. She downed her glass of wine and stood.

'We're going to bed now.' She hugged him where he sat.

Frik got up from his barstool and threw his arms around me.

'Come back anytime,' he said.

It was the closest he came to saying 'congratulations'. To him, it surely meant more.

We didn't have time to bask in – let alone contemplate the significance of – what we'd committed to in the Valley.

I didn't have time because I returned the next day to battle – the cinematic one.

Nicola didn't have much time to soak it all in because... We'll get to that.

Kevin de la Noy had prepared a thirty-page manual on how we were going to shoot the Battle for Freetown.

'If Freetown doesn't work, the movie doesn't work,' our director had said.

I stood on Bagamoyo Street with Sorious Samura and one of our dialect coaches, Alfred – two survivors of the scene we were about to film. In an earlier conversation, Sorious admitted concerns about whether 'Hollywood' could make a realistic movie about the events in his native country.

'This brings back terrible memories,' he said now. 'This is almost like reliving the whole thing.'

Alfred was so shaken, he left the set before lunch. Sorious made it through the day but wasn't around much the rest of the week.

Several of the extras were amputees who had lost limbs in the Mozambican civil war. Some were from other places. Most had known the terror of real war. Our African AD, Isaac, had been around since the movie *Zulu* and had been training troupes of stunt actors for thirty years.

'This is acting but this is also bravery,' he said of his team. 'They remember a time when the bullets were real.'

They ran for their lives amidst gunfire, explosions and vehicles full of pursuing armed rebels. At the end of the day, they embraced each other and wept. Nearly all of them returned for the next day's filming. And the next. And the next.

The main cameras followed Leo and Djimon through the chaos. Leo's knee was aching and Djimon supported him as much as the script would allow, their off-camera friendship cementing during the ten days of filming this key sequence.

But Isaac's stunt team were the real heroes in this scene.

Nicola was busy interviewing everyone in sight: the special-effects supervisor, the make-up team, the locations department, the art department, the costume department, even the director when he wasn't looking through the lenses of nine cameras covering every conceivable angle.

Nicola was so busy in part because she was doing her job and in part because she was looking for ways to avoid me.

She'd returned to Maputo a couple of days after I did, stopping off in Johannesburg to have dinner with an old lover. The former lover was recently married, she said, and they were 'mostly just friends' who'd only slept together 'a couple of times'.

She said she'd call that night. I tried phoning her at about 1:30 a.m. My call went straight to the black hole of her voicemail. The next day she explained that, after dinner, she'd gone to a lesbian bar with the woman who owned the bed and breakfast where she was staying and got in too late to phone.

Then there was the musician she met on the plane. He asked for her number. She gave it to him. I let out a small protest at that. And I may have lumped that in with a minor complaint about the ex-lover and no phone call…

'Do you really think if I wanted to do anything with him (the musician), I would've told you about him?'

Did I think that? What was I thinking? We'd just gone through a mystical experience that bound us together in sacred vows to love and to cherish – or whatever we promised in African. I mean, it was technically non-binding but if I'd felt that, I never would have gone through with it. Neither would she, right? I wanted to be bound to Nicola. Was it possible I was also still afraid of that? Wasn't it a little late for those questions now?

I'd stepped into her world, this ceremony, this… commitment, and embraced it with respect and sincerity. Was I doubting her sincerity? What kind of a first-class asshole did that make me? What were my petty jealousies about?

I had to find a new approach to our relationship.

Thus, began my defiant, 'Okay, you'll do your thing, I'll do mine.'

Those who care the most, suffer the most. My best option was not to care.

Which led to Nuno and the ambassador's wife.

CHAPTER THIRTY-FIVE: CLUBBING

Ragged, decaying and poor, Maputo had a vibrant night life. It didn't take long for the film crew to discover it.

Three-storey, thousand-capacity Coconuts was the staple for dusk-to-dawn dancing, but there were numerous other venues that accommodated hardy partiers. One of the most popular was the Railway Station, run by a suave Portuguese Mozambican named Nuno. One Saturday night, Leo rented it for a semi-private crew party. The regular gang, plus a plethora of pretties from around town, jammed the bar and dance floor for an end-of-the-work-week blowout.

Nuno was a rough-edged, pseudo-sophisticate who looked like he could break up a bar fight or quote a few lines of Hemingway with equal ease. He was running a nightclub to run in bigger circles. The Railway Station wasn't classy but it was inviting: funky-chic with a hip, artsy clientele.

I won't pretend to know anything more about Nuno than what Nicola told me – to explain why she was spending so much time with him at the bar.

'He knows all the big editors and journalists – who all adored Samora Machel – and he wants to introduce me to them. I'm a journalist. I want to meet them.'

Fair enough. If he hadn't been leaning on the bar, licking his chops like a cartoon wolf.

A few more words about jealousy here: sometimes it's as simple as 'pay attention to me, not to him/her!' Sometimes it's a fear of losing the object of your affection to a worthier suitor – the inference being you're not worthy. Sometimes it's desperate; sometimes a mere irritation. Sometimes it's a sign of affection; sometimes the hoarding of a possession. I was old enough and had enough self-regard to believe I was above all that. It was dawning on me that I wasn't.

I moved in and Nuno moved back to bartending. He returned a few minutes later with a wizened Asian man to whom he introduced Nicola.

'He was Samora's personal photographer. They were side by side during the freedom fighting with Portugal and the war with RENAMO.' To the photographer he said, 'Nicola is a journalist, here with the movie. I thought you'd like to meet.'

They were off and running and I couldn't hear one-out-of-three words standing behind her with music pounding from the adjacent dance floor.

I felt someone bump against me and a high-pitched squeal made me turn to my right. There were two attractive women drinking next to me.

'Oops. Sorry to disturb you,' said the one who'd been pushed into me. Indicating her girlfriend, she added, 'She was just being stupid.'

The tall, pretty brunette spoke perfect American English. They definitely weren't part of the film crew.

'No, don't let me disturb *you*. What were you talking about?'

They looked at each other.

'You,' my brunette said.

Nicola didn't notice when I followed them outside for a smoke.

She was American. She was here with her husband.

'Here?'

'Oh, not here. He'd never come to a place like this.'

He was a European ambassador to Mozambique.

My new friends drifted off. Leo had already left and soon most of the crew were lining up at the taxi stand.

My wife-girlfriend-fiancée was still on the dance floor.

'Dance with me,' she screamed over the music. 'Just another fifteen minutes.'

I'd heard 'just another fifteen minutes' at least fifteen times too many.

'Let's go!' I shouted into her face so there was no question about her hearing me.

She danced the dance of defiance back into the centre of the floor.

I passed up a couple of taxis at the kerb, thinking, hoping she'd come out after fifteen minutes. I wanted to go back in but I didn't. I jumped in a cab at 2:15 a.m. and headed to the Polana. I stayed awake as long as I could. At around 4 a.m., I heard Nicola fumble with the lock to our hotel door.

'I got a ride back with one of your mates who had the same last name as yours. He told me he wouldn't make a pass because he respected you – and you had the same last name.' She passed out on the bed only half undressing.

A few days later, Nicola informed me she had a lunch date with Nuno and 'some journalists he wants to introduce me to'.

She returned late that afternoon.

'How was your meeting with the journalists?'

'Their car broke down. Nuno drove me around to some of the landmarks from the civil war. They're all on the outskirts of the city and very few tourists know about them.' She was talking a bit fast.

It wasn't until her second lunch date with Nuno and 'the journalists' that I called the ambassador's wife.

We met at a café in central Maputo where it was all very public and prim. There we had a pleasant, if not completely comfortable, lunch in which the speech bubble above both our heads read, 'What am I doing here?' She was a diehard Republican who'd done her master's thesis on Richard Nixon. Still, we had a few chuckles and it was nice to talk with an educated American who had nothing to do with the film business. And, I'll admit, it was nice to be out with a nice-looking woman in whom I had no vested interest and to whom I was slightly exotic.

Feeling only a bit surreptitious about my own rendezvous, I asked Nicola about her lunch when she got home – expecting to hear another story about Nuno's 'journalist friends' being no-shows.

'It was great. They're a lovely couple. She's a writer and he's the editor of the biggest left-wing paper here. They want us to come visit them on their island this weekend. I said we would. We don't have any plans, do we?'

The Green-Eyed Monster skulked back to its dark corner. I didn't tell her about my lunch date. There wasn't much to tell.

Filming had switched to night scenes in which Jennifer and Leo meet at a beach bar. Maddy is trying to get information about the diamond-smuggling business from Archer. She flirts; he flirts back. They dance, surrounded by a hundred party-dressed extras – among whom was the ambassador's wife. She was positioned in the near background behind our stars. At a break, Nicola followed Jennifer to her chair to ask a few questions about the scene. Ambassador's Wife remained on the dance floor, chatting with two other dancers. I ambled over in their direction.

'Nice moves.'

A wide smile, a tight hug and about five minutes of banal banter followed before AD Nilo Otero called, 'Everybody back to one.'

I returned to the sidelines and Nicola returned to my side to watch another hour or so of filming. We left before wrap.

It must have been around 5 a.m. when my mobile phone rang.

'Hey, we're at Coconuts! Come join us!'

It took me a second to recognise the voice. I made a quick refusal and hung up, hoping Nicola had slept through.

She hadn't.

'Who was that?'

An extra who was at the party scene last night.

'What did she want?'

The question was more what did I want?

Where had it started?

Did it go as far back as my mother's poor health when I was a child, worrying for the first ten years of my life that she might die and leave me?

Abandonment. Betrayal. Get too close to someone and they can destroy you. Needing someone is courting cataclysm. Hedge your bets. Cover your ass. Keep up your shield.

I expressed none of this to the woman in bed beside me.

'I met her at the Railway Station when you were flirting with Nuno. She's married to some ambassador here. She was in the scene last night. She could've got my phone number from one of the crew. Let's go back to sleep.'

Of course, neither of us did.

'I was *not* flirting with Nuno.'

Even after the war ended in Sierra Leone, there were still thousands of child soldiers in Africa, some as young as seven years old.

One of our last scenes in Mozambique took place in an abandoned brickworks factory about an hour's drive outside Maputo on the squalid outskirts of Umbeluzi. It served in the film as a training camp for child soldiers. Shivering boys sat in the dank shadows of an RUF holding pen, blindfolded and terrified. Solomon's son is chosen to take an automatic weapon and fire against a wall. When the blindfold is removed, he sees he's killed a man who the rebels had set up there.

A child psychologist was on hand.

'This is the worst part of the story,' Sorious told us. 'In Sierra Leone, these kids are a lost generation. In real life, he probably would've been made to kill a member of his family.'

'That way, they can never go back,' added Quiteria Mabasso, the psychologist who worked in rehabilitation programs for the nearly 10,000 child soldiers from the Mozambican civil war.

This scene appeared to affect our director more profoundly than any of the others. His teenage son, Jesse, had left the show and flown home to return to his studies a few weeks ago. But it was apparent he was in Ed's thoughts this day.

'Movies can't change politics,' he said, 'but they can contribute to changing consciousness.'

This movie was not about De Beers.

The child was the gem.

CHAPTER THIRTY-SIX: MOVING ON

I had a farewell handshake from Louis at the car wash and gave him a crew T-shirt. He indicated he'd put it on after work but didn't want to get it wet. I also bid fond farewell to my assistant, Teresa, who was moving back to Portugal.

'This has been the best experience of my life,' she said through tears.

Some of the crew had become involved with orphanages and other local charities. Many would stay connected. Nick Laws came up with a plan for the Blood Diamond Foundation. Ed and the actors kicked in some money. I helped organise a fund drive among the crew and persuaded Warner's to donate matching funds. All together, we raised over $100,000. Nick and João would put it to good use. Here is the list:

> The creation of a chicken farm to help the disabled community (ADEMO) by creating jobs and providing a source of income.
>
> Providing sewing machines and a tailor's facility to make clothes for orphaned children.
>
> Providing 900 seed kits for cultivation in Boane, Umbeluzi and Costa do Sol villages.
>
> Building repairs and installation of cooling fans in the Casa Alegria care home for the destitute, and provision of food, milk, nappies and cleaning products.

Installation of two water tanks and repair of borehole for Goba village, and building of toilets, water fountains and shaded seating area for the village health centre.

Provision of blankets, sheets, pillows and mattresses for local hospital.

Carpentry education and construction of reed huts for the most disadvantaged in Catembe.

Building of a borehole and repair of school buildings and supply of desks and chairs.

Malaria prevention: supply of 4,000 mosquito nets and education for prevention of Malaria in Umbeluzi and Costa do Sol villages.

Others, including Jaap, couldn't wait to leave the poverty of this place and move on to the First World comforts of Cape Town.

Our company caravanned across the Mozambique border in buses, cars and SUVs toward the South African town of Nelspruit, near Kruger National Park. We arrived around noon and immediately boarded helicopters to take us to a grassy hilltop, which was once a secret meeting spot for ANC freedom fighters. On this day, it was filled with goats.

This was Leo's first scene in the movie: Archer attempts to smuggle diamonds out of Sierra Leone, tagging along with a band of goatherds, claiming he works for National Geographic. Border patrolmen stop him from crossing and our action begins.

'Hurry up, we're losing the light!' Ed screamed.

Few of the recruited background actors spoke English. None spoke agitated American. We were not moving quickly. This was an expensive half-day of filming and it was a gamble that cast, crew and equipment could travel overland here, then be transported to the hilltop with enough time to shoot a full-page scene before sunset. Kevin was rolling the dice and his end of this operation had gone smoothly.

'Get that goat out of the shot! He looks like he's giving Leo a blowjob!'

'Uh, Ed, the goat is on its mark,' Nilo noted.

We got the last shot with the last rays of sunlight. The crew helicoptered back in the dark. We were rewarded with a night at the aptly named Serenity Lodge, which featured gardens, ponds, waterfalls and a firepit at which several of us sat after dinner, reminiscing about Maputo as if it had been much longer than a day since we'd last seen it. It already felt like a distant memory.

On our final day in Maputo, Jennifer Connelly had suffered whiplash and a concussion from a low-impact crash during a driving scene in which she banged her head on the unpadded dashboard. She flew ahead to Cape Town to see a doctor who put her in a neck brace and gave her painkillers. She braved it through the pain and smiled through an EPK interview with Vic Davis who had flown in with Steve Wacks to cover five of our eight days filming in this stunning seaside metropolis.

Scenes here would be the most perfunctory for the production – no trudging up gorges, no nasty ticks, no shooting in squalor. But Cape Town was the busiest time for the publicity department. We had all our major interviews to do, plus I was repaying cooperative press with wrap stories.

Nicola had her own busy agenda here. Off set, she scheduled social engagements with several people she knew from her many years of visits to this city. On set, she was running out of time to snare Leo.

She had become friendly with some of his entourage, gaining trust, getting to be a familiar, comfortable face around the star, occasionally trying to sneak in a question here and there that she might use in her production story. But Leo had a crafty way of acknowledging you and ignoring you at the same time.

Nicola was determined to penetrate that and not only get an interview for the Warner Bros. story she'd been commissioned to write, but a by-line article in one of her British news outlets. She'd interviewed Djimon over dinner in Maputo and turned that into a sale to the *Telegraph Magazine.* She'd talked with Jennifer about her veganism and set her sights on a feature in the health section of the *Evening Standard.* DiCaprio was the elusive jewel in the crown. She was so close but still so far.

Then one social evening at a house filled with animal bones and other eerie bric-a-brac, a documentary filmmaker began talking about a movie he was making on the 'Shark Whisperer'. My darling's attention was all his.

There was a man living in Cape Town who claimed to have a special relationship with great white sharks. He could hypnotise them. Once he got a shark under his spell, he could roll it over, tickle its fins, stick his head in the jaws. He could do with killer sharks what Robert Redford could do with horses. And he gave diving tours.

One day on set, Nicola was talking with Leo's assistant Jason and friend Peter, and her interest in going shark diving with this man was mentioned. A short time later, word had made its way to Leo.

'So, tell me about this shark guy,' our star asked our in-house journalist.

We were working on the weekend, through the beginning of the week, and had Wednesday off. The next three days were at the Colonel's Farmhouse, a sprawling vineyard in Constantia, one of Cape Town's most upscale suburbs in the heart of wine country.

Vic Davis, Steve Wacks and I were reeling in most of our EPK interviews here – including Leo. He said he 'rarely does these things' until he's had time to process the experience but he'd do one this time and re-do it, if necessary, in the States. It was a gesture of respect, which I appreciated. I did not want my renegade writer taking advantage of the star's good will by pushing for her own time with him.

'You can use the EPK transcript for your production story,' I bargained.

She smiled. It was a curious smile.

'I'm going shark diving with Leo and his guys on Wednesday,' she announced.

I'm not great in the water. Nicola and I had taken a weekend trip to a resort in Inhambane, on the south-central Mozambique coast. The big thing to do there was snorkel with whale sharks. Lest that sound suicidal, a whale shark is a plankton-eating fish – not a mammal like whales, nor a carnivore like sharks. They can grow to thirty-six feet in length with the girth of a tanker truck. But they're harmless.

Nicola was an excellent swimmer and, as we know, always game for a go at something new. I don't know why I went along but it must've sounded like a good idea at the time.

Our boat found one of the huge, spotted sea creatures, crept up beside it and kept pace. When it came my turn to dive, I breathed in when I should've breathed out and had to be hauled back onto the boat choking on seawater.

I would've said 'no, thanks' to shark diving with real sharks – had I been invited.

The Shark Whisperer loaded his boat with Nicola, Leo, Jason, a couple of other DiCaprio cohorts and a tub full of chum and piloted to an area called Gans Bay – known as Shark Alley. He lowered anchor, tossed in the chum and waited. Fins began to cluster around the boat. Leo and Nicola got in a cage and were dipped into the middle of the feeding frenzy. There they shared the thrill of a great white trying to break through the bars.

'Leo was taking pictures with his underwater camera and he jumped back just in time,' she reported later – in an article for the *Mail on Sunday*. Thankfully, her story would be held until the release of the movie or the insurance bonding company would've had us both thrown in Gans Bay without a cage.

That night, she was invited to dinner with Leo and his entourage where they all relived the excitement of the day. Her new pals wouldn't let her drive home alone.

'It's too dangerous,' one of them said.

The work in Cape Town proceeded apace and Vic Davis got the last of his interviews at a trendy restaurant in a tourist area overlooking the harbour. A far cry from Mundo's Pizza. Most of the South African crew were home with their families. Foreign crew were housed at the five-star Mount Nelson, off the chic café district along Kloof Street. The hotel corridors revealed surprises about who was sleeping with who.

Our wrap party took place at the Indigo Club in Camps Bay, the most fashionable district in the Cape. It was the wrong atmosphere. Runway models mingled with production assistants, and sharply dressed dudes, who no one knew, draped themselves along the bar trying to look movie-cool. The neon, the lava lamps, the multiple tiers that separated us from each other – all wrong.

Movie time is measured in mega-numerics: a day is a week, a week is a month, a month is a year. Sometimes more, depending on the intensity of the experience. We'd been together as a unit nearly five months – five years, movie time. We'd shared the beauty and the horror of Africa, witnessed the obscene wealth gap between races, and recreated the best and worst of humanity. We needed to be together in reflection, not neon. Nicola didn't even want to stay 'til the end.

On our way out, we spotted Leo and his mother in the cordoned-off downstairs café and joined them. We chatted about endangered wildlife and the environment. This was his passion. It was good to end our time in Africa with some passion.

We had a turnaround day from night shooting, a travel day, a prep day and a rest day before beginning two days of filming in London. Michael Sheen joined the cast, playing the diamond broker who trades a suitcase full of cash to Solomon for his pink gem. The final shot of the production took place on New Bond Street with Solomon looking in the display window at Tiffany's.

The company had put us up for a week at the Athenaeum Hotel on Piccadilly Circus. The filming may have ended but I was still having meetings with groups like Global Witness and Amnesty International, so I finagled a couple of extra days' lodging.

Nicola was going back and forth between the hotel and her mother's cottage in Eversholt. I had to attend a couple of meetings with her as well. We went over the guest list with Mary, half of which were hers. Her embossed invitations were too expensive for me to send to friends and family who I didn't think could make the trip here.

'We'll have another wedding in New York,' my love promised.

How I adored this woman who fought for her independence and our relationship with equal ferocity.

CHAPTER THIRTY-SEVEN: TRUST AND BETRAYAL

It began by email. I would say 'innocently enough', but it wasn't entirely innocent: Surprise Guest wanted a favour and I wanted the attention. We hadn't communicated in almost three years when her note landed like Eve's apple in my mailbox. It was around the time of Nuno.

She wanted to know if I would co-sponsor her for an American visa. There'd been something in her past that had banned her from entry to the US for a few years, but it had been cleared up and she was ready to try again.

I don't really know you that well, I wrote back.

When is this movie coming to London? She'd learned it was coming from the party-planning outfit she worked for. Within a few days of my arrival, she wrote again, asking if we could have lunch. One rationalisation led to another and I agreed.

We met at a club in Notting Hill. It was a disco by night and an upscale lounge by day. She wore pressed white slacks, a short-sleeved blouse unbuttoned to her bra clasp and three-inch heels. We talked about the movie and she told me about a music video she'd recently been in.

'I wore a mask and a cat suit,' she said.

I'd been very clear in telling her about Nicola and our wedding plans. She told me she was 'seeing someone'. She said she wanted to show me around London. I said I would be pretty busy. She asked for my UK phone number. I gave it to her.

The texts began the morning of the day Nicola arrived back at my hotel.

Whatcha up 2?

I turned off the sound alert on my phone.

Will your girlfriend be around this weekend?

I didn't answer that one. Nicola had talked about spending the weekend with her mother in the country, going over the seating arrangement.

A few more exchanges and the mud got thicker.

Have you ever seen Bath? It's so beautiful!

Bath is an old Roman city that I'd heard was… beautiful.

I continued to flirt – at least enough to keep the game alive.

Considering your architecture, Bath might pale in comparison.

The last two texts were the ones that got me in trouble.

(her) *My body is a labyrinth!*

(me) *I think we should go back to email.*

Those were the ones Nicola saw.

Our fight was brief. In fact, it wasn't really a fight.

'I hate Becky-from-Berkeley,' she said at some point, attributing all my distrust and relationship dysfunction to the girl who dumped me in college.

She moved back to her mother's house in Bedfordshire.

I was left nakedly alone with my transgression. The gambit of you-do-this-I'll-do-that had gone too far. It was a game I'd never really wanted to play. I wasn't very good at it.

She never said, 'This is over' – or anything close.

It wasn't a question of what I'd risked. It was a question of why.

The dystopia of life in the movies is that nothing is permanent and everything moves on. The Buddha teaches us to let go of attachments. The movie business teaches us that once you start believing in that, you're lost. At least after a certain age.

Older people on film crews have either found something/someone to latch on to or are visibly drowning. Some in alcohol, some in nostalgia, most on the treadmill of the next adventure. Was that what I wanted? Of course not. Was that what I had to confront? Of course it was.

People in non-Western cultures get married for all sorts of reasons beside love. Marriage is union. Marriage is a three-legged sack race: love or not, you must both be running in the same direction.

Where were we running?

Nicola toward her fear of commitment. Me toward my fear of abandonment. Can marriage be the consequence of two people, hand in hand, turning to face their demons? If I should fall behind, wait for me?

Love is worth nothing until it's been tested by its own defeat – Rian Milan.

I wrote this to Nicola.

She wrote back.

We are married.

That was all.

My non-conformist bride wanted the most traditional wedding the village of Eversholt had ever seen. Making her mother happy was only a cover. In a dress of white lace, she even chose to wear a veil. Sam and Casey flew in and we went to be fitted for morning suits. Summer in England can be drizzly and dreary but on the day of our wedding the sky was clear blue. It was a 'sign', Nicola would say.

'It looks like that side are the colonialists.' Millard leaned over my shoulder to point out Mary's guests: white women wearing feathered hats and stiff, sombre white men.

As people were being seated, Mom approached Millard.

'Please don't do that during the ceremony.' She pointed to his camera. He put it away. I looked back and smiled.

My beautiful bride was predictably a half-hour late, processing on her brother's arm. Sam stood by my side as best man. The choir sang. The ceremony began. Nicola didn't want it to end.

'Can you have us sing "Jerusalem"?' – the unofficial anthem of England – she whispered to the vicar.

Once that had been sung.

'Can we do the hymn about…'

I glared.

'Just one more,' she pleaded.

We had one more.

We rose. The vicar proceeded with the vows. I was barely able to choke out, 'I will.'

And we were married. Again. Officially. In the eyes of God and England.

I like to think we set a record for the longest ceremonial kiss.

'I thought I was going to have to break you up,' the vicar said, laughing.

The recessional music was my choice.

Sam approached the podium. Casey's new cousin Ben guided him to the organ. Felix and Caspar stood on floor level in front of Sam. They began clapping in time. Casey started playing. And Sam, with his extraordinary voice – a gift from his mother – began to sing.

'*When the night has come. And the land is dark. And the moon is the only light we'll see. No, I won't be afraid. Oh, I won't be afraid. Just as long as you stand, stand by me.'*

And we danced down the aisle.

The reception at Berrystead was the best party we'd ever been to together. Neither of us wanted to leave early.

THE BEGINNING

EPILOGUE

Becoming a Mother

There's always another story to tell. The part of this one left untold is how Nicola became a mother.

It was 2009. We'd been trying everything from Chinese herbs to wishes on the full moon; from daily sex to sex only according to her ovulation cycle. We went to fertility doctors and both tested capable of conceiving. We went to acupuncturists and back to Angel, the psychic in Los Angeles who told Nicola she'd have two children. Finally, Nicola gave up resistance to in vitro fertilisation and subjected herself to that uncomfortable and expensive process. She once thought it might have worked – then she got on a plane to London, had a painful menstruation and that was the end of that.

I was working on the James L. Brooks comedy *How Do You Know* in Philadelphia when we got a call from Sam.

'Casey's in the hospital,' he said in barely restrained panic. 'He's screaming at the nurses that he doesn't want to be here. But, Dad, he's really sick. I'm really worried.'

I called our friends Marianne and Donald Berman, asking if they could relieve Sam at the hospital until we got to New York. It was a two-hour drive from Philadelphia. Marianne was in the ER room when we got there.

Casey had an IV drip flowing into his arm to treat severe dehydration. He was threatening to pull it out and 'walk home'.

We spent the night with him. He was more agitated with me in his room and calmer when Nicola took over. Her soft English voice soothed him. She spent most of the night by his bed.

I called Margaret. She didn't have to drive down tonight, I told her. He would be released in the morning.

'But you should find a kidney specialist here and make an appointment.'

The twenty-to-thirty-year prognosis for a transplant had turned out closer to five years. Once again, Casey had defied the odds. Margaret and I were both a match as donors. Margaret asked to donate her kidney to save her son.

'Thank you for taking such good care of my boys,' Margaret said to Nicola when they met in the hospital on the day of the operation.

It was a stew of emotions watching her wheeled into surgery. The gurney carrying Casey followed immediately after. I was terrified for both of them. But the most frightening thing had been the post-op instructions given to us by his doctor: assuming the operation was a success, his life depended upon a strict drug regimen during recovery and forever after. My rebel child would have to live the rest of his life adhering to a schedule.

I'd signed up to work as a local hire – meaning I'd have to fund my own housing – on the movie *Black Swan,* so we could be in New York to care for Casey. Margaret would recuperate back in Ithaca where her sister could look after her.

My work was mostly in the city. But Casey hated the city – this place he'd longed to be with his brother but found so aggressive and inhospitable after moving here. So Nicola found a house in the country where his auditory sense would get a reprieve from police sirens, ambulances and Brooklynites screaming outside his window. I would stay near the production and drive up on weekends.

Director Darren Aronofsky started the first day of filming, at Lincoln Center, by gathering cast and crew in a prayer circle to invoke a blessing on the production. It was a lovely and inclusive ceremony.

I asked for a more personal blessing.

Let Nicola tell the rest of the story.

The Convalescence

For a month, we move into a big windowed house on the edge of a lake near New Paltz, up the Hudson Valley, on the border of a Mohawk Reservation. The 299 Highway crests a ridge out of town toward the setting sun. It's late autumn and the trees are shedding the last of their leaves, their great skeletons pointing to the imposing escarpment on the horizon and giving the sun easy passage into our eyes as we drive toward our place of convalescence.

Sam, my youngest stepson, falls in love as we crest the ridge. 'Aaaaaahhhh!' he says, with the relief of a resident New Yorker brought up in the countryside. 'This is amazing, Casey,' he alerts his elder brother. 'This is so beautiful!'

But Casey sees nothing of this because Casey is ninety per cent blind. He can see your features if the light is just right and you are really, really close; he can read the news a few letters at a time on a specially configured computer and he can grill a salmon steak and cook pasta, but he can't tell if the girl hitting on him is pretty or find his way around New York City without a white-tipped cane.

We've just liberated him from the New York Presbyterian Hospital where he received a new kidney from his mother. I know, almost-blind with failing kidneys. I have wondered more than once why so much suffering should be vested on one human being. But right now, as we crest into the sunset, he feels liberated: liberated from the men in white coats brandishing needles and long words, the city noise and smog. Liberated from the snoring man in the hospital bed next to him and liberated from the debilitating drain on his energy that combined with his blindness to create The Worst Life Ever.

While he cannot see the trees and the escarpment exactly, he can see/sense that there is space and sky and a horizon. He feels the light of the sun on his face. Brooklyn pavements and angry taxi drivers, the hustling bustle that everyone else loves about New York City makes life outside his apartment something of a combat exercise.

I flutter around Casey, gently easing him out of the car and into the house to a sofa where I lay him down. Pale and uncommonly slim, he pretends pain isn't there even as he holds his side and grimaces. I fake a confidence I don't feel in taking care of this precious cargo. His life-saving immunosuppressant drug regime and strict instructions not to come in contact with any human being who might be carrying a virus have me terrified for his life. He already looks as though a slight breeze might carry him off into the Hudson River. Deep shadows around his eyes and sculpted hollows under his high cheekbones make him look as though he has one foot in the land of the dead already.

The key to his survival is a simple plastic drug tray with the days of the week going horizontal and times of day going vertical. Morning, midday, teatime, evening. There are eight pills every morning and every night – and some more in between. The most important are the immunosuppressants because if he doesn't take them religiously and on time, his body might start rejecting his new kidney. Then there are his vitals that I need to take in the morning and night: his blood pressure, his weight, his temperature. Nothing I have ever done feels this important.

Casey has instant and lasting memory. His survival depends on it. One recce to his bedroom, the bathroom, kitchen and living room, up and down stairs and in and out of doors and he can remember and find his way around the house alone. He remembers his drug regime far better than I do despite listening to a doctor, a nurse reading the literature and watching a video. He even knows the names of his medications, while I am still talking about the 'little white ones' and the 'big red ones'.

'Shouldn't I be taking the Valcyte every day?' he asks me, knowing that of course he should.

'No, no, no, that is only for Mondays, Wednesdays and Fridays,' I say, reading the 'Daily Schedule'.

Ever so diplomatically he says, 'I think the doctor told us that I should be taking two in the morning and two in the evening because my creatinine levels are still pretty high.'

And then I remember that he is right: the doctor did tell us that but they did not adjust the literature so me-of-little-brain did not recalibrate.

'Damn!' says his dad, full of pride, 'we are so impressed by how responsible you are with this drug regime.'

Remember that this is a 22-year-old blind kid who plays in a band and works as a piano tuner during the day. Who has very specific dietary tastes but doesn't always brush his teeth.

'I am a simple man of simple tastes,' he is fond of saying, always very apologetically, as he refuses anything that does not sit within his parameters of plain protein (white chicken breast, steak,

salmon), plain vegetables (broccoli, asparagus), plain pasta (only butter) with nothing mixed, no sauces, light on the herbs, zero complexity and lots of salt that I have given up giving him a hard time about.

'Daddio,' he says, 'it's not as if I have much else to think about right now.' Always the master of understatement.

Sam and Casey are my stepsons from a late and destined marriage. Sam is the youngest but you would never know it, and the years on his young shoulders are accounted for by looking out for his older brother.

As long as he can remember, Sam has been guiding Casey: around the school playground, into restaurants, out of clubs and, more recently, in and out of hospitals.

Casey has shoulder-length blond hair and bone structure that would make supermodels jealous. His chin is a direct derivative of his father who happens to be six foot three, dark and almost always leads from the chin. It is square and very big and seems to me to indicate a familial stubbornness and forthrightness – in a good way, in the sense of 'putting your chin forward'. Casey is beautiful rather than handsome and reminds me a little of David Bowie. His almost-sightless eyes are big and blue and they find you when you speak.

Of course, he has no idea how good he looks. Or how good anything looks, for that matter. I am finding my own liberation in being around an almost-blind guy. You are operating on a completely different playing field: it is more about feeling and touch, about the sound of your voice rather than the fact you are sitting there in a ratty dressing gown with no make-up and dodgy hair. So, because he has no idea how he looks, you can stop worrying about how you look. It means that you have to be focused, come from the heart and be especially vigilant about things you never thought about. It is liberating, somehow.

I have tried to ban the words 'sorry' and 'thank you' because Casey uses them too much. He is most uncomfortable with anyone doing anything for him – and I remember that this has nothing to do with his kidney transplant but was always there as a result of his blindness. He is constantly apologising and constantly saying 'thank you'. It drives his brother nuts and I sense his approval when I say I have tried to ban these words.

So, when he says 'thank you', I tell him that it is only because of him that we have found this place of hibernation in Upstate New York where we can also regroup our resources and our strength and be in the silence of winter and rediscover who we are and what we want, only because we are in this lovely silent hiatus between our lives in Los Angeles and our lives in God-knows-where. So, I tell him, it is us who should be thanking him but we won't because we're banning the words.

And he just reaches his sightless arm toward my cheek and says, 'Thank you, Nicky, thank you.'

He is impossible. And he is my stepson. And he might as well be my son-son. I watch over him like a mothering hawk, jumping up at every pain grimace, setting a blanket just so around his shoulders, staying up, waking up, jarring myself at every jarring moment he is experiencing on car journeys, feeling the pain in my vein when the nurse administers an IV into his milky-white, too-slim forearm.

And like a mother-mother, I would be happy to put myself in his place and suffer his pain instead of him. And I think this is really weird. Well, actually, I think it deeply magical – which is also weird. So, I ask, how come I ended up with these impressive step-children that I feel like I know? It was so immediate, so meant, so easy to connect with these teenagers who bear the imprint of their upbringing in such a noble and sweet way. There is nothing not to love, but how did they bring themselves to love me so easily and how come I am able now to stay up nights and do such intimate stuff with no feeling of strain? There is no feeling of strain or even the slightest effort: just a deep natural drawing-on-the-well kind of feeling – as though I had been a mother-mother all my life.

This was how Nicola became a mother. We never had children of our own. I couldn't talk her into adoption. She believed in fate. Fate brought her my two boys. They have embraced her like another mother. And rather than a conflict, it created a bond between her and Margaret. I never could've seen that coming.

Sam and Casey's band found their drummer, Adam Levin, in a dormitory at the New School University in Manhattan. They eventually named themselves X Ambassadors. They play to thousands of people around the world and, in 2017, founded the Cayuga Sound music festival in their home town of Ithaca.

Ever After

Imagine, if you will, a job fair. There is bunting and a banner across the entry to a barn-like building with a ceiling so high you can't see it from the floor. The banner reads: *Your Life Begins Here.*

Inside is an infinite number of folding tables; seated behind each is a pleasant-looking man or woman. One wears a lab coat, one a leisure suit, one is in shorts and flip-flops, and so on. You stop at a station where a woman in white describes entry into the medical profession. 'Learn on the job,' you are told. 'Become a doctor or a dentist, a surgeon or a scientist.' The only qualification is your inclination.

As you make the rounds, you are offered career paths in business, building, bookkeeping, beekeeping, bartending. You go through the alphabet of possibilities: hospitality, horticulture, hypnotist; marketing, management, manufacturing; teaching, tree-trimming, truck driving; zoologist, zen master, zipper repair.

When you've chosen your table, you are handed a simple form to sign. The form reads: DO NOT SIGN BEFORE READING THE FINE PRINT. Beneath the space for your signature is a single sentence: This will be your job for the next thirty years.

Now imagine Nicola standing in the doorway, scanning the room. She sees something of interest. In a shadowy corner, beyond 'Z', is a man in a pointed hat and wizard robes. She takes a seat opposite him.

'What is my destiny?' she asks him.

'You've chosen the right table,' he says. 'I can offer you dreams.'

'Dreams only lead to disillusionment,' she responds.

He reaches behind and opens a small chest.

'How about belief then?' He extends both palms to show nothing in his hands.

'I have plenty of that but it doesn't seem to get me anywhere.'

He reaches back into the trunk and comes up with a pen.

'You are a writer.' He hands her the pen, then he hands her the contract.

She clicks the pen, reads the fine print, hesitates at the thirty-year commitment. But having no other inclination, she puts pen to paper and starts to sign.

'The pen has no ink,' she says in surprise.

'Ahh!' He smiles. 'You think you can have everything.'

I'd signed my thirty-year contract, having found a job that changed often enough to satisfy my wanderlust and low boredom threshold. Nicola and I shared those inclinations and, when her career as a freelance journalist hit the wall of the electronic news age, I thought she might like to try my job. I had retired but some offers continued to come. The first one was in Uganda, the next was in Spain, then there was one in Italy, then one in India and Thailand. She became a unit publicist. She was good at it. It incorporated her journalism skills with organisational skills she never knew she had. She referred to this transition as 'going over to the dark side', the poacher had become the land owner. Then one day, an AD kicked her cameraman off set, an actor dodged an interview he'd agreed to, the studio came up with an idea for a dog-and-pony show that was going to be a nightmare…

'I'm not a unit publicist!' Nicola declared in exasperation.

Actually, she still is. But not exclusively.

Our work defines us in internal and external ways. Do we do what we are? Are we what we do? Do we become who we are through what we do? A career in the movies has taught me the answer is yes to all the above. But we are also parents, we are lovers, we are dancers, diviners and discoverers of worlds around us and inside us. We are always who we are doing what we do, learning as we go.

The trouble with love is it doesn't conquer all. It's another job – the only qualification for which is inclination and the only path to success is steep, rocky and rutted with failure. We follow it because it is breath and the alternative is suffocation. Nicola and I continue working at both love and the movies.

I still want to leave parties earlier than she does.

THANK YOU...

First and always to my beautiful wife. Then and always to my beautiful former wife. And to Ann, who died at an age younger than my boys are now. Thank you for your love and your wisdom.

This book is for the people in the borderless country in which I've lived for the past thirty-five years. It's also for their partners and loved ones who may see something of themselves in these pages. And for anyone else whose heart is left behind when the plane takes off.

The Dunbar Number – the ideal size for human groups – is 150. That's about the size of a working film crew. My thanks to all with whom I've been in that number. My gratitude also to the studio executives and publicists who have trusted me in protecting their investment, their contacts, their clients and allowed me to stretch their patience. My admiration as well as appreciation for the actors who expose their innermost selves for the film, then explain themselves for publicity. If movie-goers didn't care, it wouldn't matter.

Special thanks to my publisher Tom Perrin for his faith in this book, his wisdom, and his assigning the brilliant George Tomsett as my editor. Gratitude to the multi-talented Austin Mutti-Mewse for connecting me with Tom and Zuleika. Thanks also to Susan Salter Reynolds, Karen Krizanovich, Mary Lucas, Roger Armstrong and Robert Edsel for their comments and contributions.

Thanks to those whose input and encouragement was essential at various stages: Peter Dunne, Bob Spitz, Jason Barlow,

Anita Overland, Jan Tuckwood, Scott Eyman, Lynn Kalber, Lois Cahall, Andy Lipschultz, Katherine Hooker, Terry J. Erdman, Robert Berkeley, Donald Buckley. Also, colleagues Sarah Bradshaw, Simone Goodrich, Nick Laws, Jean Black, Alexander Siddig, Brian Cox, John Shrapnel, Barbara Huber, Nilo Otero, Daniel Petersen and others who have helped me tell this story. Love and thanks to my sister, Cynthia, for being a rock and safe harbour all my life.

Colleagues and friends who have been my ballast and my bliss in this business are too numerous to name. I won't try. You know who you are. Thank you. Filmmakers for whom I've worked multiple times – Ridley Scott, Wolfgang Petersen, Scott Rudin, Sam Mendes, Douglas Wick and Lucy Fisher, Laurie MacDonald and Walter Parkes, Ron Howard and Brian Grazier, Eric Fellner and Tim Bevan, George Clooney and Grant Heslov, John Sayles and Maggie Renzi, Ron Shelton, James L. Brooks, Richard Donner, Paula Weinstein, Duncan Henderson, Todd Hallowell, Colin Wilson, A. Kitman Ho, Joe and Anthony Russo and Mike Larocca – thanks for having me back. Hugs and gratitude to PMK and Marian Koltai-Levine for putting 'stones in my slippers', as Nicola likes to say.

'Writing is bearing witness... Bearing witness contains within itself an exposure of other people's lives,' Marci Shore wrote in the acknowledgments of her brilliant book *The Taste of Ashes.* I've tried to limit that exposure to myself and those closest to me but, inevitably, lives that have touched mine have also found their way to these pages. It was easier to ask forgiveness than permission. I hope you don't mind.

Final thanks to my sons Casey and Sam, whose own stories I have partially purloined to tell the story of us. I celebrate the love you've found with your extraordinary partners. Deepen it, trust in it, desire it, wait for each other and walk in commitment to each other. I'll love you always.

ABOUT THE AUTHOR

Rob Harris began his professional career as a freelance television writer for such shows as *Laverne & Shirley*. He moved to a staff position as head publicity writer for 20th Century Fox and, later, a brief stint as vice president of publicity in the New York office of Gramercy Pictures. He's been a publicist on nearly a hundred movies, including *Gremlins, The Goonies, The Sandlot, The Bonfire of the Vanities, Air Force One, Men in Black II, Hannibal, The Perfect Storm, Gladiator, Frost/Nixon, Black Swan, The Bucket List, American Gangster, Revolutionary Road, Extremely Loud & Incredibly Close, World War Z* and *Maleficent*. He lives in England with his wife, Nicola Graydon Harris. Their sons, Casey and Sam, live in Los Angeles – when X Ambassadors are not touring – and in Ithaca, New York, where Casey recently bought his old family home.

Photo: Millard Arnold